TEACHING
PHYSICAL
EDUCATION
in Elementary Schools

MARYHELEN VANNIER, Ed.D.

*Director, Women's Division,
Department of Health and Physical Education,
Southern Methodist University*

MILDRED FOSTER, B.S.

*Teacher of Physical Education,
Dallas Public School System, Dallas, Texas*

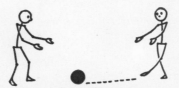

DIAGRAMMATICALLY ILLUSTRATED

W. B. SAUNDERS COMPANY
Philadelphia and London · 1954

This book is dedicated to our Mothers

MRS. MAUDE VANNIER

MRS. HILDA WEST

who taught us, among other things, to love children

"I keep six honest serving men;
(They taught me all I knew)
Their names are What and Where and When
And How and Why and Who."

RUDYARD KIPLING

PREFACE

This book is first a presentation of physical education—what it is and what its place should be in our everchanging educational system. Secondly, it is a source book of activities for children in grades one through six. Thirdly, it is a suggestion of how to teach children through these activities.

It has been written mainly for three groups: (1) the specialized physical educator, (2) the classroom teacher, and (3) the college student who is training to be an elementary teacher.

The need for such a book has arisen from great changes in educational methods that have come about in recent years, from the swing away from a tradition-bound physical education program to a modern one, and from vast environmental changes which have taken place in elementary schools themselves.

Elementary school enrollment is higher than ever before in the history of America. Few books are available at the present time to help teachers deal with bigger classes, or pupils living in a war-torn world full of fear, hatred, and insecurity. Often the specialized physical education teacher today has classes with as many as 80 to 100 pupils each class period for six periods daily in a makeshift gymnasium of 20 by 40 feet. Too often the classroom teacher is asked or forced to teach physical education along with many other subjects to her class—a field in which her only training has been two years of required college physical education for adults. The college student, likewise, too often is trained to work in an ideal teaching situation which does not exist except in a textbook or some professor's dream world.

Every activity found in this book has been used successfully with elementary school children for a number of years. Each one has long challenged and delighted youngsters and has helped them grow as individuals and group members.

v

An ideal physical education is elastic. It must fit the needs of the individual situation. No two instructors, children, or teaching situations are identical. But suggested teaching techniques coupled with a new sensitivity toward children and a willingness to try new and better suggestions tailored to fit one's own situation should prove beneficial. If so, writing this book has been worth while. It will be only as good as those using it.

It is imperative that we as teachers join with parents to develop healthy, vigorous children rich with initiative, resourcefulness, imagination, and courage. Together we must face fearlessly and honestly our great responsibility to help children help themselves be fit for and fitted into our present world.

It has been claimed that education will save the world in a mad race between education and world catastrophe. This is not entirely true, for educators of today's heritage will not get very far ahead in the struggle. To win, tomorrow's educators must be better than today's! Tomorrow's adults must be better than we are or have ever been!

For it is in the education of children, and not in the council of statesmen, that the future of the world will be determined for good or for evil, for man's crash into an abyss or his climb to glory.

MARYHELEN VANNIER
MILDRED FOSTER

Dallas, Texas
January, 1954

ACKNOWLEDGEMENTS

The authors are indebted to many persons who have made this book possible. Especial gratitude and appreciation are due to our families for continual inspiration and encouragement during its creation.

We are especially grateful to numerous students in our classes, both on the elementary and college level, who have helped us play the games, and collect new materials.

Betty Eaton and Kathleen Bivings deserve our special vote of thanks for typing the manuscript.

CONTENTS

Part One. THE WHY

Part Two. THE WHO

Part Three.   THE WHERE

Chapter 4

THE GYMNASIUM, PLAYGROUND AND CLASSROOM 49

Part Four.   THE HOW

Chapter 5

LEARNING AND TEACHING 61

Chapter 6

THE PROGRAM 75

Chapter 12

CLASSROOM AND QUIET GAMES 240

Chapter 13

CONSTRUCTED GAMES 264

Contents

Part One

THE WHY

If we would develop strong, courageous, loyal citizens, conscious of their role in society, we, as adults, must help children to do better the things they will do anyway, and teach them to do those things we can and they might do. Above all, we must enlist their enthusiasm and desire to preserve and pursue further that which man throughout history has found to be good.

Chapter 1

The Place of Physical Education in Schools

What is Physical Education?

Physical education is as old as man. The very existence of our primitive ancestors depended upon their ability to secure food, to erect crude shelters in caves, forests, or on mountain slopes, to battle successfully with changing weather elements, and to refresh their bodies through sleep, rest, and play. To know how to use their bodies meant life; failure to utilize this knowledge brought death.

In ancient Greece and Rome physical training held an important place in the educational program for boys and girls. Since then physical education has swung back and forth from favor to disregard in the eyes of the educator, churchman, and citizen. Bowed down by the narrowed vision of the man of the Middle Ages, who was concerned largely with his soul and saving it, the physical self was held to be evil, a thing of the devil. Modern man thinks differently; his vision has widened, his knowledge increased. He now sees the folly of trying to separate the mind from the body, knowing that the mind is of the body and vice versa—that it is impossible to train, educate, or use either singly. Thus, now the parent, the public school teacher, and the college professor speak of developing the "whole child" and likewise, then, the "whole man."

Physical education today is regarded as an important part of general education. However, there are those both in and outside of schools who confuse big time athletic contests for a few players with physical education for all, 1-2-3-bend type of mass exercise done to a shouted command with a wide range of games and sports, or boxers with bulging muscles and lady wrestlers seen on television shows with a full program of sports and games,

3

rhythmical activities, and recreational pursuits for all people of all ages.

Just as primitive man had to learn to use his body wisely or perish so must modern man, for biologically they are almost identical. Just as our ancestors needed vigorous activity to keep themselves fully functioning, so do we today. The difference lies only in degree. There are those among us who claim that all too rapidly Americans are becoming a race of on-looking softies rather than doers. Others claim that we let our bodies rust out rather than wear out. Man, primitive or modern, is an animal and as such his physical needs are the same. His emotional, social, and mental needs are greatly intensified. Failure to satisfy properly his physical needs, or the balance wheels, often throws him out of gear. Wise men among us declare that in this push-button age of "cocktails, canasta, and catastrophe" modern man is already obsolete. Some even claim that organic degenerate disease will destroy man providing his own created weapons of destruction do not beat the diseases to it.

Just as youth may learn more outside of schools than they do in them, and just as they often learn more from their peers than from their teachers, so do they gain through life experiences a type of physical education. Learning to play successfully a game of hide and seek with policemen is a type of physical education, learning to use harmful narcotics is another. For in spite of adults, youth will learn. Because of adults what children learn can be socially good as well as good for them. Play must be directed if desired results are to accrue. If we would develop strong, courageous, loyal citizens, conscious of their role in society, we, as adults, must help children to do better things they will do anyway, and teach them to do those things we can and they might do. Above all, we must enlist their enthusiasm and desires to preserve and pursue further that which man throughout history has found to be good. Educators have long claimed that the purpose of education is to enable people of all ages to *pass* on and to pass *on* our cultural heritage, as well as to live successfully and happily while *in* it.

Physical educators, as well as classroom teachers who teach physical activities to children, have a great as well as a grave responsibility. Educationally speaking they are in a choice spot, for they have the opportunity to play with children, to observe children at play, and to teach them the enduring lessons of life through an informal play approach. Psychologists tell us that children are their real selves when they play. Educators claim that all people regardless of age learn more, faster, and remember longer when they are doing something they enjoy, when they become absorbed in the adventure of learning. Joseph Lee, an early leader of recreation in America, held that play for children is creation or the gaining of life, whereas play for adults is recreation or the renewal of life. Other leaders declare that if adults want to know what a child is really like they should *observe* his play, but if they are truly concerned about what a child may become they should *direct* his play.

Physical education in schools is directed, purposeful activity centered around the total body, its movement, care, and use. As such it stresses the development of skills—physical, social, and mental. A good program in physical education should enable one to develop into becoming a highly-functioning individual full of zest for life, capable, and desirous to serve well both himself and society. Such a person would be able to do a number of skills. Regardless of age, he would know *how* and *want* to use these skills while working, playing, and living with others.

Forty-two states have mandatory laws decreeing that physical education must be included in the public school curriculum; the remaining six have permissive laws for its inclusion. There are forty-one state directors of physical education throughout the country. Each state has established by law minimum minutes for daily class instruction. Although the amount of time designated for daily instruction periods varies, a major portion of the states require a minimum instruction period of thirty minutes daily from grade 1 through 12. Nationally it has been estimated that one out of every twelve teachers is directly concerned with physical education and its related fields of health and recreation.[1]

However impressive these figures are, much has to be done on a national and local level to improve both the *status* and *content* of this program in the school curriculum. Laws alone will not do

[1] Nash, Jay B., Moensch, Francis, and Saubon, Jeannette, *Physical Education, Organization and Administration*, New York, A. S. Barnes, 1951, p. 223.

this, just as laws set up to punish criminals will not prevent crime, nor those established to fine speeders will prevent reckless driving. People can and will get around laws as long as they give only lip service to them or do not really believe in their value. Thus, in some states the recess period is counted as physical education. Some administrators even record the noon lunch period or the walking to and from school as physical education. Trained leaders who realize the value of directed physical education instruction must sell the real program to their colleagues, their administrators, and to the general public. Only then will state laws regarding education in general and its component parts be enforced and improved upon. Youth has the legal and the moral right to receive the best education possible.

The Aim of Physical Education

Physical education should aim to provide opportunities for the individual and the group to learn from skilled teachers activities which are invigorating, fun to do, and will lead to positive physical, social, mental, and emotional growth.

This definition implies that the resultant growth and development of children through directed physical activities should affect the total child. Social, mental, and emotional growth is closely related. The teacher of physical education must understand these interrelationships and accordingly guide learning toward their development. Small classes are essential if this worthy aim is to be fulfilled.

Such a directive also means that: (1) both the specialized and classroom teacher be trained in methods of teaching youth *through* physical activities; (2) the physical education class be no larger in size than those in English, history, or any other subject; (3) all youth be guided toward mastering skills which will help them grow in organic vigor, knowledges, appreciations, and ability to fit into groups.

Since all life is mostly group life it is vastly important for youth to learn early how to find peer status and gain adult approval legitimately as well as how to contribute and receive benefits from the group. A child adept in sports and games, in working and playing with others, will reach this goal earlier and with more ease than one lacking such skills. A good teacher somewhere along the academic ladder has helped this youth learn from and through a wide variety of experiences lessons vital to his existence.

General Objectives

The broad objectives of physical education are those of education in general. Schools should assume the responsibility to see to it that every child, regardless of sex, economic status, geographic location, or race should receive the best balanced education possible. Such an education should:

(1) Equip him to enter an occupation suited to his abilities and offering reasonable opportunity for personal growth and social usefulness.

(2) Prepare him to assume the full responsibility of American citizenship.

(3) Give him a fair-chance to exercise his right for happiness.

(4) Stimulate intellectual curiosity, engender satisfaction in intellectual achievement, and cultivate the ability to think rationally.

(5) Help him to develop an appreciation of ethical values which should undergird all life in a democratic society.[1]

Obviously these worthy objectives can best be achieved when the school, home, church, and other institutions in the community work closely together for their accomplishment.

Specific Objectives

The school has the definite function to teach the values of democracy to each individual, to instill within each person the desire to educate himself to his highest capacity in order that he might best contribute to society, and to develop in each citizen the desire to perpetuate democracy. Physical education has valuable contributions to make to this total educational program of the school. Its contribution is built upon the specific objectives of developing: (1) organic vigor, (2) skills, (3) knowledges, and (4) appreciations.

Organic Vigor

Taking part in vigorous activities contributes to organic development and general well being. If we would build strong dynamic

Educational Policies Commission, *Education for All American Youth*, Washington, D. C., National Education Association, 1944, p. 21.

youth we must plan for and work toward that goal. The muscles of the body grow in strength, size, and tonus through use or exercise.

The vital organs of the body are likewise favorably affected by exercise. Through activity the rate and force of heart beat is increased, breathing becomes deeper and more rapid, heat production and body waste stepped up. Improved appetite and sleep, accelerated energy build-up and energy breakdown results. In children physical activity serves as a stimulus to growth.

Physical fitness is the result of planned activity and regularity of exercise, sleep and rest, eating, engaging in play or recreation, keeping in the state of emotional well-being, and regularity of waste elimination habits. Abundant, buoyant health gives one the drive to work, to play, to live with zest. Children need from five to six hours of rugged big-muscle activity daily through play in the outside after school in order to develop, to be, and to stay healthy.

Skills

Skills are the result of training the whole body to coordinate properly. Children increase their ability to master certain skills as they grow older. This is known as maturation: that one will best learn to play baseball, tennis, or other sports when he is ready to learn them, or has a desire to do so. Seven-year-old George may not want to learn to play badminton, but because of urging by a doting aunt will try and fail. He throws down the racket in disgust and walks away. George at fifteen, however, may be a skilled player and rabid badminton fan. There are many sport skills a child of nine cannot do, but the same child may be a master player by the age of eleven. When teachers wait until this maturation period is reached, when the student is ready to learn, much can be accomplished. They must know what are these individual maturation points, how they can be seen, and at what age they are most likely to appear.

Skill coordinations are learned mostly through trial-error plus imitation. Jane learns to roller skate by trying to copy the movements of her older brother. She tries until she masters the skill, or, if she fails, will keep on practicing either alone or before a small group until she is an old hand at it—but will drive herself to skate, in spite of repeated falls and skinned knees only as long as she is determined to learn. The will to do is a dynamic driving force! It can both be instilled in others and guided, it can be used for learning how to do things. Children are eager to learn, to do!

Since youngsters learn sport skills largely by imitating others and practicing what they have seen, the most productive teachers of physical education know how to perform a number of skills well. They know how to throw and catch balls of all sizes, how to aim and hit targets, how to coordinate arm with leg movements, how to do the polka and other dance steps, as well as many, many other kinds of body movement.

If, however, the teacher is unskilled and unable to demonstrate to others how to do a movement correctly, she may be able to describe it in such a clear concise way that the best student in the class can do it from her description well enough for the others to copy. However, not all teachers who can perform a beautiful tennis shot can teach others to do likewise. Chances for successfully getting others to want to learn to play tennis well may be greater, however, if the player-teacher is highly skilled and has a pleasing, attractive personality.

It is important for the teacher to know that practice makes perfect only if the correct way to perform a skill is being practiced. It is harder to unlearn bad movement habits than to learn new ones. Susan tends to learn to swim faster if she is taught from the beginning by someone who knows how to teach than if she learns to do a few dog paddles on her own and in some magic way learns to stay above water. Charles will learn to make more baskets if he works with someone who is a whizz at basket shooting than if he takes a ball and practices unguided in his own back yard.

The role of the teacher in skill teaching is that of recognizing learning readiness, demonstrating the correct way to do the movements, and helping the child teach himself how to master them. Speed, strength, timing, and increased movement range can be developed through practice under skilled directions of the teacher.

Knowledges

Increasing the ability to make correct judgments, how to do things well, and knowing about other people as well as one's self is another specific objective of physical education. Children must learn early in life the meaning of signals, symbols, and how to react to them. They must learn how to move around with ease in their environment of the home, school, playground, and community. These social knowledges become increasingly important as the child moves from his primary home group to the larger secondary group of the school and the community. Furthermore they must learn to find security, love, recognition, and belonging in each of the many environments or groups they join hourly, daily, weekly, throughout life. And as they move from group to group they learn the rules of that group, of the game of life. They get to know about the other fellow. Through movement or play Johnny learns also about himself, whether his classmates consider him a "swell hitter" or an "easy out." He also soon knows what his teammates are like, if they are good or poor sports, if they will cheat in order to win or if they will play fairly. Likewise through activity Johnny learns that if he steps over this line he is out, or if he shoves and pushes other players he will be penalized. Johnny learns much about grownups, too, through games. He soon masters techniques for getting along with them with the least effort. He also discovers when is the right time to swing the bat to connect it with the ball or where to aim to hit the bull's eye. He learns how to modify games for his immediate purpose, how to play baseball in the narrow confines of the back alley or the city street. He learns to use, find, and substitute equipment in him discover what are the beautiful and the best things? Can we his environment when he wants to play a game learned at school; thus the shinny stick replaces the hockey club or the broom handle the baseball bat. Through experiences of movement, through games, through activity Johnny learns about life itself.

Can we as adults help him to learn to know, appreciate, and want the beautiful and best throughout his own life? Can we help teach him the real value of material wealth against the wealth of living a successful, abundant life which may make him and society better?

Appreciations

People continue to do throughout life things they most enjoy. Children will play baseball or prisoner's base on playgrounds, vacant lots, and in narrow city streets as long as they gain deep satisfaction from the game. This joy of playing, of participation, increases as they gain in ability. Children and adults alike choose to do the things they can do best in their leisure time. If we would build in youth a feeling of success at playing games, if we would have them like their physical education classes, we must teach physical education in such a way that coming to class, playing and learning with others is more than fun; it is a thrilling adventure.

Through games, rhythms, and other types of body movements children learn to appreciate more than the activity itself, they become cognizant of the rights and privileges of others. They may regard the adult teacher highly or they may distrust and disrespect her, for appreciations or lack of them collect and dam up within the child in whatever he is doing.

Through instruction in physical education selfish "I" drives, so markedly strong in many young children, can gradually be rechanneled to reach the deeper "We" drives. As children grow both in age and experiences of learning to share with others, to give and take, they become more mature in their social relationships. Possessing and using a "we" feeling is one sign of maturity. It must be learned if one is to live a full, happy, adjusted, and useful life.

The Value of Play

Play is one of the great physical needs of man, along with food, rest, elimination, and sex. Life abounds with the rhythm of work-play, energy breakdown—energy build-up, sorrow-joy, health-sickness. The phrase "all work and no play makes Jack a dull boy" is truer than we have been led to believe in the past. People need to get away from the drabness, dullness, and monotony of their lives whether they are six, sixteen, or sixty. They need a change to do activities that are challenging and adventurous.

What is work for one person may be play for another. The manual laborer who lays brick upon brick eight hours a day for five days is working. Winston Churchill, on the other hand, lays bricks for fun; it is one of his many hobbies. It has been said that the main difference between work and play is the degree of pleasure that comes from either. What is hard work for one is great fun for another. What one does during his hours of "off-the-job living" may be play providing it brings deep satisfaction, release from tension, is done voluntarily without pay, and gives one a change from his usual routine. Children need to be taught to play as much as they need to be taught to work, for play and work are inseparable. We work so we can play, but we play so we can work more productively. This is true of all children and of all adults.

There are three types of play: (1) motor (hitting a tennis ball, swimming, riding a bicycle, etc.), (2) sensory (watching a sunset, listening to a symphony or jazz; tasting ice cream on a hot day, etc.), and (3) intellectual (going to lectures, the movies, reading a comic book or Shakespeare). What one does during his leisure hours, as well as which type of play one favors, is largely dependent upon the amount of education he has, the place in which he lives, his age, sex, color, and sometimes his religion. But whatever be the reason one does what he does when playing, psychologists, educators, and medical authorities are agreed that regardless of age we all need to blow off steam, to get away from it all. In short, we need to play. Through activity the child and the adult are revitalized, refreshed, and recreated.

Value of Play to Children

Children are dynamic, exploratory creatures. The vast portion of their early learning comes from and through movement. One is amazed at the number of things a one year old child can do. If he is normal, throughout life he will continue to add skill upon skill until a peak limit is reached. Children find deep satisfaction in the big muscle movements of running, skipping, hopping, jumping. Joy comes in pretending, in moving to sounds, in playing tag and it, in chasing and being chased.

Some adults have erroneously believed that children, since they naturally seem to enjoy movement, pretense, and rhythms, do not need to learn how to play. These people have claimed that it is as silly to try to teach children how to play as ducks how to swim. We now realize that these oldsters knew as little about ducks as they did about children. We now believe that although play is universal, each child in each culture (whether he is a zombie, pygmy, or a freckle-faced American boy or girl) must be and is taught by adults the games of the clan, tribe, city block, plus those most favored ones of his own sex, race, religion. A boy is taught games thought best for boys. Little girls are given dolls and baby carriages. Sociologists and anthropologists call this cultural and social conditioning through play. Both tradition and education influence the child through the adult. Games such as

"Run, Sheepie, Run," "Fox and Geese," "Red Rover," are passed on down to children. They are eager to learn them, for children crave to be like grownups, to do the things adults would like them to do, to play games favored by adults. Often the cry is to "teach us a game you played when you were a little girl."

Children up until the age of three largely take part in parallel play. They are rarely interested in playing very long with other children. They refuse to share their playthings, and will scream bloody murder when the girl next door grabs their toys and runs away. As they grow older they become more social in their play interest and will voluntarily play with two or three or four others. They also become more socially conscious, more willing to share. Just how many games they will play, with how many other children they want to and can play successfully will be dependent upon their age, how well they were taught to play, when they were taught, and by whom.

Children from rural areas need directed play just as much as do city children in spite of the fact that they have wide fields in which to roam, and trees in which to climb. Indeed, among rural children this need to learn how to play with others is often intensified.

Value of Play to Older Youth

Because of differences in strength, play interests, and physical capacity, boys and girls are usually separated at the fourth grade for instruction in physical education. Boys tend to like games in which they can show their strength, while girls tend to favor rhythmical activities and team games. As each sex grows older activities are favored in which they can meet members of the opposite sex. During the adolescent period which has been often called the time of temporary disorganization, youth is awkward, ill-at-ease, moody, rebellious. He is more apt to bridge the gap successfully between childhood and adulthood if he can play several sports with more than average skill, if he has mastered some social graces fairly well or at least well enough not to be completely miserable at a social gathering. Above all, it is vastly important that somewhere between the ages of ten to fifteen skill patterns laid down in previous years be refined, reinforced, and relearned. Unless youth can dance, play tennis, swim, ride horseback or do other sport skills well, their chances for learning to do so at the age of twenty, thirty, forty or later are very small. As one grows older he is more fearful of losing face among his peers, he cannot afford to be a dub. The adult will be a most unusual person if he learns how to swim, sail a boat, or play badminton unless basic movement patterns similar to those found in these activities were learned during early life.

Value of Play to the Adult

As one grows older he tends to become sluggish and soured on life. Too often he is a victim of heartburn, headaches, or ulcers. One reason why heart disease is the chief cause of death among American people is that people burn themselves out too early; they become frustrated and unhappy, not from physical overwork, but from overworking their emotions and their minds. Some medical authorities claim that modern man works all day and worries all night. This present decade has even been called the aspirin age. *How To Win Friends and Influence People*, *The Art of Being a Real Person*, *The Mature Mind* and *Peace of Mind* have become the favorite books of this period. The American adult tends to be pleasure-mad without finding real or peace-abiding pleasure in many of the things he does or seeks. He rarely spends his leisure time leisurely. Play or recreation alone will not cure our national present-day problems or the personal problems of each citizen. It can help, however, especially if one knows how to choose the activities best suited for his age, and how to play them.

Whether or not one develops a state of physical, emotional, and mental fitness depends among other things upon the regularity of practice of good health habits. Routinized daily health habits of early childhood become habitual and tend to carry over to later life. A healthy happy childhood is the foundation upon which a healthy happy adulthood rests.

When Is One Educated?

One is never completely educated, for opportunities for more learning are everywhere at all times. When the desire for securing knowledge is lost one is at a standstill. Education involves learning, which in its last analysis means changed behavior. If a person's behavior does not change, or if his actions do not change because of the amount of education he has received, he has not learned. Time and energy have been wasted. Increasingly one is being considered educated because of what he does, rather than what he knows. Education should and must make a difference.

One is educated when he:

(1) Can communicate with others and has something of real value to communicate; when he has command of fundamental communicative arts.

(2) Can solve his own personal problems, or knows how to go about solving them and is working toward a solution, and is actively engaged in helping to solve the bigger problems of society.

(3) Knows how to live abundantly, and knows the things he can do in order to use his body best when he is a child, youth, adult, aged citizen.

(4) Can make a living doing the things which to him bring satisfaction, which to him are creative.

(5) Can accept sorrow; when he can find happiness.

When Is One Physically Educated?

One is never completely physically educated, for each year of life brings new adjustments which must be made, new techniques which must be mastered. Physical education, like education in general, is continuous. It can be measured or evaluated by what one does, how one lives, how one uses himself. Those who have taken courses in this subject in schools should act differently than those who have not had this opportunity.

As the twig is bent, so grows the tree. The kind of an education the child receives determines the kind of an adult he will be. What type of a product do we want to turn out from our schools and colleges? What kind of boys and girls do we want to put our stamp of approval on or pass in our classes as physical education teachers?

An individual is physically educated when he:

(1) Knows about his body and how to use it wisely, whether he is six, sixteen, or sixty.

(2) Knows how to do one or more individual sports with above average ability and gains satisfaction for having participated.

(3) Knows how to do one or more team sports with above average ability and gains satisfaction from participating.

(4) Knows how to move his body gracefully to rhythm, how to do one or more social, folk, or square dances.

(5) Knows how to save himself from drowning.

(6) Knows how to use his body without undue fatigue.

(7) Can move through space at different speeds with ease, can change directions, can judge distances.

(8) Can throw balls of varying sizes with a fair degree of accuracy.

(9) Can hit, strike, kick, and catch moving objects with a fair degree of accuracy.

(10) Can hit stationary and moving targets with a fair degree of accuracy.

(11) Can fit into several groups and contribute to each one.

(12) Is happy, and has a zest for living.

(13) Does a wide variety of activities in his leisure time regardless of age.

(14) Has periodic medical and dental check-ups and has remedial defects corrected.

(15) Has regulated daily health habits.

This list may be incomplete but it will serve as a guide for youth and adults, pupils and educators. Teachers of physical education, like all other educators in the public school and on the college campus need to determine for themselves *what* they are trying to do through their teaching, and *how* they are going to bring about learning or changed behavior among their students. The most difficult task may be determining those objectives, not accomplishing them.

Someone has once compared teaching to taking a trip. First you must choose the place you want to go, next you must discover how you are to get there in the most economical way in time, money, and energy, and then to gain the real satisfaction from your planning, your dreams, you must go.

Whether or not civilization will endure during our age of ever-increasing wars at more frequent intervals depends upon the greatest race the world has ever known, or seen—the race between education and world destruction. Education of the present type or kind will neither cure nor save the world. For if education will win the race it must find new and better methods of changing selfish "I" drives to "We" drives in people and in nations. It must devise new ways to change immaturity into maturity. It must help a sick society full of feelings of fear, frustration, and futility become a healthy one full of courage. It must help each person to help himself to find and live an abundant life. This is a challenge education must accept.

Suggested Readings

Brownell, Clifford and Hagman, Patricia, *Physical Education— Foundations and Principles*, New York, McGraw-Hill Co., 1951.

Conant, James B., *Education in a Divided World*, Cambridge, Massachusetts, Harvard University Press, 1948.

Cowell, Charles, *Scientific Foundations of Physical Education*, New York, Harper Brothers, 1953.

Educational Policies Commission, *Education for All American Youth*, Washington, D. C., National Educational Association, 1944.

LaSalle, Dorothy, *Guidance of Children Through Physical Education*, New York, A. S. Barnes, 1946.

Menninger, K. A., *Man Against Himself*, New York, Harcourt Brace, 1938.

Mitchell, Elmer and Mason, B. S., *The Theory of Play*, New York, A. S. Barnes, 1948.

Nash, Jay B., Moensch, Francis, and Sanborn, Jeannette, *Physical Education, Organization and Administration*, New York, A. S. Barnes, 1951.

Oberteuffer, Delbert, *Physical Education*, New York, Harper Brothers, 1951.

Plant, James, *Personality and the Cultural Pattern*, New York, Commonwealth Fund, 1939.

Rugg, Harold and Shumaker, Ann, *The Child Centered School*, Yonkers, New York, World Book Company, 1928.

Samuels, Gertrude, "Too Much Murder or Not Enough?", Magazine Section, *New York Times*, November 30, 1947.

Sharmon, Jackson, *Introduction to Physical Education*, New York, A. S. Barnes, 1934.

Williams, Jesse Feiring, *Principles of Physical Education*, 5th ed., Philadelphia, W. B. Saunders Co., 1948.

Part Two

THE WHO

Good teaching is guiding people to help themselves. It can be a conducted tour shared by teachers and children through a world of thrilling experiences.

Children are not miniature adults. We, who are older, must increasingly help them to develop their own personalities. Above all, we should help them to find true happiness.

Chapter 2

The Teacher

The teacher of physical education on the elementary level may be the regular classroom teacher or the specialized physical educator. Often in smaller schools it is the teacher, who in a self-contained classroom assumes the responsibility of teaching all subjects offered in the curriculum. In the larger city system, however, it is the trained physical educator who is in charge of the program. It is also customary in larger public schools to separate the sexes from the fourth grade level on through high school for instructional purposes, and for the girls to be taught by a woman and the boys by a man. However, the sexes should not be completely separated at and following the fourth grade level. There are many coeducational activities which should be included in the program. Just how often coeducational classes should meet depends upon desired objectives to be realized.

Who Should Teach Physical Education In Primary Grades?

There are arguments pro and con to this question. Some educators believe that it is better for the children in the primary grades to have their physical education classes and playground periods supervised by their own classroom teacher. Those who believe in this school of thought claim that since play is so significant it is important for the teacher, who will be with the children for the longest period of time, to see how they play so that she can best guide them into desirable physical and social growth patterns. Other educators hold that only those persons trained and certified to teach physical education activities do so. Those who cling to this line of thought believe that children learn faster when they are taught correctly from the beginning by a trained physical educator.

In smaller schools the classroom teacher usually is the only one available to give instruction in all subjects offered in each grade. This includes basic skill in the broad fields of language arts, physical education, art, and music. In schools organized under the self-contained classroom plan the teacher must be a jack of all trades. Too often she is master of none, or of fewer than she might be, had she less responsibilities.

It is imperative that the person selected to teach physical education be the best one available. The teacher above all should be the one most skilled in methods of teaching children through physical activities. Such a person may well be the classroom teacher, especially in the first three grades.

Throughout the country the generally accepted plan is for: (1) the physical education classes to be taught by the classroom teacher under a qualified supervisor; (2) classroom teachers with special preparation or special teachers of physical education for elementary schools; and (3) special teachers for secondary schools.

Teacher Preparation

Physical educators must be certified to teach this subject by the state in which the training was received. Although states vary considerably in specific requirements to be met, the majority of them require over twenty hours of specialized training for a major in this field. Broad training areas center around theory and practical courses in activities, organization and administration, principles and methods of teaching physical education. Ten to twelve hours in the biological sciences including anatomy, kinesiology, physiology, and hygiene are usually required. Supervised practice teaching is required in most states for certification. Gradually teacher certification standards are being raised throughout the country on both the elementary and secondary levels. This is a hopeful trend, for better selected and prepared teachers should produce better educational results.

In-Service Training

Granted that a trained physical educator would be more apt to teach this subject successfully than one untrained in this area, classroom teachers can and often do a splendid job teaching physical education on the elementary level. If the teacher is sincerely interested in helping children grow into becoming healthy citizens, well rounded in physical and social skills, she will seek help in order to learn more about the field. Summer school courses can be of great value if they are taken in the area of physical education for elementary schools and are taught by experienced leaders.

The teacher can also gain aid from writing to the director of physical education at the local state university, as well as to the state director of physical education at the state capitol. She can also receive helpful suggestions from the Executive Secretary, American Association for Health, Physical Education, and Recreation, 1201 Sixteenth Street, Northwest St., Washington, D. C. Subscribing to the monthly Journal of Health and Physical Education, the official publication of this association, should prove most helpful. Trained physical educators in her own locality can often be found who might be of great assistance. People usually like to help others.

The Role of the Supervisor

It is increasingly becoming the practice in many American schools for the classroom teacher, who may be unprepared to teach physical education, to be under the supervision of a highly trained and experienced teacher. This form of guided in-service training can be of invaluable assistance. Together the expert and novice in this specialized field should plan, carry out, and evaluate a physical education program for which each particular grade teacher has responsibility. All such teachers in the entire elementary school should have regularly scheduled group conferences with the supervisor to establish goals to be accomplished, program content for each grade, and testing procedures to be used. In this way each grade teacher can see the relationship and contribution her program has with that of all other teachers in the school.

The role of the supervisor should be that of guiding the teachers, and as such he or she will be most successful if democratic methods of leadership are used. Guidance in its broadest sense means helping others to help themselves. Democratic leadership rests upon the principle that a real leader makes more leaders. As the expert consultant the supervisor should help all teachers grow in their understanding of the importance of skills in teaching children through physical activities. The supervisor should periodically visit each classroom teacher to observe the effectiveness of both her teaching and program—their strengths and weaknesses—and acting in the role of a co-worker aid the teacher to improve in those areas in which assistance is needed. The regular classroom teacher should be visited under her poorest and best teaching situations. Above all no special program should be prepared to impress the supervisor. A friendly atmosphere should prevail throughout the supervisor's visit. In modern education "snoopervision"—as supervision was once called and practiced—is as outdated and passé as teacher-dominated classes and dictatorial school administrators.

Qualities Necessary for the Physical Education Teacher

The qualities most desired in a physical educator are the same as those desired in any other teacher. All good teachers in any field must have technical skills, personality, integrity, and good health. They must have a genuine and sincere feeling for people, in contrast to a feeling for things. They must know how to use desirable methods of democratic leadership, realizing that a good leader is also a follower at times, and that a real leader aids others to develop good leadership traits. A teacher is like a good parent —both want to help children to help themselves to grow into strong, healthy, useful individuals and group members.

Teaching requires much stamina. One has to be physically fit to withstand the wear and tear of being with children over a long period of time. Too often weary, foot-sore teachers project their own feelings of fatigue, disappointment, and angered pent-up emotions upon children. This is a fairly safe victim choice, for children are less apt to fight back than adult colleagues. Teachers, like their youngsters, need to be able to get away from it all through recreative play. Increasingly, they must do themselves what they want others to do. Emerson's phrase of "what you *are* sounds so loudly in my ears that I cannot hear a word you are saying" is well worth remembering! If one wants to teach physical education she must herself be physically educated, as well as have a deep desire to help others become educated in this field.

Desirable Principles and Philosophy

Principles, or basic beliefs regarding what is known from all fields of knowledge, should guide all teachers; these are the foundations upon which one's philosophy of teaching, of education, and of life are built.

Teachers continually search for short cuts in their work, practical ways in which to solve their problems. Such solutions come best out of each individual's experiences. They cannot be passed on too successfully from one person to another. Bernard Shaw believed that if you teach a man anything he will never learn. Materials in this book can be valuable to the readers only when tried and improved upon, modified, or reshaped to fit into their own unique situation, and when they are added to things learned from their own experiences. Suggested teaching methods, materials, and books will be, however, most valuable to readers when they have been rooted in educationally sound principles. Both basic beliefs and objectives require continual modification as we push further back to explore into regions previously marked "unknown." One's philosophy must keep pace with the result of man's eternal quest to *know*, and to find out *why*.

Principles of Teaching

Teaching is both an art and a science. To some, it is a struggle, a bore, a job in which one does too much work for too little pay. To others teaching is a joy, an adventure, a challenge. To still others it is a service to be rendered to mankind.

Each teacher's philosophy—whatever it is—governs, colors, spurs on or retards her results in working with others. The best and most fruitful gleanings can come only from those in the profession who enjoy working with others. Such teachers improve constantly in their methods and continue to grow professionally. Principles basic to education are:

(1) People are educable.
(2) Every experience from which people learn involves their whole being.
(3) Education goes on wherever there is life. It can be good or bad depending upon the teacher in the learning environment.

Principles basic to teaching are:

(1) Everyone can learn something.
(2) Learning means changed behavior.
(3) The learner masters materials more readily if he shares in the planning, doing, and evaluation of what he is to learn.
(4) Teaching is largely motivating people to want to do things.
(5) The learner, in reality, teaches himself. The role of the

teacher is to help him find short cuts toward mastery and satisfaction in accomplishment.

(6) Good teaching is guiding people to help themselves.

(7) Teaching can be a conducted tour shared by the teacher and learner through a thrilling world of experience.

(8) The most fruitful results accrue in a warm, kindly, friendly atmosphere, in which the learner feels secure.

(9) Good teaching is progressive. Skills, knowledges, and appreciations are built upon each other.

(10) Good teaching develops initiative, self-reliance, confidence, and independence.

Each teacher should discover her own methods based upon these and other educational principles. It is this leader who is the key to successful accomplishments in physical education, more so than adequate or elaborate facilities and equipment, small classes or sufficient time given to the program. Often the best instructors in the field have the poorest equipment with which to work, the most crowded room space. Creative master teachers are few. Resourcefulness, coupled with enthusiasm, can sometimes produce better results than superior technical knowledge and training.

Integration

Physical education offers many opportunities for integration with other subjects, such as with:

(1) Arithmetic—counting, scoring, laying out courts.

(2) Art—making costumes, posters, scenery, charts, and creating dances.

(3) Language arts—speaking distinctly in games, dramatizing stories, choral speaking, reading and writing game rules, keeping squad records.

(4) Music—working with rhythms of all types, making and playing various kinds of instruments.

(5) Social studies—folk dances, playing period games, developing understanding and appreciation of other persons and groups, developing group consciousness, leadership-followership activities.

(6) Science and health—building desirable health habits and attitudes, developing physical fitness, good body mechanics, planning one's rest, work, and play daily schedule.

(7) Practical arts—making and repairing game equipment, laying out play areas.

Class Organization

Physical education classes are often vastly overcrowded. The ideal number of pupils per class is thirty-five. Lack of sufficient time, poor facilities and inadequate equipment coupled with large numbers of pupils present gigantic problems to the teacher. Careful planning for the best type of class organization possible will result in more fruitful results. Pupils should assist the instructor in planning, conducting, and evaluating the program on each grade level. Primary children can gradually be given more responsibilities in determining what they will do, how they will learn the subject matter, and finally in evaluating their results.

The Use of Squads

Squads can be started as early as the end of the first half of the first grade. Ideally they should be started when the pupils have reached that stage in their social development which enables them to move easily in groups. The squad leader may be selected for the first time by the teacher but the children should be given opportunities to select their own leader by the second and/or third week of each semester. The length of the leadership period can best be pupil-teacher determined. Elements of leadership are superior knowledge and skills. These take time, patience, and determination to develop. Some children are seemingly born leaders but others can be taught how to lead, too. It is important, however, that every child be given an opportunity to be in a key position in the class several times each semester, either as the squad leader or the leader of some specific activity.

Duties of the squad leader include:

(1) Checking the attendance of squads.
(2) Assisting the teacher in planning the daily weekly, and semester's program.
(3) Assisting the teacher with demonstrations, and helping each squad member learn each activity.
(4) Assisting the teacher and squads to evaluate the program.
(5) Setting patterns of example for the others to follow of good sportsmanship, and fellowship.
(6) Checking equipment in and out to squad; assisting in repairing the equipment.

A good teacher becomes progressively unnecessary. After the pupils have been taught a number of games they can be given opportunities to play their favorite ones during the supervised free play period on the playground or in the gymnasium. Suggested techniques for letting the children choose what they want to play are:

(1) Assign a play space to each squad leader who will remain at the space while each squad rotates around each leader who will lead the same game to each squad which has been assigned to him by the teacher.

(2) Assign a play space to each group of ten to fifteen children who want to play a specific game. The entire squad would play the game all period. A variation of this method would be to have each squad made up of three who want to play two or three of the same specific games throughout the period.

(3) Assign each squad leader to a specific area and give one an opportunity to choose the game or games he would like to play. Other pupils who also want to play those games with that particular leader can join his group.

(4) Assign each squad and their leader to a specific piece of equipment and have all squad groups rotate around to each piece during the period.

Use of Student Leaders

A good teacher often leads from behind. If teaching is guiding people to learn how to help themselves to become independent and to grow as citizens, then boys and girls must learn early in life how to solve their own and group problems, how to cooperate, choose leaders, how to follow, as well as how to lead others.

The use of a squad leader can produce more efficient, effective teaching. It can also enable the teacher to work more in the role of a supervisor. As soon as possible, however, the pupils should select the leader they believe to be most qualified. A Leader's Club may be organized at the fourth grade level as a means of teaching pupils how to lead. This group should meet regularly with the teacher to plan and evaluate the work to be done with the rest of the students. The group may also learn new activities to be presented later in class. Squad leaders may serve for a semester's term, or be changed more frequently. The former method adds unity to the program as well as increased leadership skill, whereas the latter passes leadership opportunities around, just as a ball is passed from one to another.

Younger children often tend to dominate rather than democratically lead others. All groups in our culture, regardless of age, must have additional training and experience in choosing leaders wisely, in leading and following others. Mankind has always felt the need for good leadership, for the history of the world shows that we have never had enough leaders in the right places at the right time. The elementary school is the rich soil in which children can develop those traits necessary for good leadership.

Suggested Readings

Broady, Lois and French, Esther, *Health and Physical Education in Small Schools*, Lincoln, Nebraska, University of Nebraska Press, 1942.

Bucher, Charles, *Foundations of Physical Education*, St. Louis, C. V. Mosby, 1952.

Clarke, Harrison, "Select Your Physical Education Teacher With Care," *Education*, 68:465–468, April, 1948.

Davis, Elwood and Lawther, John, *Successful Teaching In Physical Education*, New York, Prentice-Hall, 1948.

Department of Supervisors and Directors of Instruction, *Leadership at Work*, Fifteenth Yearbook, Washington, D. C., National Education Association, 1943.

Manley, Helen, *Health Education for the Elementary School*, Washington, D. C., United States Office of Education, 1947.

Oberteuffer, Delbert, *Physical Education*, New York, Harper Brothers, 1951.

Prall, Charles and Cushman, Leslie, *Teacher Education in Service*, Washington, D. C., American Council on Education, 1944.

Report of the National Conference on Undergraduate Preparation in Physical Education, Health Education, and Recreation, Jackson's Mills, West Virginia, May 16–27, 1948, Chicago, Illinois, Athletic Institute.

Sharmon, Jackson, "Preparation for the Professors of Physical Education," *Journal of Health and Physical Education*, 6:11–13, 58–59, December, 1935.

Sharmon, Jackson, *The Teaching of Physical Education*, New York, A. S. Barnes, 1936.

Troester, Carl A., "A Specialized Curriculum for Training Elementary School Teachers," *Journal of Health and Physical Education, 16*:250–251, 285–286, May, 1945.

Woodward, R. S. and Marquis, D. G., *Psychology*, New York, Henry Holt, 1947.

The Child

Each child reacts to others according to his own growth patterns. Although teachers have long claimed allegiance to this belief, too often many of them compare Johnny, age ten, with Jackie, age ten, or Mary, age six, with Alice, age five, or lump all children in one grade together as a group comparing this year's batch with last.

If it is true that each child is an individual then we must teach him individually and know his own unique growth pattern. Johnny, age five, may be an uncooperative bully, but his social growth by his tenth year, when compared to behavior patterns of the five previous years, may show remarkable progress.

Growth is influenced by many environmental and physical factors. Proper development can be retarded by sibling rivalry, constant criticisms and rebuffs, unbalanced by lack of praise for things done well or even tried, or feelings of guilt welling up within from being called "bad" or "naughty." Lack of the right amount of proper foods, not enough sunshine and rugged outdoor play can hold a child back from developing along lines in his own unique growth channels. Increasingly parents are wearing their children out by pushing them into too many activities. Boys and girls who are going to school have room in their already full lives to work and play for one or, at the very most, two additional activities a week. Foolish is the parent who has her child taking dancing, music, and figure skating lessons or other outside activities during the busy school year, for childhood is the time for few responsibilities and the high adventure of discovery.

Growth might be compared to a ladder, each rung representing a developmental stage. Each child must progress up three such ladders, one marked physical growth, the second social growth, the third mental growth. Every boy and girl must climb up to, and pass, each developmental rung, for there can be no skipping. The best adjusted youngsters are those whose progress up all three growth ladders is relatively even. Thus adults will claim a child reacts like most other ten year old children if that child is ten years in physical growth, socially advanced to levels of behavior characteristic of the average ten year old child, and can learn materials suitable for his mental age. Other youngsters may be five in chronological age and physical development, may be eight from the standpoint of mental age, but only comparable to the average three year old child in social development. It is imperative that all teachers study the special needs and growth patterns of each individual child. Although growth cannot be forced it can be encouraged, for children, like plants, grow best in a warm, favorable environment. Both plants and children suffer from neglect and overnourishment. Skillful, wise handling can aid all growing things to find the best that life contains.

Teachers need to learn more about each pupil, his rate of development, as well as where he is in his own developmental stage. Chronological age of a single year's space is of little help. Age groupings which include a two or three year span may be more accurate and meaningful. Although it is relatively easy for the teacher to distinguish between boys and girls, colored and white children, it is more difficult to see maturation levels. Thus, not all children in the first grade can and will learn to skip correctly even though a majority may do so. The child who has difficulty may not learn to skip until he reaches the third grade, but meanwhile he may learn to do other motor skills better than anyone else in his class. It is imperative that the teacher discover with each child things in which he can excel. This will yield more fruitful results than if she concentrated on trying to bring all pupils up to an unobtainable average in a chosen activity. Each child needs to be helped to accomplish the best he can do according to his own ability. Teachers should study each one carefully to discover what his maturation levels are as well as his differences, for these provide the basis upon which a rich personality may be built. A sign of a well taught class is the number of varied personalities of the pupils who have been allowed to remain as each one is—unique and individual.

The age span during which most children attend the elementary school is a difficult one to study. In seeking greater independence children often become hostile toward adults, or listen more to their peers than to their parents. Motives for actions are often concealed. From their point of view, children are more removed from any other age groups than their own. Mere babies are children a year younger, adults are but one or two years beyond. Faced with the dichotomy of "acting like a man" and being treated as a baby, of being "too big to cry" and not being trusted out of sight, children are more confused than we adults realize we have made them. Although grownups, including the teacher, may count for little in the eyes and world of the child, adults must provide much more guidance and help him grow in his own sight and his own world. Greater knowledge is needed to help children in their stages of confusion and *when* to keep hands off. Teachers, if they are worthy of the name, push children gently away from them— they do not keep them clutched to their breasts. Man cannot fly if he is chained to an abyss—learning how to fly can only come from learning how to stay aloft, from having tried.

It has often been said that the difference between an adult and a child is the difference between *being* and *becoming*. This implies that one must grow into adulthood, and that children change into becoming adults slowly and often painfully.

Basic Needs of All Children

Needs basic to all children are: (1) physiological, (2) social, and (3) ego or self needs. If children can best grow in the friendly, warm, healthy environment of school, gymnasium, and playground, answers to these inward pressures must be met. If and when these needs are ignored, submerged, or thwarted the child becomes disturbed, rebellious, delinquent. Although ideally the home, community, and school should work together as a team to provide for these inward urges, there are some cases of alarming neglect from any or all of the three in many of our public schools. When home and/or community factors exert negative influence the school must assume greater responsibility. Teachers need be much more informed of the background of each pupil than they are; only then behavior otherwise unexplainable suddenly can become understandable.

Physiological Needs

Food, elimination, rest, exercise, and fresh air are the center of all human needs. Proper balance between rest and activity is of great importance to the health of the elementary school youngster. Children must have daily from four to six hours of big muscle activity that involves running, jumping, and hopping. They need eight to ten hours of sleep nightly, plus one hour daily of quiet, restful activity. Many elementary schools provide cots or pallets for mid-morning and mid-afternoon naps. Wisely, little if any homework is assigned so that the children are free to choose what they want to do in their leisure time after-school hours. It is important that children use this time to explore, roam, wander, and play games in which there are no set rules nor anyone giving them directions. It is vital that they play with their peers. Children who can play together away from watchful adults grow as individuals and as group members. It is the lonely isolated child suffering from deep fears of insecur'ty who often is frail and sickly.

In a study made of children in elementary schools in New York, it was found that 42 per cent of them got less than eight hours sleep, and that only one half of the group had any form of outdoor recreation. The same study discovered that 75 per cent drank insufficient milk, that 50 per cent had poorly balanced diets, and that 25 per cent of the children drank tea and coffee regularly.[1] These figures are typical of the situation throughout the country and have been found to be approximately the same in numerous similar studies of later date. Each teacher should check the health habits of all pupils in order to gain further insight regarding their health habits.

Social Needs

These needs are especially strong among all people of all ages. We all need to (1) belong, (2) feel secure, (3) gain recognition, and (4) be loved. These inner pressures are often intensified among children.

Behavior patterns are laid down early in life. Personality prob-

[1] F. O. O'Neill and M. G. McCormick, "*Everyday Behavior of Elementary School Children*," Albany, New York, University of the State of New York, Bulletin No. 1057, 1934.

lems among adults usually are traced back to early home or school conditions or incidents. Children, regardless of age, need to belong, to be a part of a group. Those who have few, if any friends, who are always alone, or are the last one chosen, who are crowd fringers rather than joiners are greatly in need of a friend. The teacher can best help such a child belong by aiding him to develop extra skills and abilities. She can push the youngster gently forward in the eyes of other children. Care must be taken that the child does not cling to the teacher friend, but gradually be weaned away.

Children must feel secure in what they are doing if they are to do their best. Two circumstances contribute greatly to insecurity: (1) feelings of not being wanted, and (2) a disturbed home life. Instability resulting from either or both can literally wreck a boy or girl, or an adult.

Day-by-day relationship with adults can build feelings of security. Teachers must, like parents, be consistent in methods of dealing with youth. One can not laugh on one occasion at conduct which two days later may bring punishment or disapproval. Insecure adult teachers who vacillate between being "a good egg" and "a sour puss," a friendly advisor and a hostile enemy confuse children. They cause those who are already insecure to be more so.

Studies show that children favor teachers who are firm, strict but fair, who do not show favoritism, and who are friendly and really like them. They dislike most teachers who are bossy, who do not know what to do in a situation but try to bluff their way out of it, and who are careless in their own appearance.

Children crave to be noticed, to be "first," and to be singled out. When this need is thwarted and they fail to gain such recognition legitimately, they will get it by negative methods. Deceitfulness, tattling, bragging, stealing, or other such measures may be resorted to in extreme cases. "I can run further than *you*" or "my Dad can lick *your* Dad" are expressions of this normal need. Recognition should be given to all not only by the adult but by the other children as well. This can be made in the form of simple phrases such as "Johnny, you are really getting that step now" or "Mary did the best in this group today," or "Alice learned how to do this faster than anyone yesterday." It can also be given by posting names on bulletin boards of those who won class honors and class events, or squad members who played most coopera- tively for a two week period. Children are not as interested in elaborate awards, such as cups or pins, as they are in receiving earned praise from adults and their peers. Although youth craves the approval of adults still more they crave recognition from their friends.

Children also need love—the kind that says "I trust you," "I know you can do it," "Let's figure out how we can do that better," the kind that is consistent. Boys and girls need the security of knowing that adults will be available for help if they need it. They need to feel that the adult cares about their welfare and their pressing problems. Adults need to remember that love or friend- ship is not a weapon, a big stick, or a favor to be used, denied, or removed when "Johnny is bad." We need in our society today to love each other truly, using love in the religious sense and not as in the popular songs or radio advertisement. Love, the highest emotion of the human being, is too often expressed by our cheapest phrases. Thus, foreigners find it difficult to understand how we can *love* that flavor or *adore* that book.

The American school has too long neglected to answer these basic needs of pupils. Too frequently little balance between ac- tivity and rest has been maintained; frequently only the superior children or the motor morons are singled out for praise or ridi- cule; all too often the extreme pressing concern of the pupil for the approval of his classmates is overlooked; all too readily we like children only when they do what *we* want them to do, or perform according to our adult standards.

Children are *not* miniature adults. They are children who can and will grow into becoming adults. As teachers we can help them or we can be their stumbling block. We can aid them by provid- ing for their basic needs. We can retard them or even be their albatross when we teach games, sports, or facts, and not primarily teach children through activities.

Ego or Self Needs

The need to be loved, to feel wanted, and to have a sense of security which is pressing among all children should be met in the school as well as the home. Children must also develop a sense of pride in themselves, a type of self-respect without egotism. They will acquire this self-respect from others according to their achievements. Teachers are morally responsible to see that each pupil receives praise for what he has accomplished each class period.

Youth must be aided to accept and make necessary compromises with life. They must know how to accept limitations and how to work, play, and live effectively within these boundaries. Those who are physically handicapped need to learn early in life how to compensate for their handicap and how to work around it.

Conflicts That Arise from Unfilled Needs

Physical, egotistic or self, and social needs fuse together and become closely interwoven to cause behavior. If a child's needs are gratified, he is a happy, well-balanced individual; when they clash, become thwarted, or submerged, atypical behavior often results unless the child can be taught to sublimate or re-channel these drives into socially approved patterns. Regression, introversion, segregation, rationalization, dissociation, and projection are escape mechanisms through which the child may avoid self-realization or insight.

Regression means returning or going back to childish behavior. First graders who do not get their way with their playmates often resort to foot stamping, temper tantrums, or other antics characteristic of three year olds.

Introversion frequently results from deep fears of inadequacy from which the child may escape reality through excessive day dreams. Children unskilled in play techniques often wander off from the group and sit watching others have fun. Basically such children often want to join their peer group but are held back by fears of failure.

In all children there is the ever-present possibility for the flood waters of pent-up feelings to gush out when ideas and emotions clash. Unless they have mastered the fine art of self-control, mere trifles that exert pressure upon an emotional sore spot can send them flying off into a rage. They become upset, broken up, or dissociated at tiny incidents that previously untouched them. They may not only "fly off the handle" but strike back at classmates verbally and otherwise. A pupil who is teased by his peers because he is afraid to be at bat in a baseball game may suddenly turn on them and lash out at these tormentors. The child may or may not be aware that he is afraid to bat but also of many other things as well. Because he wishes to hide his "horrible secret" from others he may suddenly charge at them like a wild animal. This action expresses a form of dissociation common among children.

At school the child who deeply distrusts or resents the adult teacher may be afraid to show these feelings. He feels safe, on the other hand, in releasing his pent-up frustrations upon his classmates. They, not the teacher, become the butt of his pugnaciousness. Prejudice, intolerance, excessive criticism, and cynicism are closely related to projection. One becomes adept in discovering those discrepancies others display that he knows are also his own, regardless of age.

Wise is the teacher who recognizes sudden antisocial behavior in pupils as an expression for a need for adventure. Allowing the child to get away with it is not the answer if the actions are repeated. However, the child has had the thrill of trying, and usually passes on into his next growth pattern stage. The teacher's attitude toward the child here again is the most important. Getting the other children in on finding how they can help the offender solve the problem is suggested.

Recognition

This wish is apparent in all age groups. Some gain it in socially approved ways, others find it through exceptional or antisocial behavior. In class some children will early gain peer recognition by being fair or cheaters in their play, physically adept or poorly coordinated, a willing follower or a rebellious leader. This drive to display or improve skill mastery is intensified in some children. Pupils must legitimately receive recognition and praise from adults and their classmates. Every child can do some things better than anyone else, and should receive recognition for that ability providing it is one socially approved.

Characteristics of Children

The following chart shows the characteristics of children age five through twelve.

Table 1

CHARACTERISTICS OF CHILDREN, AGE 5–12

AGE	PHYSICAL	SOCIAL
5–7	Soft bones Rapid growth Best in big muscle activities Extremely active Emphasis upon energy and speed Rapid development in eye control Narrow stance Heart growing rapidly	Questions continually Craves attention Independent Seeks adult approval Selfishly egocentric Slight interest in groups Slight desire to share Sex interests beginning to differ

MENTAL	PLAY ACTIVITIES
Lacks ability to concentrate Short attention span Imaginative Initiative Intense on "my or mine" Exchanges ideas with peers	Running Slides Balls (large) Climbing Balls, beanbags Jumping ropes Singing games Tag and "It"

AGE	PHYSICAL	SOCIAL
8–10	Rapid growth—average 2″ per year Frequent fatigue Nutritional disturbances Gaining control of small muscles of hands, feet, and body Body movement more rhythmical Medium height for age 8—49″ medium weight 55 lbs. Medium height for age 9—51″ medium weight 64 lbs. Medium height for age 10—54″ medium weight 70 lbs.	More group conscious Evidence of cooperation Eager to learn Adventurous Attitudes and appreciations developing Interested in accomplishing things begun

MENTAL	PLAY ACTIVITIES
Initiative Imaginative Creative Craves to know why Rapid development of motor co-ordinations Skill in judgment and timing	Puzzles Marbles Stunts and tumbling competition

Table 1 (continued)
CHARACTERISTICS OF CHILDREN, AGE 5–12

AGE	PHYSICAL	SOCIAL
10–12	Rapid growth, change in organs Girls developing faster than boys Skill growth marked Sex characteristics developing Increased muscular coordination Heart growing rapidly	Gang stage Loyalty Appreciates team play Self-conscience Little interest in the opposite sex Desire to be independent, strong Adventurous Developing into individual Strong attachment to an admired adult

MENTAL	PLAY ACTIVITIES
Rapid growth in ability to concentrate Struggle between being realistic and idealistic Can see through things more rapidly Increased ability to judge things well Interested in own growth patterns and physical development	Rhythmic activities Interest in gaining skill proficiency More coordinated movements Individual stunts and self-testing activities Strength tests

Not all children will fit into the growth characteristics listed above according to his age. However, the majority of them will. The teacher should realize that a child of 5 to 7 is undergoing a most important transition. Because of his boundless energy, never-ending curiosity as a "doing" creature, adults must be on the lookout with him that he maintains a careful balance between active and passive play.

As children grow in age, skill, and ability to play with others they should not engage in competition with children less advanced. The transition from early childhood to adolescence is one of remarkable progress. In schools, children should have increased opportunities for real responsibilities, as well as increased freedom to select, do for themselves, and evaluate their own progress. Growth, like education, is a long, tedious process.

The characteristics of a healthy child are: an abundance of vitality, bright, clear eyes, lustrous hair, good muscle tone, clear skin, good teeth, a hearty appetite, and freedom from remedial defects. Such a child gains progressively in weight and height. A healthy child is happy: he radiates and sparkles. An unhealthy child tires rapidly, is irritable, seems and is dull.

The Six Year Old

Six year olds are eager to learn! They are often overactive and tire easily. Although they are less cooperative than they were at five, they are beginning to learn how to use their whole bodies. Often they are boastful and eager to show others how well they can fight. Interest periods are relatively short but are gradually increasing in length. Acting things out, as well as all other such forms of spontaneous dramatizations, are favored pastimes.

Children of this age need increased opportunity to take part in big muscle activities of many kinds. Teachers can best work with them by giving them indirect supervision with minimum interference. Increased opportunities for making decisions might well be provided.

The Seven Year Old

The seven year old suddenly seems to become sensitive to the feelings and attitudes of adults. Fear of their disapproval causes him to be less anxious to try many things than to do a few well. Fairy stories, rhymes, myths, nature stories, comic characters bring delight to him. Although he is becoming increasingly more capable of some abstract thinking he learns best in concrete terms and through activity. Boastfulness and exaggerated cocksureness show that he often prefers the word fight to fighting.

Both teachers and parents should help the seven year old find the right combination between independence and dependence. Warm, encouraging, friendly relations between the child and the adult are imperative.

The Eight Year Old

Although the eight year old regresses to becoming dependent upon Mother or Teacher again, he also is gradually becoming more interested in others. Gang life becomes a part of his play pattern. Although he may appear to be noisy, aggressive, and argumentative to adults, he tends to favor adult supervised activities. Collections of all kinds fill his pockets, his bedroom, or den.

He may have more accidents than when seven due to his increased daringness.

Special needs of the eight year old include receiving much praise and encouragement from adults. Wise supervision from friendly grownups can help him belong to groups. Opportunities to develop control over small intricate muscles should be provided. Wood carving, making model airplanes, sewing, sketching, and other forms of arts and crafts can furnish channels for needed creative urges.

The Nine Year Old

By the age of nine most children have formed a reasonably strong sense of right and wrong although they may argue long and loud over fairness in games, or decisions of referees. Prolonged interest and carefully laid out plans become increasingly apparent. Stories of other lands and people and love for his country cause him to desire to become a good citizen, to do a good deed daily. Much time is spent with gang members discussing people and events in his own environment. Active rough and tumble play keeps the nine year old on the go.

Children of this age need to be given frank answers to their questions about sex; they need to belong to a gang they can be loyal to, and should have increased responsibilities around home, school, and community. Training in the advanced skills, such as learning to kick a ball or hit a target in the correct way, should gradually be included in the physical education program for both sexes.

The Adolescent

Although there is a wide range of individual differences in maturity levels among this age group, certain generalizations can be made of the adolescent. He prefers his gang to his girl friend and will be often more loyal to this gang than to his own parents. Although there is a marked interest difference between the sexes, both tend to like best team games, pets, television shows, radio programs, and comic books. Teasing and other forms of antagonism between boy and girl groups is a favorite pastime. Although the majority of adolescents tend to be overcritical and rebellious, and have an "I know it all" attitude, some few do not display these characteristics. Nail-biting, day-dreaming, and often impudence show a regressed return to habits characteristic of younger children. Fear of ridicule, of being different becomes a nightmare.

The adolescent needs to know about and understand emotional and physical changes happening within him. A sense of belonging to a peer group coupled with increased opportunities for independence are paramount. Adult guidance which is friendly and unobtrusive enough not to threaten his need for freedom is necessary. Increased opportunities for the adolescent to earn and spend his own money, pick out his own clothes, and set his own daily routine should be provided. Membership in clubs which work toward a "worthy cause" should be encouraged.

Skill mastery is one of the great desires of youth. They long to surpass others in strength, speed, and accuracy. Strict physical training to gain team membership is willingly accepted and should be encouraged.

Atypical and Exceptional Children

The majority of children attending public schools are normal. However, there is a small percentage who suffer from physical, emotional, and mental handicaps. These children require additional attention. Since all children should take physical education no student should be excused from his class because of defects. The social values of play are greater than adults have formerly believed. A neurotic, psychotic, or disturbed child first shows evidence of emotional illness when he withdraws from the crowd and refuses to play. Yet psychiatrists tell us that, oddly enough, the first sign of recovery from emotional involvement among all ages is the sudden desire to be active, to play with others. Physically handicapped children can profit often even more than normal youth from the social aspects of physical activities. The crippled child needs to be accepted. His chances for being taken into groups will be increased through the play approach. Every child can and should be taught to master some type of physical activity. An individual program should be tailored to fit his physical case should he deviate from normal.

Enlisting the Cooperation of Others

Teachers sometimes need help in understanding each child more fully. Cooperation with the parents, teachers, and other pupils can often prove fruitful. Frank discussions should be held with parents, but these should be carefully planned by the teacher. Suggested techniques for successful parent-teacher conferences are:

(1) Quickly establish the feeling that, like the parent, you want to help the child, that you are working together.
(2) Find out as much about the child as you can without probing or prying.
(3) Visit the parents in their home, if possible.

The Use of Behavior Records

Driscoll[1] offers the following suggestions to teachers for observing children in play:

(1) Watch for the children who maintain leadership after the activity or game has been continuing for five or ten minutes.
(2) Watch for the children who are noisy, but who are on the side lines rather than in the center of activity.
(3) Are there children in your class who are remaining in group activity only as long as they can have their own way?
(4) Which children are always on the fringe of activity?
(5) Are there some children who are using teasing as a source of power?
(6) Are some children so considerate of others that they have little time to attend to their own work?

All children reacting to the type of behavior described are problem ridden, many of them are preneurotic. If growth is a slow process, the teacher must know more about ways in which the child needs to develop and aid him to help himself. If the teacher would teach the child, he first must know where his developmental level is in as many areas as possible.

In appraising the developmental rate of each child the teacher should make, keep, and carefully study cumulative behavior records of each pupil. Although this is time consuming it leads to better pupil understanding and teaching.

The following is a suggested chart for recording and studying pupil behavior:

[1] Driscoll, Gertrude, *How to Study the Behavior of Children*, Bureau of Publications, New York, Teacher's College, Columbia University, 1941, pp. 15–59.

PUPIL BEHAVIOR SHEET

Name ————————————————— School Year ——— Age ———

Physical Education Class ——————————————

Does the child:

	FREQUENTLY	SELDOM	NEVER
Take an active part in planning group activities?	————	————	————
Take an active part in playing?	————	————	————
Express himself confidently?	————	————	————
Accept criticisms and suggestions from his peers?	————	————	————
Accept criticisms and suggestions from adults?	————	————	————
Take turns with others?	————	————	————
Show above average leadership ability?	————	————	————
Have many consistent friends?	————	————	————
Change friends often?	————	————	————
Play fairly?	————	————	————
Seem interested in improving skills or learning new ones?	————	————	————
Assume responsibility without being reminded or threatened?	————	————	————
Seem happy and well adjusted?	————	————	————

Comments

1. ————————————————————————————
2. ————————————————————————————
3. ————————————————————————————
4. ————————————————————————————
5. ————————————————————————————

Areas in which the child needs help:

1. ————————————————————————————
2. ————————————————————————————
3. ————————————————————————————
4. ————————————————————————————
5. ————————————————————————————

What I will do to help him help himself:

1. _____

2. _____

3. _____

4. _____

5. _____

Signed _____

Date _____

These records can be of invaluable help to the teacher in gaining insight of all of her pupils. Changes in behavior which indicate growth and improvement should be noticed and commented upon to the pupil by the teacher.

Children are not miniature adults. We, who are older, must increasingly help them to develop their own unique personality. Above all, we need to help them find true happiness.

Suggested Readings

Brownell, Clifford L. and others, *Adventures in Growing Up*, New York, American Book Company, 1941.

Humphreys, Alice Lee, *Heaven in My Hand*, Richmond, Virginia, John Knox Press, 1951.

Isaacs, Helen, *Social Development in Young Children*, New York, Harcourt, Brace & Company, 1934.

Jenkins, Gladys, Shacter, Helen, Bauer, William, *These Are Your Children*, New York, Scott, Foresman Company, 1951.

Jersild, Arthur, *Child Psychology*, 3rd Edition, New York, Prentice-Hall, 1947.

Jersild, Arthur and Tasch, Ruth, *Children's Interests and What They Suggest for Education*, New York, Bureau of Publications, Teacher's College, Columbia University, 1949.

Keliher, Alice, *Life and Growth*, New York, D. Appleton-Century, 1938.

Lewin, Kurt and others, "Patterns of Aggressive Behavior in Experimentally Created Social Climates," *Journal of Social Psychology*, May, 1939.

Lippitt, Rosemary and Zander, A., *Child Behavior and Development*, New York, McGraw-Hill Book Company, 1943.

Patri, Angelo, *How to Help Your Child Grow*, Chicago, Rand-McNally, 1948.

Rogers, James, *What Every Teacher Should Know About the Physical Condition of Her Pupils*, Pamphlet 68, Washington, D. C., United States Office of Educators, 1945.

Strecker, Edward and Appel, Kenneth, *Discovering Ourselves,* New York, Macmillan, 1944.

Wallace, Edythe Thomas, *Pointers for Parents,* Oklahoma City, Oklahoma, Crosby Press, 1946.

Witty, Paul A. and Skinner, Charles E., *Mental Hygiene in Modern Education,* New York, Farrar and Rinehart, 1939.

Part Three

THE WHERE

Mankind has always felt the need of good leadership, for the history of the world shows that we have never had enough leaders in the right place at the right time. The elementary school is the rich soil in which children can develop those traits necessary for positive leadership.

Chapter 4

The Gymnasium, Playground, and Classroom

Usually physical education classes are held in a gymnasium or outside on a play field. Most public schools are fortunate enough to have one or the other. The schools which use the playground for play periods and the gymnasium for physical education class work usually have the best programs. The use of the classroom, auditorium, stage, or school corridor has been found to be inadequate and results in a make-shift program fitted into a make-shift space. A well equipped gymnasium, adequate playground space, sufficient time for a minimum of 30 minutes daily class instruction plus another 30 minutes scheduled play or recess period provides an ideal teaching-learning environment.

The Gymnasium

A well lighted, ventilated, clean gymnasium is of prime necessity in all modern schools. The gymnasium should not be known as a "playroom," but rather as the gymnasium—the place where children receive instruction not in play but in physical education. In certain large city systems where so-called playrooms have been provided they often are nothing more than a dark, tiny basement room full of wildly screaming children who are playing to *let off steam.* This is an adult coined phrase. Although physical activities relieve tension, children are not in the least concerned about the therapeutic values inherent in play. Screaming in play may be therapeutic but it is not in accordance with accepted social technique or play refinement. Play is the process through which the social objectives of physical education are implemented.

In determining the size of the gymnasium, the immediate concern must be for:

(1) Adequate teaching space, with a minimum of approximately

49

41 by 66 feet for 66 children. For larger classes there should be an increase of 40 square feet for each pupil.

(2) Official size courts for pupil and adult use with a ceiling height of 22 feet under all beams, tresses, or hanging obstacles.

(3) Good sunlight and ventilation. The ratio of 1/4 window space to 1/5 floor space with windows preferably placed along the two long sides of the room rather than at the end; room temperature maintained at 60 to 65 degrees.

(4) Clean walls.

(5) A clean, smooth surfaced floor marked with permanent lines for playing areas, marked with colored chalk or removable tempera paint for playing areas.

(6) The room should be free from all removable hazards; unremovable hazards, such as posts, radiators, pipes, etc., should be covered with mats.

(7) Accessibility to drinking fountains, either outside in the corridor or recessed in the wall.

(8) An acoustically treated ceiling.

(9) Spectator seating.

(10) Single type doors which swing out away from the playing area.

Locker and shower rooms should join or be beneath the gymnasium. The size of the school and pupil enrollment determine the number of lockers needed. Two common types of lockers are the (1) half-size or full-length metal, or (2) wire baskets. Each student should have a standard combination lock; the teacher should file away two copies of master sheets of all combinations. Pupils should be urged to keep their uniforms clean and sanitary. Each locker room should also contain stationary long benches, mirrors at the end of each row of lockers, scales, and hair dryers if the school has a swimming pool.

The shower room should join the locker room; preferably it should be a separate unit. Gang showers are recommended for boys; semi-private or individual showers usually are best for girls although some gang showers may be found suitable.

Pupils should be encouraged rather than required to take showers after class periods at the fourth grade level when they begin wearing special uniforms for class instruction. Required showers are not only hard to enforce but can lead to serious teacher criticism from some parents. Pupils should be sold on the idea that taking a shower is a privilege as well as a social obligation to fellow students in the next class to which they will go following physical education, rather than a requirement. The positive approach provides for positive action. Sufficient time should be allotted to include showers in the daily program. For some few, taking showers will be a big part of their physical education program.

The Playground

Playground space should be planned so that there is opportunity for the greatest number to play at one time. At least five acres should be provided for elementary schools. A minimum of 100 square feet per pupil should be an absolute requirement. Separate acres should be set off for the primary grades for safety purposes. Space should be planned for use by as many age groups as possible. For example, baseball diamonds may be used for kickball with the lower grades and for softball with the upper grades at different periods of the day. The area should also be enclosed by a metal fence.

Activities for the playground should add to the pleasure of the moment and enrich the recreational life of the child so that he uses new activities in his leisure time away from school. By teaching obedience to rules and regulations, games help teach children to get along with others. Activities should be selected which are suitable to the sex, playing space, clothing and weather, as well as age level.

Some suggestions to assure proper conduct on the playground are to:

(1) Provide a varied program appealing to all.
(2) Have a few concise rules and enforce them.
(3) Make frequent tours of the playground with pupils looking for hazards.
(4) Always maintain a spirit of fairness and justice.
(5) Foster a spirit of self-government by giving children a share in the making of rules on the playground.
(6) Use student leaders and pupil-game rotation plans.

For recess and supervised free play periods pupils should be assigned to a specific play space. Those in the primary grades should be given a section near the building and have certain pieces of fixed equipment such as swings, slides, and a jungle gym for their exclusive use.

Children in the upper elementary grades should also have a section of the play field which is their own. Boys should not be allowed to monopolize the baseball diamond or soccer field but should rotate with the girls the privilege of using all marked areas. A weekly schedule of play space assignments should be worked out by a student committee and teacher. Coeducational games can be encouraged when at least one assigned weekly period is set aside for them.

Handling Equipment

There should be a definite set of rules and procedures for handing out and returning all equipment. A good plan is to have each squad leader do this. The teacher should make certain that all equipment is ready before each class enters the gymnasium or goes out to the playground. All bats, balls, squad cards, and other needed items should be easily accessible with as many items as possible placed together. Baseballs should be stored near bats, croquet mallets and wickets near balls.

A complete inventory of all items should be made at the beginning and end of each semester's work. Worn-out equipment may be sent to charitable institutions if the items are in good enough shape to be repaired and used.

Supplies and Equipment Needed

The materials listed below are minimum essentials needed to conduct an adequate program in elementary schools. The amount and variety to be purchased will be dependent upon class size. Rubber balls are cheaper than leather ones and may prove to be just as serviceable.

SUPPLIES	EQUIPMENT
Balls:	Ball inflator
Indoor 12″	Bases
Rubber 5″, 6″, 8″, 10″	Blackboard, portable and permanent
Soccer, official	Bulletin board
Soccer, rubber	Cabinet, steel
Volley, official	Canvas bags in which to carry balls
Volley, rubber	Hurdles, 12″, 15″, 18″, 20″
Basketball, official	Jungle gym
Basketball, rubber	Junior jump standards
Football, official	
Football, rubber	

SUPPLIES	EQUIPMENT
Baseball gloves	Mats 33″ x 60″
Beanbags 6 x 6	3′ x 5′
Chalk	4′ x 6′
Deck tennis rings	Net standards
Five pin bowling sets	Nets
Indian clubs	Portable phonograph
Jump ropes, 3′8″ sashcord	Stop watch
Individual 6′, 7′, 8′	Storage cabinets or lockers
Long, 12′, 15′, 20′, 25′	Targets
Phonograph needles	
Phonograph records	
Shuffleboard sets	
Squad cards	
Tape measure, 50′	
Tempera paint	
Tom toms	

All equipment should be carefully selected, kept, and repaired. The pupils can aid in oiling balls, repairing nets, and sewing ball rips. Sporting goods companies can usually provide better equipment for money spent than local department stores.

Each teacher needs to have a yearly budget provided for the purchase of equipment, rather than being given a certain sum upon the sudden whim or urge of the school principal.

Uniforms Desired

Beginning in grade 4 it is desirable for both sexes to wear regulation uniforms for their class work in the gymnasium or on the playground. One piece suits of dark material, white tennis shoes and socks are recommended for girls. Dark trunks, a white "T" shirt, high tennis shoes, and heavy socks are recommended for boys.

In order to secure the cooperation of the parents, letters may be sent to them explaining the costume requirement and places from which the clothing may be bought. They should also be informed that the clothing may be used for several years, and that provisions will be made to re-sell used garments. Upon request, parents from low income groups and mothers who sew should be sent patterns for making the uniforms.

Companies which sell regulation gymnasium uniforms usually provide superior garments at lower cost than can local stores. Recognized serviceable companies are advertised monthly in the Journal of Health, Physical Education and Recreation.

Regulation class uniforms aid in building desirable attitudes regarding the program; they also allow for freedom of movement, and build group unity and morale. Then, too, this is one way to encourage boys and girls to keep and be clean, since part of their bodies are seen by their classmates.

Accident Safeguards

Physical education contains activities wherein children can have adventurous, joyful experiences. Many of the games and sports can be dangerous if improperly supervised. Under proper guidance and good teaching a physical education class, however, need not be any more potentially dangerous than one in any other subject. One way of safeguarding against accidents is to be sure that pupils engage only in those activities for which they are prepared in both strength and skill.

Children are not as interested in safety or being careful as they are in taking chances, in being daring. Consequently, adults must help them see that they can have the most fun over a longer period of time if they can avoid handicaps which may result from injuries. Safety education is learning to take chances wisely.

Accidents, when they do happen, can often be the best teachable moments to instruct youngsters to be careful. A boy, who sprained his ankle while running in the shower room, may help impress upon his classmates the importance of obeying the no-running rule. However, it must be remembered that parents whose children are hurt at school often develop negative attitudes toward the school, or the teacher in charge of the activity wherein the child was injured.

All teachers of physical education can safeguard against accidents by:

(1) Checking all apparatus and equipment periodically and keeping both in good repair at all times.
(2) Finding and marking all hazards with the pupils.
(3) Directing all pupils and especially squad leaders in safety measures.
(4) Using plans, materials, and programs which will reduce the possibility of accidents.
(5) Insisting that all pupils wear suitable apparel for all activities.

(6) Organizing and classifying pupils for class participation according to the results of physical examinations and motor ability tests.

(7) Insisting that all rules for playing games be obeyed at all times.

(8) Never leaving an assigned class or group.

All children injured at school should receive first aid attention by the school nurse or teacher. In small schools the teacher usually has to give first aid and suggest the purchase of needed supplies to the school principal. First aid equipment for all schools should include:

(1) 1-inch compress on adhesive in individal packages.

(2) Sterile gauze squares—3″ by 3″—in individual packages.

(3) Assorted sterile bandage compresses in individual packages.

(4) Triangular bandages.

(5) Sterile gauze in individual packages of about 1 square yard.

(6) Picric acid gauze.

(7) Burn ointment—such as 5% tannic acid jelly.

(8) Iodine, mild.

(9) Aromatic spirits of ammonia.

(10) Inelastic tourniquet.

(11) Scissors.

(12) 3-inch splinter forceps.

(13) Paper cups.

(14) 1-inch and 2-inch roller bandage.

(15) Wire or thin board splints.

(16) Castor oil or mineral oil for use in eyes. This should be sterile: it may be obtained in small tubes.

Teachers should remember that they are not medical doctors and can neither diagnose nor treat injuries. A complete record must be kept of all accidents. Accident reports should be filled out in duplicate or triplicate, depending upon the size of the school. The school teacher should keep one copy on file and send remaining copies to her administrators. Each accident report form might well include:

(1) The name of the person injured and date of the accident.

(2) The place of the accident and condition of the environment.

(3) What the teacher did for first aid.

(4) Names and addresses of two or more witnesses.

A suggested form follows:

SUGGESTED ACCIDENT REPORT FORM

Name of injured student _____ Sex _____

Age _____ Class _____ Address _____

Phone _____

Description of the accident _____

_____

_____

Condition of the environment _____

_____

What was done for first aid treatment _____

_____

Name and address of witnesses _____

_____

_____

Additional comments _____

_____

Final disposition of the case _____

_____

Signature _____

Date _____

The Classroom

The specific objectives the teacher may well have in mind when conducting physical education activities in the classroom are to:

(1) Use all available space to the best advantage.

(2) Set up rules of conduct with the pupils while playing so that people in other classes will not be disturbed.

(3) Discover with the pupils hazards in the room to be avoided.

The general objectives the teacher may well have when teaching active games and contests in the classroom are to:

(1) Develop within the child those knowledges, skills, and appreciations favorable to his fullest and wisest use of free moments in the present and future.

(2) Guide toward mastering social response in a variety of situations.

(3) Familiarize the pupil with a wide variety of activities.

(4) Develop understandings and abilities involved in the planning, selecting, and conducting of games.

Although the classroom is not very suitable as a place in which to do physical activities it can be used during bad weather, provided the children have their physical education classes outdoors whenever weather permits. All children need, among other things, plenty of fresh air and sunshine.

Suggested Readings

Broady, L. P. and French, Esther, *Health and Physical Education for Small Schools*, Lincoln, Nebraska, University of Nebraska Press, 1937.

Cole, Luella, *Teaching in the Elementary School*, New York, Farrer and Rinehart, 1939.

Garrison, Charlotte, *Permanent Play Materials for Young Children*, New York, Charles Scribners, 1926.

Kaurn, Ethel, *The Wise Choice of Toys*, Chicago, University of Chicago Press, 1938.

LaSalle, Dorothy, *Physical Education for the Classroom Teacher*, New York, A. S. Barnes, 1937.

Nash, Jay B., *Teachable Moments*, New York, A. S. Barnes, 1938.

Playground and Recreation Association of America, *Play Areas, Their Design and Construction*, New York, A. S. Barnes, 1938.

Sharmon, J. R., *Introduction to Physical Education*, New York, A. S. Barnes, 1934.

Stock, Herbert and Siebert, Elmer, *Education for Safe Living*, New York, Prentice-Hall, 1945.

Voltmer, Elmer and Esslinger, Arthur, *The Organization and Administration of Physical Education*, New York, Appleton-Century Crofts, 1949.

Williams, Jessie F. and Brownell, Clifford L., *The Administration of Health and Physical Education*, Philadelphia, W. B. Saunders, 1934.

Part Four

THE HOW

A good teacher becomes progressively unnecessary.

Chapter 5

Learning and Teaching

Learning

Learning takes place wherever there is life. It is a growth process which results from activity. One learns when he acts differently or when his behavior changes. This mastery through experience comes as the resultant interaction of the individual and his environment. One learns all over, for the whole body is engaged in the process. Feelings and emotions determine not only how much and how rapidly one will learn but also the depth and span of retention.

MOTOR SKILLS

Skill is developed largely through trial and error. Children learn largely from their mistakes. Through experience they learn how to meet responsibilities and how to solve problems in their own way. Youth needs to know that adults, be they teachers or parents, are there to help if and when assistance is needed. However, learning from mistakes should take place in a friendly relaxed atmosphere. Children should not be unduly embarrassed, ridiculed, or humiliated because of errors they make while learning. This connotes that the teacher must be patient and allow the children to muddle through experimental attempts until they catch on. This is called insight or the time when the learning or mastery actually occurs. Encouragement from the teacher will hasten its arrival.

Motivation is aroused desire to learn. It is that potent quality which spurs the learner on. Pupils respond quickly to praise, to feeling secure, to being accepted, especially when they, too, can see their own improvement. False motivation in the form of undue emphasis being placed upon grades, or eating the spinach in order to have the ice cream, has been compared to placing a setting hen on hard-boiled eggs. Learning an activity because it is fun or because it will make one a better and more totally-functioning person is positive motivation. It is more valuable and enduring to both the learner and the group.

One learns largely through doing, and not by seeing a movie which shows how a certain skill is done nor from hearing how to do one. Although the teacher can demonstrate a skill correctly and through it show the preferred patterned movements, the pupil will learn only when he himself imitates, copies, and thus creates his own movement patterns.

Since the teacher of physical education is largely concerned with teaching pupils through activity, this goal must be kept constantly in mind. If she wishes to increase organic vigor, skills, knowledges, and appreciations she cannot risk emphasizing any one of these more than the others. If teachers will be willing to experiment, or try new methods or re-test the value of old ones in the light of these four objectives, chances for their attainment are greater.

In reality the learner teaches himself. The teacher brushes aside retarding influences that might act as a hindrance to the learning rate; she motivates the learner on to new discoveries and helps him evaluate his own progress.

The best learning results will accrue when:

(1) The activities are child-centered.
(2) The individual needs, interests, and capacities of each pupil are fully understood.
(3) Teachers aid children to explore and discover things for themselves.
(4) Pupils are free to create their own responses in a situation.
(5) Pupils are guided by teachers who are sincerely interested in them.
(6) Pupils believe in what they are to learn and believe that it will be valuable to them.
(7) That which is learned will increase the pupil's power to make intelligent choices.
(8) That which is learned will build and refine new meanings.

Basic Learning Principles

It is important for the teacher to realize that the learner does control the learning situation. This is expressed in the folk saying that "you can lead a horse to water but you cannot make him drink." However, the child will want to learn when properly motivated or when he wants to if the teacher will follow these principles basic to all learning:

(1) There is learning wherever there is life, it is not confined to school houses or imprisoned only in books.

(2) The child learns all over and likewise is affected all over from what he learns.

(3) Learning means growth which is a long slow process.

(4) One's will to learn can be developed or can be forged into a burning desire by the adult, the group, or by the child himself.

(5) Learning is best when the child has definite goals in mind, can select what is to be learned, plan his procedure, and judge the results.

(6) All learning is based upon a theory of good human relationships.

(7) The child seeks to satisfy his wants; he attempts to do so when he learns.

(8) One acts largely because of what he feels, not because of what he knows.

(9) Short practice periods increase the rate of learning.

Kinds of Learning

Physical education activities should be selected which will develop vigor, endurance, and resistance to fatigue. Neuromuscular skill, or total body coordination and habits, are developed only through activity. Body balance, accuracy, speed, coordination, rhythm, agility, sensory perception, and reaction time develop through guided experience. All learning is of three types: (1) technical or skill learning, (2) associated or knowledge learning, and (3) concomitant or attitude and appreciation learning. Skill mastery alone is of little value without accompanying knowledge concerning the skill; both need to be reinforced by the shaping of proper attitudes. This implies that the teacher who helps children learn how to improve their soccer skills should also aid them to learn all they can about this sport, as well as to develop desirable traits of good sportsmanship, fairness, and opponent consideration. All three learnings are equally important and should receive balanced stress.

(1) *Primary Learning.* This type of learning is concerned with total body or organic neuromuscular development. Youth is that skill-hungry doing period of life where organic power is built through activity involving muscular work and recovery. Youth needs to learn vigorous, joyful activities during these skill-hungry years that have high carry-over value. In doing so, the foundation is laid for present and future leisure-time activity choice. Children should be aided to shop around when choosing activities and to

become skilled enough in those selected to desire to continue doing them when away from school. One of the best ways to evaluate the effectiveness of any program in physical education is to observe whether the children play the games they have learned at school, when playing in their own back yards.

(2) *Associated Learning*. This learning results from an accumulation of meanings that come through participation. Taking part in activities develops new insights that center around the activity itself, a knowledge of playing rules, a knowledge of one's own ability in relationship to that of others, and the environment, or playing conditions. Such learning results in one's ability to know his own skill in activities, and those of his peers.

(3) *Concomitant Learning*. Concomitant or attitude learning develops socially approved concepts, conduct, and appreciations. Teachers need to know better how to analyze program activities in terms of inherent values that contain elements of positive character and habit formation. Such development takes place only under positive leadership.

Character standards are socially determined. Positive character in America contains many of the same elements as democracy. Despite the claims made by administrators and school teachers of the character values inherent in sports and games, systematic methods and definite procedures for fostering right conduct receive too little emphasis in too many schools. Although games contain numerous opportunities for the development of self-direction according to commonly accepted moral and social standards, these opportunities and this development must be analyzed and encouraged or they remain untapped, unused. Educators need to become sensitized to viewing activities in terms of probable means of character education. As adults they must place in the child's environment those things that will aid him to grow as a self-directing individual who has much to contribute to group welfare.

Teaching

Every good teacher discovers for herself the most effective teaching methods. The best method for each is the one that gets the job done provided it is used in socially approved ways. A football coach may play his injured quarter-back in order to win, but educators, medical authorities, and other adults would frown upon this method of producing a winning team. The end result rarely, if ever, justifies the means when human beings are used in the process.

The following techniques for teaching physical education are suggested for trial and each teacher's revision.* In each class:

(1) Explain briefly what the class will do.
(2) Establish a need for learning by having pupils experiment. (In the case of learning to throw and catch a ball by having the pupils throw and catch balls, or listening and moving to music to get the rhythm of the dance before teaching actual steps.)
(3) Demonstrate the correct way to do the whole activity. (Show the class how the complete dance looks, or the complete bat swing.)
(4) Use squad leaders to demonstrate to their squads likewise.
(5) Demonstrate the correct way individually again to those having difficulty.
(6) Explain how to do the skill as simply as possible. ("Hook" elbows rather than "bend your arm and then place it through the bent left arm of your partner.")
(7) Encourage pupils to keep trying until they master the skill by praising what they do correctly.
(8) Integrate isolated skills in a game, dance or other activities as soon as possible. (In a soccer class, for example, five minutes may be spent on learning how to kick, dribble, and trap the ball; the remainder of the period should be spent in playing a game so that these skills will be used. No class period should be devoted entirely to practicing isolated skills.)
(9) Work toward 100 per cent pupil participation throughout the class period.
(10) Choose, whenever possible, activities which relate to the season, weather, day or interest.
(11) Keep plans flexible; overplan rather than underplan.
(12) Have a high degree of expectancy for each child and stimulate him through it to do his best.
(13) Analyze classes that did not go well; realize the reason may be your fault more times than not.
(14) Build skill upon skill.
(15) Employ techniques which will help each child learn something new every day.

Pitfalls to Be Avoided

(1) *Verbiage.* Teaching is *not* telling; it is getting others to do, to teach themselves.
(2) *Faulty Planning.* Provide enough equipment or activity so

* Specific techniques for teaching various parts of the total program are given in each of the following chapters.

that all are active. Physical education is a *doing* process, not a watching one. Ten pupils may use the baseball equipment but one hundred others should not stand and watch them have all the fun. If there is insufficient equipment, use what you have to the fullest degree but add squad play and squad rotation of games which do not require equipment. Give each group a chance to use what you do have.

(3) *Shot Scattering*. Do not attempt to talk *above* groups, or while pupils are talking. Make a direct hit every time you do talk and/or give directions by training the pupils to be quiet when you are speaking. Insist upon this rule being observed but be wise enough to know *when* to talk, *what* to say, and *how* to say it.

(4) *Let George Do It*. Do not pass the *buck*, or send an offending pupil on to the principal. Handle discipline cases when they occur in a firm but fair fashion. Group pressure and group discussions can work sometimes when teacher's reprimands fail.

(5) *Dressing for Class*. Teachers should not attempt to teach physical education wearing street clothes except in the primary grades where the classroom teacher conducts playground activities. If pupils are required to wear special costumes, so should the teacher. Like the pupils, the instructor should be neatly dressed and clean. Soiled sweat shirts and pants are out for men, as much so as baggy bloomers and middy blouses for women. All white shorts, shirts or blouses are recommended for both sexes.

(6) *Being Too Palsy-Walsy*. Physical educators are usually the most popular teachers in the school system. Some few gain their reputations for being "good Joes or Janes," by being back-slap happy, and too friendly with pupils, especially the highly skilled ones. A leader often loses the respect of the group if and when he comes down too near the group level. All youth need to have heroes and teachers worthy of emulation. Big Brothers or Sisters or Buddies who are also their public school teachers often are not followed by children over a long period of time.

(7) *Failure to Plan or See Relationships*. Growth follows patterns. Teachers can help children build shacks or temples, make mud pies or bake cakes—but only when they utilize building blueprints. Skills must be built upon skills. Daily, weekly, monthly, yearly plans are the blueprints of this creation.

(8) *Window Pecking*. When children have playground periods and physical education classes the teacher assigned to teach the physical education cannot do this by remote control. Some older teachers, as well as some few unprepared younger ones, believe physical education is staying in one's own warm classroom peering out of the window to watch the children playing on the cold playground and pecking on the icy glass at them

when they get into fights. Teachers of this type are gaining experience in the fine art of window pecking, while the children are being cheated out of a real educational opportunity.

(9) *Becoming Whistle Happy.* The whistle may be used as a means of gaining group attention at the beginning of each year's work, semester, or class. Children can be trained to be quiet when the whistle is blown. But whistles can also become a nuisance, as well as a source of annoyance when used too often. Children can be taught to be automatically quiet when the teacher speaks. A gymnasium of 100 or more children *can* be a controlled teaching-learning environment. The teacher who has something exciting for children to learn has little trouble gaining their attention if she has also trained them to react to her leadership position and ability. However, whistles are recommended for playground use when the children are scattered over large areas where it may be difficult for them to see or hear the teacher.

(10) *Throwing Out the Ball.* Too often boys in elementary grades are taught physical education classes by the coach. His primary duties too often are to produce winning teams, not teach unskilled boys how to play. Too often he is not as interested in teaching all boys as he is in training the few who are highly skilled. Coaching takes time and energy spent in after-school hours. It is easier to sit in one's office to conserve energy by drawing up plans for team practice than to teach classes. So the ball is thrown out on the gymnasium floor, like a wee bone to a pack of howling wolves, and physical education classes are taught by remote control. Luckily such practices are diminishing in our better schools. Physical education in schools for all is quite a different thing from high pressured athletics for a few.

Planning with Pupils

Pupils should work closely with the teacher in developing weekly programs. The approach may well be for the teacher to have suggested activities to present to the group, rather than asking "Well, what shall we do today and the rest of the week?" Children tend to like most the things they can do best, and to get into a rut consisting of old favorite games. Weaning them away from favored activities will lead to growth. The teacher may have to use initiative coupled with force in order to incorporate new activities. However, she need not superimpose all her ideas upon the group; as the adult leader she should eagerly be followed by the pupils. She will be as long as they have enjoyable experiences learning to master new skills.

Some techniques of evaluating outcomes are observation, comparison, questions, class discussions, analyses, and tests, both skill and written. Children can be taught to appraise what they have accomplished. So can the teacher. Evaluation, which is a method of thinking through an accomplishment so that one can revise purposes and procedures for the next effort, is an important part of teaching. When the teacher and pupils share in evaluating outcomes, democratic procedures are being used.

The process of thinking through a project is a valuable achievement in education and life. It can be used effectively with young children, for in spite of their age they have an uncanny way of seeing through things, of sizing up others as well as themselves. Their charming frankness can be utilized for individual as well as group development.

An illustration of how planning and evaluating appears in a physical education lesson follows:

Objectives. To teach children how to play "end ball."
Procedure
   (1) ORIENTATION. Give the class a preview of the game by observing an upper class play a demonstration game.
   (2) PLANNING. Discuss with the class the object of the game and help them to identify skills used, team position, and the rules. Form color teams of squads and let players take assigned positions on the playfield.
   (3) EXECUTING. The pupils will walk through or explore their team positions and then play the game.
   (4) PUPIL'S EVALUATION. Following the playing of the game, the teacher will lead the children to consider what they should have done to play the game more effectively. They may compare the way they saw the demonstration game played with the way they played it or analyze only their play and establish their needs. The children will discover through this procedure what they need to learn or practice in order to play more skillfully. Thus they will discover their need for learning, which through increased interest will cause them to learn more rapidly than if the teacher had pointed out what she thought they needed to learn. Through such evaluation, teacher and pupils share a new purpose and agree upon objectives for the next lesson. They may have included:

   (a) To practice a straight throw for distance.
   (b) To practice catching while standing, while running.
   (c) To play "end ball" again.

Teacher Evaluation

Periodically, the teacher should evaluate the results of her teaching. This may be done by:

(1) Motor ability tests

(2) Skill tests

(3) Paper and pencil knowledge tests

(4) Health records

(5) Continuous observation

(6) Check sheets

The following check sheet for the teacher's use may be helpful:

Table 2

TEACHER'S EVALUATION OF THE PROGRAM IN PHYSICAL EDUCATION

	ALWAYS	FREQUENTLY	SELDOM	NEVER
1. Do the majority of my students enjoy their class work with me?				
2. Do the students respond to my directions willingly and quickly?				
3. Do the students feel that I am their friend?				
4. Is the program full of varied activities, yet all balanced properly?				
5. Does every child leave the class feeling secure in what he is learning, and feeling that he has accomplished something worthwhile?				
6. Are the majority of pupils growing in play skills?				
7. Are the majority growing into becoming good citizens?				
8. Am I providing enough opportunities for the highly skilled children to accomplish skill mastery?				

The following form might also well be used:

Table 3

TEACHER'S PERSONAL EVALUATION SHEET

	ALWAYS	FREQUENTLY	SELDOM	NEVER
1. Am I patient with the motor morons and poorly coordinated pupils?	_____	_____	_____	_____
2. Do I enjoy teaching?	_____	_____	_____	_____
3. Am I making the best use of student planning and leadership?	_____	_____	_____	_____
4. Do I utilize all space wisely in the gymnasium?	_____	_____	_____	_____
5. Do I utilize all playground space wisely?	_____	_____	_____	_____
6. Do the activities I teach have real carry-over value for after-school play?	_____	_____	_____	_____
7. Do I keep in mind and work toward the objectives I set up when school began this year?	_____	_____	_____	_____
8. Do I try to understand my pupils through their play; am I observant enough?	_____	_____	_____	_____
9. Do I overplan my work?	_____	_____	_____	_____
10. Do I underplan my work?	_____	_____	_____	_____
11. Do I teach the children something new or how to do old skills better every class period?	_____	_____	_____	_____
12. Do I really try to build skill upon skill?	_____	_____	_____	_____

Things I can do to make my program better are:

a. _____   e. _____
b. _____   f. _____
c. _____   g. _____
d. _____   h. _____

                              Date: _____

My progress on this so far has been:

a. _____   c. _____
b. _____   d. _____

Pupil Evaluation

Pupils can do much to help evaluate the program. One of the best ways to know their true reactions to the program is the amount of happiness radiated by the group. Classes should be fun and will be if there is a good feeling of rapport between the teacher and the children. Another means of evaluating the results is to check how many and what activities learned in class the children play in their leisure after-school hours.

Pupil suggestions for class improvement can be gained informally through individual or class discussions. This method works best with groups experienced in evaluating if the pupils feel free to say what they really think. Children learn early in life to give back to adults answers sought. Their charming grace, however, is their blunt frankness used among adults they consider as friends.

The pupils may feel freer to speak truthfully if they are asked to write suggestions for class improvement and turn them in unsigned. Another method is to have each child fill in the following suggested check list:

Table 4
PUPIL EVALUATION SHEET

	ALWAYS	FREQUENTLY	SELDOM	NEVER
Do you enjoy classes in physical education?	_____	_____	_____	_____
Do you feel as though you are getting enough individual attention in learning to do new things?	_____	_____	_____	_____
Do you play the activities learned in class after				

Table 4 (continued)

PUPIL EVALUATION SHEET

school and during your
leisure time? _____ _____ _____ _____

Do you like to take show-
ers after class? _____ _____ _____ _____

Do you feel as though your
class gives you enough opportunities to get to know
a number of activities and
people? _____ _____ _____ _____

Do you feel as though you
have gained in skills? _____ _____ _____ _____

List the things you like most about physical education.

1. _____

2. _____

3. _____

List the things you like the least about physical education.

1. _____

2. _____

How do you think our class could be made better?

1. _____

2. _____

Evaluation with the Principal

The school administrator should be aware of the work accomplished by all teachers during the school year. He should visit each teacher regularly and offer suggestions for improvement. As the chief administrator of the school system, he often must be the go-between for teachers and the general public. By observing classes in physical education and reading reports submitted by the teacher he may gain insight upon the program.

The task of teaching also includes that of educational diagnosis. The teacher's analysis of each class should include consideration of what the children accomplished during their class period, learning problems that were evident with the entire group as well as with individuals, and possible solutions for learning stumbling blocks.

Tests are useful tools for evaluating learning in skills, rules, and attitudes. Each unit of work should include a written and skill test. These should be easily administered and not be too time consuming to grade or record. Not more than two class periods should be taken for these tests.

Written Tests

Objective tests should include true and false questions, matching questions, blanks to be filled in, and multiple choice questions. It is recommended that such written tests be included in the program beginning at the fourth grade level. Tests can be an aid to teaching if they are used to: (1) measure individual as well as group improvement; (2) serve as a means of comparison between pupils, classes, or schools; (3) aid the teacher to diagnose pupil weakness; and (4) help the teacher see flaws as well as strengths in her own teaching methods.

Written tests are of greatest value when the teacher fully understands what it is she wants to test, knows what she will do with the results, and has found the best measuring instruments for these purposes.

A sample test in Hit Pin Baseball for sixth grade pupils follows:

PART I. *True* (+) *False* (0)

0 1. Five Indian clubs are used in this game.
0 2. Each run scores 2 points.
+ 3. The ball, when kicked fair, must be sent to first, second, third, home base, in this order.
0 4. The bowler may throw the ball to the kicker.
+ 5. The kicker is out on the third strike.

PART II. *Matching*

1 Knocks down any Indian Club   1. Player is out
2 Player misses a fair bowl   2. Strike
1 Foul ball caught   3. Scored run
1 Fair ball knocks down field club
1 Player does not touch all bases in order
1 Kicker fails to stand on one foot within the circle when kicking
1 Accurately bowl the ball over the kicker's plate.

Skill Tests

Such tests should measure the amount of mastery of the basic skills of a game, dance, or activity. In an area of rhythmical activities demonstrating the ability to do the dance or move to rhythmic beats is considered the best type of test. Kicking, throwing, hitting, and batting for distance and accuracy are suggested skill tests for the upper elementary level. Teacher observation and rating of each pupil's ability to play the game in which these skills are utilized are also recommended.

A sample skill test in Hit Pin Baseball for sixth grade pupils might well include demonstrating the ability to:

1. Accurately bowl the ball over the kicker's plate.
2. Accurately throw and catch the ball as it travels from home plate around all three bases.
3. Accurately kick the ball to center field, right field, left field.
4. Play the game.

Other Tests

Other methods of evaluating include check lists, rating scales, motor ability tests, physical fitness tests, interviews, case studies, group discussions, and self-rating. Also included are standardized tests of strength, cardiac and respiratory function, physical efficiency and ability, endurance, speed, posture and body type.

Suggested Readings

Bovard, John, Cozens, Frederick, and Hagman, Patricia, *Tests and Measurements In Physical Education*, Third Edition, Philadelphia, W. B. Saunders, 1949.

California State Curriculum Commission, *Teacher's Guide to Child Development, Intermediate Grades*, Sacramento, California, California State Department of Education, 1936.

Cowell, Charles, *Scientific Foundations of Physical Education*, New York, Harper Brothers, 1953.

Davis, Elwood and Lawther, John, *Successful Teaching in Physical Education*, New York, Prentice-Hall, 1948.

Hopkins, L. Thomas, *Interaction, the Democratic Process*, Boston, Heath and Company, 1941.

Kozman, Helda, Cassidy, Rosalind, and Jackson, C. O., *Methods in Physical Education*, Second Edition, Philadelphia, W. B. Saunders, 1952.

Lee, Mabel, *The Conduct of Physical Education*, New York, A. S. Barnes, 1931.

McCloy, C. H., *Tests and Measurements in Physical Education*, New York, F. S. Crofts and Company, 1937.

Oberteuffer, Delbert, *Physical Education*, New York, Harper Brothers, 1951.

Prescott, Daniel, *Emotion and the Educative Process*, Washington, D. C., American Council in Education, 1938.

Scott, M. Gladys, and French, Esther, *Better Teaching Through Testing*, New York, A. S. Barnes, 1945.

Chapter 6

The Program

The Total Program

The total program for both the lower and upper elementary grades should be a balanced one containing a wide range of activities. Broad areas around which the program should be built are:

(1) Rhythmical activities
(2) Games of low organization
(3) Relays
(4) Mimetics and story plays (grades 1, 2, 3)
(5) Camping and outing (grades 4, 5, 6)
(6) Athletic team games
(7) Aquatics
(8) Stunts and self-testing activities

Tables 5 and 6 show the suggested time percentages for a balanced program from grades 1 through 6. Sexes should be separated at grade 4 since physical differences in boys and girls, varying interests, and performance ability become marked after the age of ten.

Table 5

TIME PERCENTAGES FOR THE PHYSICAL EDUCATION
PROGRAM IN THE PRIMARY GRADES

	GRADES		
	1	2	3
	%	%	%
(1) Rhythmical activities	25	25	25
(2) Fundamental play skills	20	20	15
(3) Relays	10	10	10
(4) Mimetics and story plays	25	20	10
(5) Athletic team games	0	0	15
(6) Aquatics	5	5	5
(7) Apparatus, stunts and self-testing activities	15	20	20
Total	100%	100%	100%

Table 6

TIME PERCENTAGES FOR THE PHYSICAL EDUCATION PROGRAM IN UPPER ELEMENTARY GRADES

| | GRADES | | | | | |
	4		5		6	
	Boys % Girls		Boys % Girls		Boys % Girls	
(1) Rhythmical activities	20	30	15	30	15	30
(2) Fundamental play skills	20	15	15	15	10	10
(3) Relays	15	15	10	10	10	5
(4) Athletic team games	20	15	30	20	35	30
(5) Aquatics and camping activities	10	10	15	15	15	15
(6) Apparatus, stunts, and self-testing activities	15	15	15	10	15	10
Total	100%	100%	100%	100%	100%	100%

In as much as possible these suggested percentages should be used in order to develop a broad program. In some geographical areas where aquatics are impossible because of lack of facilities, hiking and camping may well be incorporated, or used as activities suitable for children even in the primary grades.

PLANNING THE PROGRAM

Points to consider when building the daily, the weekly, monthly, or semester's program in physical education include:

(1) The specific grade level.
(2) The number of pupils in the class.
(3) The age and sex.
(4) The interest and needs of the pupils.
(5) The carry-over value of the activities.
(6) The available facilities and equipment.

The teacher should make general and specific objectives for the class to accomplish. General objectives may be to increase:

(1) Organic vigor.
(2) Skills.
(3) Knowledges.
(4) Appreciations.

Specific objectives the teacher wishes to accomplish with the group may include to:

(1) Develop good health, happiness, character, and the democratic spirit in each child.
(2) Develop leadership and followership techniques.
(3) Develop basic skills in as many kinds of activities as possible.
(4) Develop in each child abilities to plan, conduct, and evaluate the things he can do as an individual and as a class member.
(5) Develop good safety habits.
(6) Develop proper attitudes toward playing, winning, and losing.
(7) Develop the ability to reason and to give directions.
(8) Develop independence.
(9) Integrate health and safety education with physical activity.
(10) Develop courage and initiative.
(11) Develop vigor and physical fitness.
(12) Develop skills in games and activities suitable for after school play.

Period Divisions

Children in the elementary grades should have a total of one hour daily devoted to physical education. On the primary level at least 30 minutes daily should be given to class instruction, the remainder of the time to supervised play on the playground. It is customary to have the morning time given over to the former, and the afternoon to supervised free play. Grades 4 to 6 should also have one hour daily for physical education. The suggested time division is 40 minutes for class instruction with the remaining 20 minutes for supervised playground work later. Some schools devote three 60 minute periods weekly to physical education and two 60 minute periods weekly to health instruction.

Regardless of the period divisions established by school administrators, the physical education class period should be carefully planned in order that there be a spread of activities or that more skill mastery can be accomplished. Suggested plans are:

PLAN I

Primary Level (Grades 1, 2, 3)
Free play .... 5 min.
Rhythms .... 10 min.
Games of low organiza-
  tions .... 10 min.
Discussion or evaluation 5 min.
         Total   30 min.

PLAN II

Free play .... 5 min.
Teaching new activities 15 min.
Reviewing games .... 10 min.
         Total   30 min.

PLAN III

    Free play .... 5 min.
    Stunts and tumbling .. 5 min.
    Lead up team games .. 15 min.
    Discussion or evaluation 5 min.
          Total   30 min.

PLAN IV

    Free play .... 5 min.
    Mimetics and story
      plays .... 25 min.
          Total   30 min.

PLAN V

    Upper Elementary Level
        (Grades 4, 5, 6)
    Undressing .... 5 min.
    Rhythms .... 20 min.
    Class evaluation ...... 7 min.
    Dressing and showering 8 min.
          Total   40 min.

PLAN VI

    Dressing .... 5 min.
    Teaching new activities 25 min.
    Practicing and playing 7 min.
    Dressing and showering 8 min.
          Total   40 min.

PLAN VII

    Undressing .... 5 min.
    Review of previous day's
      lesson .... 15 min.
    New games .... 10 min.
    Evaluation .... 5 min.
    Dressing .... 5 min.
          Total   40 min.

PLAN VIII

    Undressing .... 5 min.
    Aquatics .... 30 min.
    Dressing .... 5 min.
          Total   40 min.

Emphasis in the primary grades should be placed upon joyful activity; small children are not as interested in learning how to do intricate game skills as they are in being active. On the upper elementary level, however, the teacher should begin to place emphasis on skill realizing that her pupils will receive greater pleasure from games when they can play them with better than average ability.

Instead of including a wide variety of activities in the beginning of the year the teacher should start with games familiar to the pupils and gradually introduce new ones into the program. She should go from the known to the unknown, reviewing the familiar and gradually including the new.

Pupils and the teacher should evaluate together their weekly and daily progress. Time allotment for this purpose may be 5 minutes daily or 20 to 30 minutes weekly. During this period, the group should plan with the teacher the ensuing work, check progress made toward reaching desired goals and objectives, and discuss problems which have arisen during class time.

Lesson plans for each grade should be made both weekly and for the term. Activities suitable and recommended for each grade level include:

GRADE 1

Rhythmical Activities
Folk Dances
  I See You
  Shoemaker's Dance
  Danish Dance of Greeting
  Chimes of Dunkirk
  Farmer in the Dell

Singing Games
  A Hunting We Will Go
  Did You Ever See a Lassie
  How Do You Do, My Partner
  London Bridge
  Hokey Pokey
  Muffin Man
  Soldier Boy

Dance Fundamentals
  Walk to music or rhythm
  Skip to music or rhythm
  Slide to music or rhythm
  Hop to music or rhythm
  Gallop to music or rhythm
  Creative movements to chang-
    ing beats

Games of Low Organization
  Have you seen my sheep
  Crows and cranes
  Dodge ball
  Fox and geese
  Flying Dutchman
  Cat and rat
  Squirrel and trees
  I say stoop
  Slap Jack
  Circle pass ball
  Old mother witch
  Jump the brook
  Statues

Stunts, Tumbling and Self-
    Testing
  Log roll
  Forward roll
  Push up from knees
  Running
  Jumping

GRADE 2

Rhythmical Activities
Folk Dance
  Bleking
  Kinder Polka
  Gustaf's Skoal
  Seven Jumps
  The Crested Hen
  Broom Dance
  Rovenacka

Singing Games
  Farmer in the Dell
  Hippety Hop to the Barber Shop
  Thread Follows the Needle
  Jolly is the Miller
  I'm Very, Very Tall
  The Muffin Man
  Old King Cole

Dance Fundamentals
  Combinations of movements
  Skip-hop-glide
  Changing directions
  Changing tempo

Relays
  Back to back
  Automobile relay
  Head balance relay
  Rope skip relay
  Passing relay
  Stiff legged relay
  Gunny sack relay
  Three legged race relay
  Running
  Skipping
  One leg hop

Run-up, walk-back
Running backwards
Up and over
Balance relay
Up and under
Box relay
Sack relay

Mimetics and Story Plays

Rope jumping
Figure skating
Branding cows
Fishing
Bicycling
Acting out sports
Animals
Follow the leader
Building a house
The trip to the country
Cowboys and Indians
Christmas tree and Santa
Playing in the wind
Going to the grocery store
Modes of travel

Stunts, Tumbling and Self-Testing Activities

Bear walk

Duck walk
Elephant walk
Seal walk
One leg hop, changing directions
Log roll
Rope jumping
Wheelbarrow
Measuring worm
Crab walk
Leap frog
Rocking horse
Chicken fight

Games of Low Organization

Do this—do that
Midnight
Call ball
Charley over the water
Steal the bacon
Poison tag
Garden scamp
Squat tag
Red light
Wood tag
Line dodgeball

GRADE 3

Rhythmical Activities
Folk Dance

Polka
Ace of Diamonds
Green Sleeves
Indian War Dance
Norwegian Mountain Dance
Tantoli
Finger Polka

Singing Games

A-Hunting We Will Go
Captain Jinks
Indian Braves
Looby Lou
Pop Goes the Weasel
Rig-A-Jig
The Needle's Eye

Dance Fundamentals

Singing
Gallop
Slides
Fox trot
Polka
Dances created to songs, poems, and stories

Games of Low Organizations

Caboose
Stride ball
Bull in the ring
Three deep
Boiler burst
New York
Target throw
Last couple out

Hill dill
Circle blub bowls
Line dodgeball
Hopscotch
Loose caboose

Mimetics and Story Plays
Actions for poems and stories
Song titles
A bus ride
A train trip
The aeroplane
Gardening
Acting out sports

*Stunts, Tumbling, and Self-
    Testing*
Knee dip
Cartwheel
Nip-up
Coffee grinder
Push-up
Cross leg stand
Foot clap
Walrus walk
Backward and forward roll
Chimney

Fish hawk dive
Twister
The swan

Team Games
Soccer keep away
Capture the flag
Kickball
Dodgeball
Boundary ball
Kick it and run
Throw it and run
Line soccer
Corner dodgeball

Relays
All four relay
Throw and sit relay
Down and up relay
Soccer dribble relay
Run and throw back relay
Automobile relay
Goal butting
Basketball pass
Horse and rider

GRADE 4—BOYS AND GIRLS

Rhythmical Activities
Folk Dance
Minuet
Broom Dance
Highland Schottische
Seven Jumps
Sellinger's Round
Sailor's Hornpipe
Maine Mixer

Square Dance
Grand March
Virginia Reel
Red River Valley
Take a Little Peek
Jump Jim Crow
Soldier's Joy

Dance Fundamentals
Walk, run, jump, hop to even
    rhythm

Skip, slide, gallop, leap to un-
    even rhythm
Creative movements of work,
    play, sports
Creative dance to records
Waltz
Schottische

Games of Low Organization
Hook-on
Streets and alleys
Vis-a-vis
Animal chase
Red Rover
May I
Charades
Club snatch
Bronco tag
Ankle tag
Prisoner's base

Nine-court-keep away
Field ball
Skills of baseball

Relays

Rescue relay
Rope climb relay
Kangaroo relay
Leapfrog relay
Run, throw, catch relay
Goal shooting relay
Zigzag relay
Skip rope relay
Family relay
Rabbit jump relay
Soccer relay
Basketball couple passing
Goal shooting
Football pass couple relay

Stunts, Tumbling, and Self-Testing

Chinning
Rope jumping
Goal shooting
Soccer kick for distance
Soccer kick for accuracy
One-leg-squat
Jump the stick
Push and pull ups
Skin the snake
Merry-go-round
Simple pyramids
Headstand
Nip up

Cartwheels
Running
Jumping

Camping and Outing

Hiking
Compass reading
Trail blazing
Fire building—tepee
Wood gathering
Menu planning
Outdoor cooking
Garbage disposal
Blanket rolling
Crafts from native materials
Camp project
Fishing

Team Games

Soccer dodgeball
Pin soccer
End-ball
Kickball
Corner kickball
German batball
Newcomb
Captain ball
Base football
Schlagball

Aquatics (Minimum Skills)

Fear elimination
Floating
Crawl

GRADE 5—BOYS AND GIRLS

Rhythmical Activities
Folk Dance

Starlight Schottische
Highland Schottische
Irish Washerwoman
Varsovienne
Kerry Dance
Troika
Sextur
Trip to Helsinki
Sicilian Tarantella

Square Dance

Oh, Johnny
Sally Goodin
Around That Couple, Take a Peek
Chase the Snake
Swing the Girl Behind You
Arkansas

Dance Fundamentals

Fox trot

Waltz Hesitation
Skip, slide, gallop
Jump and hop
Space aspects of movement
Striking and dodging
Dance creations

Games of Low Organization

Keep it up
Pinch-O
Cross tag
Fire on the mountain
Wood tag
Buddy spud
Keep away

Relays

Siamese twin relay
Jump the stick relay
Human croquet
Rope jumping relay
Running at increased distances
Squat, jump relay
Juggle relay
Pony express relay
Base running relay

Aquatics

Crawl
Backstroke
Sidestroke
Elementary diving
Elementary life saving

*Stunts, Tumbling, and Self-
Testing*

Russian bear dance
Jump the stick
Hand wrestle
Human bridge
High kick
Dive
Handstand
Seal slap
Jump over fool

Track and field events
Indian leg wrestle
Stick wrestle
Rope skipping for speed and
time
Bar hanging by arms, knees
Turn over on low bar

Camping and Outing

Hiking
Compass reading
Trail blazing
Fire building—reflector oven,
criss cross, travels
Wood chopping
Wood sawing
Menu planning
Outdoor cooking
Garbage disposal
Blanket rolling
Fishing-hunting
Crafts from native materials
Simple shelter construction
Camp soil conservation project
Overnight camping

Team Games

Progressive dodgeball
Volleyball
Schlagball
Base football
Softball
Touch football
Double dodgeball
Volleyball
Basketball—twenty-one, horse
Drop in, drop out
Circle goal shooting
Basketball pass variations
Soccer
Tennis
Speedball
Softball

GRADE 6—BOYS AND GIRLS

Rhythmical Activities
Folk Dance
  Kerry Dance
  Sicilian Circle
  Irish Song Dance
  Jesse Polka
  Badger Gavote
  Raatikko
  Cherkessia
  Road to the Isles
  Jarabe Tapatio
  Trilby
  Laces and Graces
  Ranger Polka

Square Dance
  Arkansas Traveler
  Birdie in the Cage
  Heel and Toe Polka
  Cotton-Eyed Joe
  Rye Waltz
  Dive for the Oyster

Dance Fundamentals
  Slide
  Schottische variations
  Waltz
  Waltz variations
  Congo
  Lifting and carrying
  Swinging
  Propulsive and sustained move-
    ments
  Dance creations

Games of Low Organization
  Stealing sticks
  Ante over
  Horseshoes
  Hand tennis
  Box hockey
  Tug-of-war
  Broom hockey
  Keep away
  Giant volleyball
  Overtake softball
  Long base
  Target toss

Relays
  Shuttle-pass-soccer relay
  Obstacle dribble relay
  Dribble and pass relay
  Bounce, pass, and shoot relay
  Base running relays

Stunts and Tumbling
  Throwing, batting, kicking for
    accuracy
  Throwing, batting, kicking for
    distance
  Base running
  Standing broad jump
  Hop, step and jump
  Sprinting
  The top
  Knee spring
  Handstand
  Floor dip
  Dives
  Push and pull ups
  Pyramids
  Simple apparatus

Camping and Outing
  Hiking
  Bicycle trip camping
  Use of two-handed axe
  Making things with knife, with
    hatchet
  Overnight camping utilizing all
    skills learned for sleeping,
    playing, and cooking in the
    woods
  Fire building, alter fire, char-
    coal stove
  Wood chopping and sawing
  Blanket rolls
  Menu planning
  Outdoor cooking
  Garbage disposal
  Fishing-hunting-trapping
  Construction of three types of
    shelter
  Camp soil conservation
  Crafts from native materials
  Lashing

Team Games
    Captain ball
    Basketball
    Fongo batting
    Hit pin baseball
    Soccer
    Soccer dodgeball
    Volleyball

    Softball
    Touch football
Aquatics
    Diving
    Breast stroke
    Advanced skills in all swim-
       ming strokes

The teacher should set up a weekly time schedule after she has chosen the broad classifications of the program and is aware of the various time percentage to be alloted to each phase. A sample weekly program for grades 1 through 6 follows:

Table 7
SAMPLE WEEKLY PROGRAM

GRADE	MONDAY-WEDNESDAY-FRIDAY	TUESDAY-THURSDAY
1	Stunts and self-testing activities. Games of low organization	Relay and circle games
2	Rhythmic activities	Supervised free play
3	Team games	Stunts and self-testing activities
4	Stunts and self-testing activities	Rhythmic activities
5	Rhythmic activities	Self-testing activities
6	Aquatics	Rhythmic activities

A more detailed calendar of the activities to be included under each of the broad classifications should follow this initial plan. As the teacher becomes more skilled in planning and teaching she may gradually eliminate the initial sample weekly plan with its broad classifications, and go directly into detailed planning for each week.

The teacher should devise a daily and weekly calendar listing under each day's column activities to be taught or reviewed. Over-planning is wiser than underplanning for it allows for greater flexibility.

A sample semester's program for boys, grade 6, and one for girls. grade 6, follows:

Table 8

PROGRAM FOR 6TH GRADE BOYS—FORTY MINUTE CLASS PERIOD
FALL SEASON

	MONDAY	TUESDAY	WEDNESDAY	THURSDAY	FRIDAY
First Week	Discuss class routine—dress, shower, squad, etc. Assign lockers.	Brace motor ability test.	*Circle Games* Circle tag. Circle relay. Two deep.	*Tag Games* Partner tag. Hook on. Chain tag.	Organize squads and squad leaders. Relays. Run, jump, hop.
Second Week	Discuss body mechanics. Posture test. Running relays.	*Rhythms* Fundamental rhythms: hop, skip, walk, run, jump.	*Touch Football* Instruction in passing and catching two lines practice.	*Rhythms* 1. Review of rhythms. 2. Hokey Pokey.	*Touch Football* Review Wednesday's skill. Teach punting.
Third Week	Touch football. Play.	Review rhythms. Teach Schottische.	Relay-run and throw back (football). Play touch football.	Review Schottische. Hokey pokey.	Review of Wednesday. Teach centering ball. Play touch football.
Fourth Week	Touch football. Relay. Duck walk.	Rhythms. Teach Green Sleeves.	Teach drop kick.	Rhythms. Green Sleeves. Teach Gustof's Skoal.	Review Wednesday. Squads alt. at centering, kicking, and receiving.
Fifth Week	Play touch football.	Rhythms. Teach Crested Hen Polka.	Passing to an end. Emphasize passing, catching, centering.	Rhythms. Crested Hen Polka.	Review Wednesday. Add a defensive man. Play touch football.
Sixth Week	Review running, catching, passing. Play touch football.	Review. Teach Jesse Polka.	Review rules. Play touch football.	Review all dances learned.	Test. Review Wednesday. Add a defensive man to dodge.

SECOND SIX WEEKS

	MONDAY	TUESDAY	WEDNESDAY	THURSDAY	FRIDAY
First Week	Review running and change of direction. Relay—In and out. Crows and cranes.	Review. Thursday. Teach Csebogar Rye Waltz.	Soccer skills. Play.	Review Csebogar Rye Waltz.	Soccer rules. Zig zag pass. Relay. Play soccer.
Second Week	Hunting game. Two and three deep, catch of fish.	Review rye waltz. Teach polka variations.	Soccer skills. Play.	Review polka variations. Teach Grand March.	Soccer rules. Shuttle pass. Relay. Play soccer.
Third Week	Hunting game. Cross tag. Prisoner's base.	Rumunjsko. Kolo, Mexican Mixer.	Soccer dribble relay. Review soccer basic skills. Play soccer.	Review Tuesday. Forward & back. Swing partner. Grand right and left. Allemande left.	Review dribble relay. Play soccer.
Fourth Week	Combative stunts. Indian hand wrestle, others.	Review square dance steps, promenade. Teach Dive For the Oyster.	Teach kick. Relay-soccer dribble kick. Play soccer.	Red River Valley. Review Grand March.	Introduce trapping relay. Lateral pass. Play soccer.
Fifth Week	Tumbling. Forward roll. backward roll.	Review Thursday. Take a Little Peek.	Review trapping. Circle soccer tag. Play soccer.	Review Tuesday. Sally Goodin.	Review dribble, kicking, trapping. Pin soccer. Play soccer.
Sixth Week	Review rolls. Introduce cartwheels, headstands.	Review Sally Goodin, Red River Valley.	Play soccer.	Review last three weeks rhythms.	Play soccer.

THIRD SIX WEEKS

	MONDAY	TUESDAY	WEDNESDAY	THURSDAY	FRIDAY
First Week	Review rolls. Introduce individual stunts. Cane grinder. Crab walk. Others.	Students choose dancers for review.	Test: Soccer kick for accuracy each boy four tries. Soccer dribble. Dribble and pass ability to play the game.	Test given by squads on folk dances and and square dances.	Test: Soccer dribble (obstacle). Each boy two tries. Test each boy's ability to play soccer game. Test knowledge of rules.
Second Week	Couple stunts. Chinese get-up. Siamese twins. Others.	Hunting games. Club snatch, last man out.	Introduce volleyball. Demonstrate. rules, teach skills.	Elimination dodgeball. Shuttle relays.	Review Wednesday. Teach serve, volley, return, keep it up.
Third Week	Stunt races: Crab race. Seal race. Others.	Games. Poison circle. Hit pin baseball.	Demonstrate spiking. Set up juggle. Teach positions.	Games: Chinese wall. Last man out. Bombardment.	Review rules. Play volleyball.
Fourth Week	Pyramids.	Hunting games. Water sprite. All up relay.	Play volleyball.	Relays. Over and under. Arch goal goal	Play volleyball.
Fifth Week	Pyramids.	Paddle tennis. Dodge ball relays.	Volleyball skill test.	Couple stunts. Individual stunts.	Volleyball skill test of playing ability.
Sixth Week	Pyramids.	Box hockey. Review of soccer skills.	Volleyball squad tournament.	Review basketball skills.	Volleyball squad tournament.

Table 9

PROGRAM FOR 6TH GRADE GIRLS—FORTY MINUTE CLASS
PERIOD
WINTER SEASON

	MONDAY	TUESDAY	WEDNESDAY	THURSDAY	FRIDAY
First Week	Physical examination	Organization of classes.	Team game. Alley soccer.	Team game. Alley soccer.	Co-ed folk dance. Green Sleeves.
Second Week	Posture test. Bancroft's triple posture test.	Group games. Crows and cranes. Cock fight. Hook on.	Team game. Alley soccer.	Team game. Alley soccer.	Co-ed folk dance. Green Sleeves. Hokey Pokey.
Third Week	Brace motor ability test.	Stunts. Chinese get-up. Cock fight. Indian hand wrestle.	Team game. Soccer.	Team game. Soccer.	Co-ed folk dance. Hokey Pokey. Dance of Greeting.
Fourth Week	Stunts. Indian hand wrestle. Jump the stick, kangaroo fight.	Team game. Soccer.	Team game. Soccer.	Team game. Soccer.	Co-ed folk dance. Dance of Greeting. Come Let Us Be Joyful.
Fifth Week	Stunts. Rocking chair. Skin the snake. One over.	Team game. Soccer.	Team game. Soccer.	Team game. Soccer.	Co-ed folk dance. Review of all dances learned. Crested Hen.
Sixth Week	Group games. Hook on. Cross tag. May I.	Team game. Soccer test. Dribble punt. Dribble pass.	Team game. Soccer test. Ability to play the game.	Team game. Soccer test. Ability to play the game.	Co-ed folk dance. Crested Hen. Gustaf's Skoal.

SECOND SIX WEEKS

	MONDAY	TUESDAY	WEDNESDAY	THURSDAY	FRIDAY
First Week	Stunts. Wheel-barrow. Flying angel. Review.	Team game. Basketball. Lead up. (End ball.)	Team game. Basketball. Lead up. (End ball.)	Team game. Basketball. Passing relay.	Co-ed folk dance. Crested Hen. Sandy Land.
Second Week	Stunts. Wheel-barrow. Race. Stomach balance. Neck flip tandem.	Team game. Basketball. Lead up. End ball. Horse.	Team game. Basketball. Teach rules and skills of passing.	Team game. Basketball. Relay of skills of passing, throwing, catching.	Co-ed folk dance. Square dance. Red River Valley. Sally Goodin.
Third Week	Group games. Streets and alleys. Catch the caboose. Red light.	Team game. Basketball offense. Relays of game skills.	Team game. Basketball defense. Relays game skills.	Team game. Play basket-ball.	Co-ed folk dance. Square dance. Red River Valley. Sally Goodin.
Fourth Week	Group games. Three deep streets and alleys. Tag and it.	Team game. Basketball. Foul shooting.	Team game. Basketball. Field goal.	Team game. Play basket-ball.	Co-ed folk dance. Square dance. Sally Goodin. Texas Star.
Fifth Week	Group games. Family takes a walk. Turkey trot. Forty ways of getting there over and under.	Team game. Basketball. Game strategy. Play basket-ball.	Team game. Basketball. Game strategy. Play basket-ball.	Team game. Basketball. Review play.	Co-ed folk dance. Square dance. Texas Star. Take a Little Peek.
Sixth Week	Group games. Electric shock. Boundary ball. Japanese tag.	Team game. Basketball. Test-shooting. Pass-dribble.	Team game. Basketball test. Ability to play.	Team game. Basketball test. Rules.	Co-ed folk dance. Square dance. Take a Little Peek. Texas Star.

THIRD SIX WEEKS

	MONDAY	TUESDAY	WEDNESDAY	THURSDAY	FRIDAY
First Week	Stunts. Centipede. Human Ball. Wring the dish rag.	Team game. Volleyball. Lead up. Newcomb.	Team game. Newcomb.	Team game. Newcomb.	Co-ed folk dance. Wagon Wheel. Pop Goes the Weasel.
Second Week	Stunts. Wring the dish rag. Rocking chair. One over.	Team game. Volleyball. Basic skill. Play.	Team game. Volleyball. Net play. Play.	Team game. Volleyball. Back field play. Play.	Co-ed folk dance. Pop Goes the Weasel. Starlight Schottische.
Third Week	Stunts. Stomach balance. Skin the snake. Chinese get-up.	Team game. Volleyball. Game strategy. Play.	Team game. Volleyball. Game strategy. Play.	Team game. Volleyball. Game strategy. Play.	Co-ed folk dance. Starlight Schottische. Sentimental Journey.
Fourth Week	Group games. Japanese tag. Midnight. Crows and cranes.	Team game. Volleyball. Squad tournament.	Team game. Volleyball. Squad ournament.	Team game. Volleyball. Squad tournament.	Co-ed folk dance. Sentimental Journey. Ten Pretty Girls.
Fifth Week	Group games. Midnight. Stick tag. Bear in pit.	Team game. Volleyball test. Serve, net.	Team game. Volleyball test. Pass, play.	Team game. Kick ball. Basic skills. Throw it and run.	Co-ed folk dance. Ten Pretty Girls. Mexican Mixer.
Sixth Week	Group games. Bear in pit. Pigs in pen. Have you seen my sheep?	Team game. Kick ball. Basic skills. Play.	Team game. Kick ball. Basic skills. Team play.	Team game. Volleyball. Written test on rules.	Co-ed folk dance. Review of all dances learned.

Suggested Readings

Brace, Daird, *Measuring Motor Ability*, New York, A. S. Barnes, 1927.

Evans, Ruth and Gans, Les, *Supervision of Physical Education*, New York, McGraw-Hill Co., 1947.

Irwin, L. W., *The Curriculum in Health and Physical Education*, St. Louis, C. V. Mosby, 1951.

Jerschild, Arthurs and Others, *Child Development and Curriculum*, New York, Teacher's College, Columbia University, 1946.

LaPorte, William, *The Physical Education Curriculum*, Los Angeles, University of California Press, 1949.

LaSalle, Dorothy, *Guidance of Children Through Physical Education*, New York, A. S. Barnes, 1946.

Neilson, N. P. and Van Hagen, Winifred, *Physical Education For Elementary Schools*, New York, A. S. Barnes, 1932.

Chapter 7

FUNDAMENTAL AND CREATIVE PLAY

Fundamental Play

Although environmental conditions and standards of living change, the urge to play remains a dominant characteristic found in every race and in every country. Geographical location does not alter the original theme or idea, for games are built around age old urges of running, jumping, hopping, chasing and fleeing, hiding and seeking, hunting, guessing and dodging. One may find hundreds of variations of these themes, with as many different names, but the original theme remains the same. Thus, we hear of Indians in Mexico playing a game which resembles the all familiar "London Bridge Is Falling Down" and of South Pacific Islanders playing an aboriginal version of "Hull Gull, Hand Full, How Many?" with sea shells.

The counterparts of the games to follow may be found of ageless vintage in many lands but are still popular with American youngsters today.

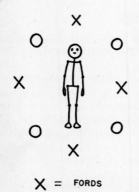

X = FORDS

O = CHEVROLETS

AUTOMOBILES OR AIRPLANES

Type: Running   Formation: Circle   Players: 30 to 40   Gym, playground   Grades: 1, 2

1. Players number off, one to four or six according to the size of the group.
2. No. 1's are Fords, No. 2's are Chevrolets, etc.
3. "It" calls the name of an automobile as Ford and all Fords run counterclockwise around the circle and return to their original place and dash to the center to touch "It."
4. The first runner to touch the starter wins the Ford race.

92

5. When each type of automobile has been called and the race run, the starter calls, "all winners" and this race determines the big winner.
6. Variations—Use names of race horses or airplanes.

FACE TO FACE   BACK TO BACK

BACK TO BACK

Gym, playground   Players: 12 to 16

1. "It" calls "back to back." Players must back up to partner.
2. "It" calls "face to face" and partners face and shake hands.
3. On the next call of "back to back" and each time thereafter, all players must change partners.
4. "It" tries to get a partner during the change and the player left out becomes "It."

BEATER GOES ROUND

Gym, playground, playroom   Players: 12 to 20   Grades: 3, 4
Formation: Circle

1. One player is outside the circle and carries a knotted cloth or folded newspaper. He walks around the circle and gives it to a player.
2. Receiver turns to his right and beats player lightly on back.
3. Player runs around circle to own place with beater chasing him.
4. Original starter has stepped into place of first receiver.

BIRD, BEAST, FISH

Gym, playground   Players: 18 to
24   Grades: 1, 2, 3   Formation: Circle

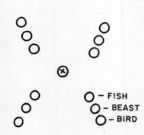

O – FISH
O – BEAST
O – BIRD

1. Group forms a three deep circle.
2. Inside player is a Bird, middle player
   is a Beast and the outside player is
   a Fish.
3. "It" is in the middle; he will call a
   name—bird, beast or fish. The group
   which he names must all change
   places.
4. When the group is changing, "It"
   runs to an empty place and the person left without a place becomes "It."

CATCH THE BAT

Playground, playroom, gym
Players: 8 to 16   Grades: 2, 3, 4
Formation: Circle   Wand or bat

1. Players form a circle and number off.
2. One player stands in center and bal-
   ances bat or wand with the fingertips.
3. Center player calls a number and releases the bat.
4. Number called tries to catch the bat
   before it falls to the floor or ground.
   If he succeeds, he becomes "It," and
   if he fails, he returns to his place in
   the circle while "It" calls another
   number.

CLUB SNATCH

Gym, playground   Players: 12 to
18   Grades: 1, 2, 3

1. Divide players into teams, numbering each player
2. Place an Indian club or any type object in the center between the two
   teams.
3. Instructor calls a number and the
   members of each team, corresponding with the number called, run out
   and try to get the club.

4. The member of the team that gets the club and gets across the restraining line without getting tagged wins the point for his team.
5. Team with the most points wins.

DOG CATCHER

Gym, playground   Players: 20 to 80   Grades: 1 to 4

1. Name three or four kinds of dogs. Each child chooses the kind he wants to be. All go to one kennel.
2. Dog catcher calls one kind of dog. They run to opposite kennel. If caught, they are put in the pound.
3. After the dog catcher has had three turns, he tells how many dogs he has caught and chooses another to take his place until all are caught. The last one caught starts the new game.

DOUBLE CIRCLE

Gym, playground   Players: 8 to 24   Grades: 1, 2, 3   Formation: Double circle

1. The class is arranged in two concentric circles, one having one more member than the other.
2. On signal they begin to skip around in opposite directions until the whistle is blown or the music stops, then each player endeavors to secure a partner from the other circle.
3. One player is left without a partner. If any player is left out three times he must pay a penalty—do some stunt, sing a song, etc. Repeat.

FOXES' DEN

Playground   Players: 10 to 18   Grades: 1, 2, 3   Formation: Circle

1. One player in the center is the hunter.
2. The circle players are the foxes and

attempt to change positions by running along the spokes.
3. If the hunter tags a fox, he becomes
the hunter, if not, the hunter remains
until he tags a fox.

FROG IN THE SEA

Gym, playground   Players: 8 to 16
Grade: 1   Formation: Draw a circle 3 feet in diameter.

1. Frog is sitting cross-legged in the
center of the circle.
2. Children tease him and cross line
back and forth but the frog must remain sitting.
3. If the frog is successful in tagging
anyone, that one becomes the frog.
4. Children tease by chanting—"Frog
in the sea, can't catch me."

HAVE YOU SEEN MY SHEEP?

Playground, gym, playroom
Players: 8 to 12   Grades: 1, 2
Formation: Single circle

1. One player is "It" and walks around
circle and asks any player, "Have
you seen my sheep?" The player
queries, "What does he look like?"
2. "It" describes his sheep (a player
as to eyes, hair, dress, etc.)
3. If the player guesses correctly the
sheep runs and he chases and tries
to tag the sheep before he can run
around the circle and return to his
place.
4. "It" steps into the vacated place in
the circle.
5. The player, if caught, becomes "It"
and if he is not caught the chaser
becomes "It" for another game.

HIGH WINDOWS

Gym, playground   Players: 8 to 12
Grades: 1, 2, 3   Formation: Single
circle with "It" in center

1. "It" runs around inside of circle and tags a player.
2. "It" runs outside of circle attempting to run around the circle 3 times before being tagged by player chasing.
3. When he completes 3 rounds, players in circle raise their hands (joined) and cry, "High windows."
4. Runner comes into the circle and is safe. He continues to be "It."
5. If "It" is caught, chaser becomes "It."

HILL DILL

Gym, playground   Players: 12 to 30
Grades: 1, 2, 3

1. Two parallel lines are drawn 50 to 75 feet apart.
2. All players but "It" stand on one line, while "It" stands halfway between the lines.
3. "It" calls, "Hill dill, come over the hill or I'll catch you while you're standing still."
4. At this signal all players must run for the opposite line.
5. All those that "It" can tag help him in the next game. When all are caught, a new "It" is chosen.

HOPSCOTCH

Playground, tennis courts and sidewalks
Grades: Girls 1 to 4; Boys 1 and 2
Players: 4 to 6 to court

This game is enjoyed by all children but is particularly suitable in remedial cases where limited activity is recommended.

1. Second through fourth grades.
   Player throws pebble into square 1, hop in on one foot, picks up pebble and hops out.
   The pebble then is thrown into square 2, the player hops on one foot

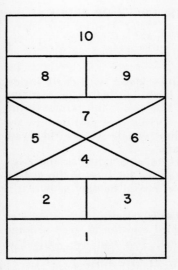

into 1, straddles 2 and 3, picks up the pebble, puts weight on left foot and hops into 1 and out. The player may continue until the pebble fails to land in the proper square or he steps on a line or puts a foot down when he should not. He hops on one foot into 1, 4, 7, and 10 and straddles the lines to retrieve the pebble in 2, 3, 5, 6, 8, and 9.

2. First graders like more activity so they follow the above instructions but hop to the end and back each time.

HOOK ON

Playground, gym   Players: Entire class   Grade: 3

1. Pick four children to go to one end of gymnasium. Others go to opposite end. Both line up.
2. Leader blows whistle.
3. All try to hook on to one of four.
4. Try to keep back end of line away from children trying to hook on.
5. Move fast. Chain with fewest "hooks on" wins.

JUMP THE CREEK OR BROOK

Playground, gym, playroom
Players: Entire class   Grades: 1, 2, 3, 4

1. Two lines drawn with chalk inside, or a stick outside, represent the creek.
2. The last child over gets to draw the new line which widens the creek each time.
3. Any child who lands in the creek must take off his shoes and put them back on before he can re-enter the game.
4. For inside activity, it is suggested that third and fourth graders jump with both feet together. (Standing broad jump.)

JUMP THE SHOT

Playground, gym   Players: 8 to 12
Grades: 2 to 6   Formation: Circle

1. Knot the end of a long jump rope or attach a weight as: bean bag or ball in a sack.
2. Teacher in lower grades, any player in upper grades stands in the center of the circle and turns, taking the rope under the feet of the players who jump over it.
3. Any player who touches the rope is out of the game.
4. The player who stays in the circle longest wins.

LOOSE CABOOSE

Playground, gym   Players: Entire class   Grades: 2, 3
Formation: Circle

1. Players stand in groups of three in a circle.
2. First player is Engine; second is Chair Car; and third is the Caboose.
3. There are two (or any number) of Loose Cabooses who try to attach themselves to the end of a line.
4. When this occurs, Engine becomes Loose Caboose and game continues.

MIDNIGHT

Playground, gym   Players: 20 to 80
Grades: 1, 2

1. The Fox stands in his den and the Sheep in their fold.
2. The Fox wanders out into the meadow, and so do the Sheep.
3. The Sheep ask "What time is it?" and the Fox answers, "Two o'clock, ten o'clock," etc. The Sheep keep milling around, but when he answers "Midnight," they scamper for the fold.
4. All the Sheep that are tagged be-

come Foxes, and the same procedure is repeated.

5. The last Sheep caught becomes the new Fox and a new game starts.

NUMBERS CHANGE

Playground, gym   Players: Entire class   Grades: 1, 2, 3   Formation: Circle

1. All players are given a number and one is chosen to be "It."
2. The players stand in a circle with "It" in the center.
3. He calls any two numbers.
4. The players whose numbers he calls exchange places, while the one who is "It" attempts to get one of their places in the circle.
5. The one of these left without a place is "It" for the next time and he calls the two numbers to change.

PLUG (An Old Broken Down Horse)

Playground, gym   Players: Entire class   Grade: 3   Rubber Ball

1. Five players make Plug by locking arms around waist of player in front.
2. Others are Throwers. Thrower tries to hit Plug's tail. When hit below waist—Tail becomes a Thrower. Player that threw hit becomes Head.
3. Repeat.

POISON

Playground, gym   Players: 8 to 12   Grade: 2   Formation: Circle

1. Players join hands and form circle with Indian Club in center.
2. One player, chosen as the Leader, signals for the start of the game.
3. Players try to pull each other toward Club to knock it down.
4. The player who knocks down the Club is eliminated and the Leader replaces the Club.

5. If the circle is broken, players on either side of the break are eliminated.
6. The last player to be eliminated is the winner and the leader in a new game.

POM-POM PULLAWAY

Playground, gym   Players: 12 to 20
Grade: 2

1. All players but "It" stand behind Goal Line.
2. "It" stands in the middle of the area and calls, "Pom-Pom Pullaway, come or I will pull you away."
3. All players run to opposite Goal Line.
4. Those tagged help "It." Last one tagged becomes next "It."

RED LIGHT

Playground, gym, playroom
Players: 20 to 40   Grades: 1, 2, 3

1. One player chosen as the Traffic Cop stands on the finish line with his back to the group.
2. The cop calls "Green Light," and the players advance cautiously while he counts.
3. The cop may call "Red Light" at any time and turn quickly and face the players. Any player in motion must return to the starting line.
4. The first player to cross the finish line becomes the traffic cop.
   This game can be used in teaching safety.

RED ROVER

Playground, gym   Players: 16 to 36
Grades: 1, 2   Formation: Line, Running

1. Players join hands and form two

lines facing each other, about 20′ apart.

2. One player in each line is the Leader or Caller.

3. The Leader in Line B calls "Red Rover, Red Rover, let Johnny (any child) come over."

4. Johnny runs from Line A and tries to break through Line B. If he succeeds, he returns to his own line. If he fails, he stays with Line B.

5. Line A calls and so on alternately.

6. The side that finishes with the most players wins.

7. Callers should be changed at intervals.

SARDINES

Playground   Players: Entire class
Grades: 3, 4

1. Sardine is a hide-and-seek game. It differs from the usual hide-and-seek game in that "It" hides and all of the other players set out to find him.

2. "It" is given time to hide and then, at a given signal, the others start to hunt him.

3. Any player finding him, must hide with him.

4. The last one finding the hiding place is "It" for the next game.

SKIP TAG

Any sizeable room with seats
Players: 20 to 80   Grades: 1, 2, 3

1. Group is seated around sides of room with right hands extended.

2. "It" skips around and slaps palm of one player.

3. The chosen player skips after "It." If he is successful in tagging, he becomes "It" and the tagged player takes his seat; otherwise he returns to his seat.

4. If "It" is not tagged in three tries, he chooses a new "It."
5. In mixed groups, girls should tag boys and boys tag girls.
6. Players must skip and cannot cut corners.

SQUIRRELS IN TREES

Playground, gym, playroom
Players: 16 to 80   Grades: 1, 2

1. Number off by 3's. Nos. 1 and 2 form Tree by facing and holding hands. No. 3 is the Squirrel inside the Tree. Odd players are the Homeless Squirrels.
2. At a signal, all Squirrels must change Trees, and in the scramble the Odd Squirrels try to find a Tree.
3. Variation: In small groups play as tag with one Odd Squirrel and one Chaser (Hunter). The Odd Squirrel ducks into a Tree and the other Squirrel must vacate and find another Tree. If the Squirrel is tagged, he becomes Chaser.
4. Change positions of Trees and Squirrels often to allow running for all.

TAG IN BRIEF

Playground, gym   Players: Entire
class   Grades: 1, 2, 3

NOSE-AND-TOE TAG
Runners cannot be tagged when holding nose with one hand, toes with other hand.

HINDU TAG
Safe when kneeling, with forehead touching ground.

OSTRICH TAG
Safe when holding nose with right hand, with right arm under right leg.

HANG TAG
Safe when hanging onto something, such as tree limb, post.

STOOP TAG

Safe when stooping down.

SQUAT TAG

Squat for safety.

HOOK-ON TAG

Hook onto arm of another player to keep from being tagged.

COLOR TAG

Safe when touching a certain color, as red, blue, green, etc.

ARMS LENGTH TAG

Playground, gym, playroom
Players: Entire class   Grades: 1, 2, 3

1. Two players stand each with an arm extended at full length at shoulder level.
2. Each tries to touch the other above the wrist without being touched in return.
3. A touch on the extended hand does not count.

THREE DEEP

Playground, gym   Players: Entire class   Grades: 1, 2, 3   Formation: Circle

1. Players get into double circle.
2. The chaser ("C") chases runner ("R").
3. "R" may save himself by getting in front of a group making it three deep.
4. When group is three deep, outside person becomes "R."
5. If and when "R" is caught, he becomes "C."
6. "R" must go into circle from outside when making it three deep. When being chased, he may cut through.

Variations may be made to this game by making it Two Deep, or Four Deep, depending upon number of group.

WEATHER COCK

Playground, gym, playroom
Players: Entire class   Grades: 1, 2, 3
Children should know directions North,
East, South and West.

1. One player represents weather bureau and stands in front of others
   and tells the way the wind blows.
2. Weather bureau says, "The wind
   blows north," the players turn
   quickly to the north, etc.
3. When he says "whirl wind," the
   players spin around three times on
   right heel.
   Play rapidly for interest.

Creative Play

The beginning of the century found a child with few toys and
the capacity to play for hours on end with "findings." A pile of
sand, a few bits of broken glass or china and twigs furnished materials for full scale villages complete with houses, barns, schools,
and churches. Tea parties of mud pies were served with great for-
mality from a pedestal table made of dirt. From large leaves and
twigs young designers fashioned hats, capes, skirts and dresses
which were modeled with an amusing exactness of adult patterns.
Labor saving devices were few and mothers kept too busy, except
to call children for meals, naps and baths.

Today, the infant lies in a toy-bedecked crib and collects more
toys as birthdays and Christmases pass. Sand is to be had by the
load, and woe to the child who dares pluck a leaf from a guarded
and nurtured tree. Labor saving devices have left mothers leisure
time to play nurse-maid, a job made easier by access to parks, well
equipped libraries, recreation centers, nursery schools, neighborhood movie houses, radio, and, more recently, television sets. Urban
children are gradually being deprived of all stimuli which once
enabled them to play without direct instruction and supervision
and mothers complain that the children cannot amuse themselves
over a thirty minute period without being bored.

Today's teacher is completely aware of the short span of attention present in the newly acquired pupil, which is characteristic
of the age level, but not entirely physiological or psychological. The
class room teacher and the special teachers have tried to remedy

this and to give the child a measure of security and self-sufficiency by equipping him with the tools for living. It cannot be said that real effort has not been made to develop the "whole" child mentally, physically and emotionally, but how near have we come to meeting this objective? Paté de fois gras is palatable, but is the process good for the goose? We still stuff children and expect magic results in the way of initiative. How many of us ask, "Is there a child in the class who could create from his own background of experience, an enjoyable period of play acceptable to his classmates?" It is far easier with age, poise and experience to direct play than to develop in one child the ability to do the same thing, "free hand!" The art teacher can take potential talent and draw from it the maximum in imagination, reality, or originality. Play is laughter, high spirits, and joy unlimited. In this field where sheer enjoyment is the key it would be shameful if teachers did not meet the challenge of the children's needs and at least give them the CHANCE to be ingenious leaders.

Creative play is not new but its possibilities are comparatively untouched. There are several reasons which explain this fallow corner in a field rich with all the newest trends in progressive education, the most prevalent being overcrowded conditions which exist in the majority of public schools. The average teacher finds it difficult to deal with a class two to four times the normal load without assuming full or partial leadership. Creative play calls for small, intimate groups, managed in the most informal manner. The ideal group would not exceed twenty, where each child would have frequent chances for expression, but creative play can and has been developed in large groups of 80 to 120.[1] A certain amount of regimentation is required in all large schools, especially where the platoon system is used, and, while it is necessary, the routine subdues latent creativeness. The time element is another reason why creative play has not flourished. Creativeness cannot be nurtured by bells. It takes a gifted teacher to hold on to a vision gained and reproject it into the minds of the participants with sustaining and refreshing enthusiasm the next day.

There can be no static method for developing creative play. The group, its individual characteristics and dominant field of expe-

[1] Foster, Mildred, *Creative Play at the Margaret B. Henderson Elementary School*, Dallas Public School System, Dallas, Texas, 1950.

rience, will dictate to the resourceful teacher the plan of procedure. An imaginative six year old child may invent a game that will keep a class engrossed for thirty minutes. There are also people who play a piano by ear, while others must learn scales and notes before tackling the simplest of piano selections. Thus, one may find a group of fourth graders who must be re-introduced to the fundamentals of play, i.e., chase, flee, tag, seek, dodge, guess, follow, etc., before one child comes forth with an original game. However, we as teachers, cannot complain too loudly, since we have leaned with monotonous regularity on tried and true game books for years. One must face innumerable presentations of questionable originality. Tact and patience will reward the persistent teacher. In any case, the reward will be adequate when the child can competently lead a game—the day Jimmie teaches a game that he calls, "I Gotcha." It *is* different! All of the children eye Jimmie with open admiration slightly tinged with envy, one even wisecracks, "Whatcha know, right out of his little pointed head." On this day you, teacher, have arrived and can take proper pride in your fledgling.

This does not mean that every child will immediately burst forth with new and exciting games. The neo-dubious will still crop up, but the group will become more discriminating and take the criticizing chore out of the hands of the teacher by observing, "Ah, I learned that at Daily Vacation Bible School or we learned that at Camp." The hard sledding is over. From then on original ideas will start appearing with encouraging regularity. Do not be too critical and, above all, try to gear your evaluation to the grade level.

Children are innately creative but the current, consuming interest will always be reflected in the games. At the present writing the "Cowboy" is "It." Children from Spokane to Los Angeles, Dallas to Duluth, and New Haven to Key West are roping, cutting calves,[1] chasing rustlers, packing six shooters, slapping leather,[2] and addressing playmates as "podner." Sex does not enter into the picture. There is an "Annie Oakley"[3] for each "Hopalong."[4] Even now cowboys are becoming "old hat," for youthful "sargents" are beginning to industriously search out atomic materials with 5 or 10

[1] Round-up—Separation of calves from stock ready for market.
[2] Hitting leather chaps with bridle reins to urge on horses and cattle.
[3] Real life character who was crack shot.
[4] Current cowboy hero.

Geiger Counters. This does not make any difference as long as the child is creating a type of play which includes mental and physical activity, and is guided into democratic channels.

Creative play involving movement fundamentals will be found in its most productive form from the first through the fourth grades. New games will still appear which concern themselves largely with skills in lead-up games, but the interest has shifted to team sports and creativeness is manifested through methods for improving offensive and defensive play. However, games related to subject matter may be created through the eighth grade and on into high school as a method for motivating learning.

Below are listed games which have been presented by elementary children and show creativeness influenced by background experience.

COLOR BALL
High Grade 1

An imaginary basket is filled with rubber balls of many colors. "It" decided on a color and lifts a ball from the basket. Three children get to guess the color of the ball. If one guesses the color, he becomes "It," otherwise he continues until one is successful.

JUNGLE JIM
Grade 3

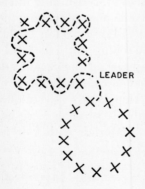

(Jungle Jim is a comic strip character read by many children.)

Twelve children form a hollow square. Leader winds in and out of the square tapping children who identify themselves as certain animals or birds. As each child is tapped he follows the leader in a snake-like line until the entire group is drawn into a circle. The group sings, "We Went to the Animal Fair." The leader then calls upon each child to give an imitation of the animal he represents. The child who gives the best imitation becomes the next leader.

RADAR SCREEN
Grade 5

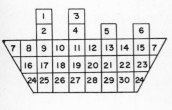

Class is divided into two teams who make out questions on any subject. Teacher reads and directs questions or better team leaders do same. When a question is answered correctly, a block is hung on that team's screen. The team that fills its screen first is the winner. Colored blocks hung on eye screws, 2 half squares equivalent to one whole square.

WASH DAY
Grade 2

Numbers 5, 6, 7 and 8 decide what piece of laundry they will represent as: sheet, towel, shirt. Number 1 pin gets two guesses as to what he is holding on the line. If the guess is correct, he changes places with Number 5. The questioning goes on down the line. If a clothes pin misses three times he must drop out of the game and a new player takes his place. The players representing the wash decide on a different article after each round of questioning.

Suggested Readings

Carlquist, Maja and Amylong, Tora, *Balance and Rhythm in Exercise*, New York, Viking Press, 1951.

Carlson, Bernice, *Do It Yourself*, New York, Abingdon-Cokesbury, 1952.

Cleveland Public Schools, *Physical Education Course of Study*, Cleveland, Ohio, Primary Division, Board of Education, 1946.

Hunt, Sarah and Cain, Ethyl, *Games the World Around*, New York, A. S. Barnes, 1950.

Kepler, Hazel, *The Child and His Play*, New York, Funk and Wagnalls, 1952.

LaSalle, Dorothy, *Guidance of Children Through Physical Education*, New York, A. S. Barnes, 1946.

Mitchell, Elmer and Mason, Bernard, *The Theory of Play*, Revised Edition, New York, A. S. Barnes, 1948.

Mulac, Margaret, *The Playleader's Manual*, New York, Harper Brothers, 1941.

Neilson, N. P. and Van Hagen, Winifred, *Physical Education for Elementary Schools*, New York, A. S. Barnes, 1939.

Radir, Ruth, *Modern Dance For The Youth of America*, New York, A. S. Barnes, 1946.

Richardson, Hazel A., *Games for Elementary Grades*, Minneapolis, Burgess Publishing Company, 1936.

Salt, E. Benton; Fox, Grace I.; Douthett, Elsie M.; Stevens, B. K., *Teaching Physical Education in the Elementary School*, New York, A. S. Barnes, 1942.

Sehon, Elizabeth I.; Anderson, Marion H.; Hodgens, Winifred W.; and Fossen, Gladys R., *Physical Education Methods for Elementary Schools*, Second Edition, Philadelphia, W. B. Saunders Company, 1953.

Whitlock, Virginia, *Come and Caper*, Creative Rhythms, Pantomimes, and Plays, New York, G. Shirmer Company, 1932.

Chapter 8

Relays

Relays are a boon to the teacher with oversized classes. A large number may participate with a minimum of organization but the end results are manifold. Most children enjoy this activity and learn skills and team cooperation while developing large muscles and coordination.

Organization of Teams

Boys and girls on the primary level should compete on the same teams. On the upper elementary level it is best, generally, to have the boys compete with boys and the girls with girls. However, when there is an equal sex distribution and class members do not wish to be separated, mixed competition is highly desirable. Other helpful suggestions are:

1. Permanent teams, where there is an equalization of skill and size, are organizational time savers.
2. Change team captains at regular intervals.
3. Train and assign student officials.
4. Divide your class by counting off 1–2, 1–2, etc., with all the ones being in one line and all the twos in another line. It is unwise to let the children choose their team members too often, for one child tends to always be the last one chosen. Another suggested way of dividing the class would be to have all children whose name begins with A–L to be on one side, all the ones whose name begins with M–Z on the other. Or have all whose birthday is from January–June be on one team, all those whose birthday is from July–December be on the other.

True Relay

1. Establish the type of formation, starting line, turning line, method of touching off, signal for starts, and objective of relay. (Right hand to right hand is most accepted touch-off.)
2. Possible fouls should be discussed and a penalty set. A team should

111

not be disqualified because a member commits a foul, but a point for each foul should be subtracted from the place won.

Team	A	B	C	D
Place	1st	2nd	3rd	4th
Points	5	3	2	1
Fouls	3	0	1	1
	2	3	1	0
Score	2nd	1st	3rd	4th

3. Start relays by a signal, whistle, or oral command. (1–2–3 go! Emphasize the word *go!*)
4. Completion of relay may be indicated by the first member of each team raising hands high, by sitting down, or the whole team may squat or sit down.

Modified Relays

The modified relay can be used with primary grade children where the details of the true relay seem too complicated. This type

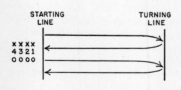

of relay is run in heats and each child who comes in first in his heat wins a point for his team. The team scoring the most points wins the relay. Otherwise, directions for the true relay may serve as an adequate guide for organization.

Relays which use the line or file formation are more suitable and the type will be governed by the skill of the group.

Relay Formations

SINGLE FILE OR DOUBLE LINE

8 to 16 per team

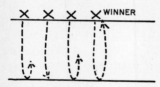

No. 1 runs, turns, runs back and touches off No. 2 and goes to foot of line. No. 2 runs etc.

SHUTTLE

16 to 24 per team

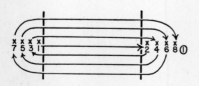

No. 1 runs to opposite line and touches off No. 2 and goes to foot of line. No. 2 runs etc. All runners end up on opposite sides.

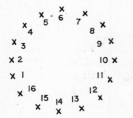

CIRCLE

8 to 16 per team

No. 1 runs around circle clockwise or counterclockwise and returns to place. Nos. 2, 3 etc. run circle until all have run.

Types of Relays

Most of the relays listed below use a parallel line or file formation. Distance indicates the number of feet from the starting line to the goal or turning line. The grade level for which relay is best suited is also given. The types of relays described include:

1. Relays using skills and stunts learned in self-testing activities.
2. Relays using locomotor skills.
3. Relays requiring equipment.
4. Relays related to team sports.
5. Obstacle relays.
6. Novelty relays suitable for special event days and parties.

RELAYS USING SKILLS AND STUNTS LEARNED IN SELF-TESTING ACTIVITIES

Grades: 1 to 6   Distance: 15 to 20 feet.

Children race, using the prescribed stunt from the starting line to turning point and back. These stunts are described fully in the chapter on stunts and tumbling.

Bear Walk	Kangaroo Hop	Log Roll
Crab Walk	Lame Puppy Walk	Double Line Formation
Duck Walk	Monkey Run	Wheelbarrow Relay
Frog Jump	Rabbit Hop	

RELAYS USING LOCOMOTOR SKILLS

Grades: 1 to 6   Distance: 20 to 40 feet.

Galloping.
Hopping—Hold one foot at front or back.
Jumping—Feet close together. Take small jumps with little knee flexion.
Skipping—Low and High Skip.
Sliding.
Running.

These locomotor movements are described fully in the chapter on Rhythms and Dance.

1. Running Relay

Race using command for start: On your mark, get set, go! First through third grade use standing start.

Fourth through sixth grade use crouch start.

2. Line Relay

Grades: 4 to 6

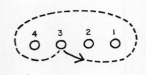

Teams number off consecutively from front to back. Teacher or leader calls a number. This child steps out of the line to his right and runs counterclockwise around his team, returning to his original place in line. Winner scores a point. Team with the highest score wins.

3. Rescue Relay

Grades: 3 to 6.   Distance: 30 to 50 feet

GOAL LINE

A leader stands behind a goal line facing his team which is lined up behind the starting line. On a signal, the leader runs to the first player of his team, grasps him by the wrist and runs back to the goal line. The rescued player then runs back and gets another player etc. until all have been rescued.

Walking: Grades 1 to 6. Arms are bent and elbows are held close to sides.

RELAYS REQUIRING EQUIPMENT

All Up Relay

Grades: 4 to 5   Equipment: 1 to 3 Indian clubs for each team   Distance: 20 to 40 feet

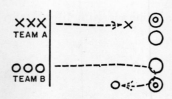

TEAM A

TEAM B

Chalk two circles the desired number of feet from the starting line. Place one, two or three Indian clubs in one circle. First in line runs and takes the club out of one circle and places it in the second circle, and runs back and touches off the second player who returns the club to circle No. 1. If a club falls over, the player must return and stand it upright.

Balance Relay

Grades: 2 to 6   Equipment: Bean bags, erasers, or books   Distance: 20 to 30 feet

Walk erectly, arms at side, balancing one of the listed objects on top of the head. If the object falls off, the player must stop in his tracks and replace it, then continue.

Bowling

Grades: 4 to 6   Equipment: 6 Indian clubs and one baseball for each team   Distance: 20 to 40 feet

Assign one child on each team to replace pins and call out score. Place pins 6 inches apart in a triangle. Roll the baseball and knock over as many pins as possible. A player gets one point for each club knocked over. Each bowler retrieves the ball and passes it to next in line.

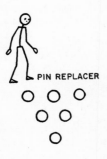

PIN REPLACER

Cap Transfer

Grades: 4 to 6   Equipment: 3 sticks and one cap for each team   Distance: 20 to 40 feet

The first three children on a team are given sticks. No. 1 is stationed at the turning point. No. 2 places a cap on the end of his stick and runs to No. 1 and transfers the cap to his stick. No. 1 returns to the starting line, transfers the cap to No. 3, gives his stick to No. 4 and goes to the foot of the line, etc. until all have run. The team regaining its original position first wins. If a cap falls off, it must be picked up with the stick without the aid of hands.

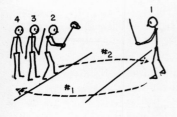

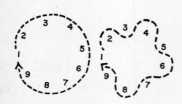

Circle Relay

Grades: 2 to 6   Equipment: Handkerchief or bean bag for each team

Give starting player handkerchief. On signal player runs around the circle and passes the handkerchief to person in front of him. First circle to finish wins.

Variation: Zigzag in and out between members of team.

Driving the Pig to Market

Grades: 4 to 6   Distance: 20 feet
Equipment: Wand and dumbbell for each team, chair or stool

STILE

Dumbbell must be rolled up to and around stile (stool). Dumbbell is controlled by sliding the wand back and forth along the hand grip.

Fetch and Carry

Grade: 4   Equipment: 3 bean bags
Distance: 20 feet

Draw a 15 inch circle about 5 feet in front of each team's starting line. 20 to 30 feet from the starting line draw 3 crosses about two feet apart. No. 1 picks up bean bags one at a time, making three trips to place them on the crosses, and runs back and touches off No. 2 who returns the bean bags to the circle in three trips. 3 does as 1, and 4 as 2 etc.

Goat Butting

Grades: 3 to 4   Equipment: Any large ball, as a basketball   Distance: 20 feet

Start in crouch position with ball on starting line, butt ball to turning line and back over starting line.

Hoop Rolling

Grades: 4 to 6   Equipment: Hoop and flat board for each team   Distance: 40 to 50 feet

Roll hoop to turning line, pick up, roll back.

Merry Go Round or Izzy-Dizzy

Grades: 3 to 6   Equipment: Baseball bat for each team   Distance: 30 to 50 feet

First player stands bat up straight, places palms down on top and head on back of hands. Walks around bat 8 times, drops it and runs to turning line and back on foot of line. No. 2 picks up bat as soon as it is dropped and repeats action of No. 1.

Over and Under

Grades: 2 to 6   Equipment: Volleyball, soccerball or basketball

UNDER   OVER

Stand in stride position, about 14 inches apart. No. 1 passes ball over head to No. 2 who passes it through his legs to No. 3 etc. No. 4 runs to head of line and starts ball overhead to No. 1. When No. 1 returns to head of line, relay is finished.

Push Ball

Grades: 5 to 6   Distance: 20 feet
Equipment: Any large ball, 6 inches in diameter or over

Push ball with stick over goal line, pick it up and carry back to next player.

Skip Rope Relay

Grades: 1, 2, 3   Equipment: Short
rope   Distance: 30 to 50 feet

Skip to turning line and back. Children
learning to jump a short rope find it
much easier to run than to stand still.

Stride Ball

Grade: 4   Equipment: Volleyball
or soccerball for each team

Teams stand in deep stride position
and pass or roll the ball between legs
to the back of the line. Last player in
line carries the ball to the head of the
line, passing the team to the left, and
starts the ball again through the legs.

RELAYS RELATED TO TEAM SPORTS
Soccer and Touch Tackle Football

1. SOCCER RELAYS

Soccer Relay

Grade: 6   Equipment: Soccerball
Distance: Soccer field   Formation:
Double line

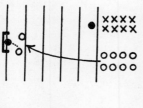

On signal, couples pass the ball back
and forth to each other down the field,
make a goal and pass the ball back to
the starting line. Only the feet may be
used and neither player shall play the
ball twice consecutively.

Line Relay

Grades: 5 to 6

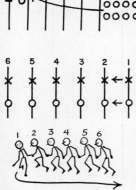

Divide group into teams of six. Draw
parallel lines 10 yards apart. Teams
line up on parallel lines with one team
player on each line. On signal, No. 1
runs to the first ten yard line and catches
the hand of No. 2 who runs and catches
the hand of No. 3. When No. 5 has the
hand of No. 6 all continue to the start-

ing line. The team that crosses the starting line first wins.

Run and Roll Relay

Grade: 4   Equipment: Soccerball for each team   Distance: Total 35 feet, 12 feet to first line

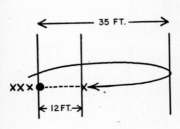

First player runs to and across the turning line, returns to the 12 foot line and rolls the ball to No. 2. If the waiting player cannot reach the ball, No. 1 must retrieve the ball, return to the 12 foot line and roll it again.

Soccer Relay Variations

Grades: 4 to 6   Distance: 40 feet

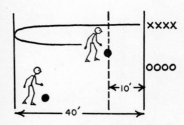

Dribble to turning line and back to within 10 to 12 feet of line and pass with the inside of the foot. In the fourth grade the waiting player shall be allowed to stop the ball with his hands. In the fifth and sixth grades the waiting player should trap the ball.

Zigzag Relay

Grades: 4 to 6   Distance: 40 feet Equipment: Soccerball for each team, 3 Indian clubs

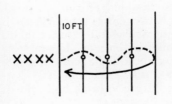

Space Indian clubs 10 feet apart between starting and turning lines. Dribble in and out between clubs to turning line, pick up ball and run straight back to team.

2. FOOTBALL RELAYS

Refer to *Cross Over* and *Baseball Relay* in softball section of relays. Refer to *Circle* and *Zigzag Volley* in volleyball section of relays.

Run and Punt Relay

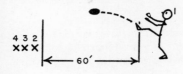

Grade: 6   Equipment: Football for each player   Distance: 60 feet

First player is given a ball. On signal,

he runs to turning line and punts to waiting player and moves back to make room for him. The team that gets all team members to the opposite side first wins.

Center Pass Relay

Grade: 6   Distance: 10 feet
Equipment: Football for each team

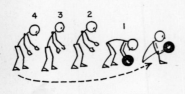

Teams line up on parallel lines spaced about 8 to 10 feet apart. The first player places the ball on the ground and on signal passes the ball between his legs to the player behind him. Number 2 places the ball on the ground and repeats the action. The last player to receive the ball runs to the front of the line and sits. The line that finishes first wins.

3. VOLLEYBALL RELAYS

Throw and Catch

Grade: 4   Equipment: Volleyball for each team, long rope and jump standards   Distance: 30 feet

In front of teams stretch a rope across standards at a height of 6 to 8 feet. On signal, the first player runs forward, tosses the ball over the rope, catches it on the other side and returns to his team, hands the ball to player No. 2 and passing to the right goes to the foot of the line. *Fouls:* Failure to throw ball over rope; failure to catch ball after it has cleared the rope.

Circle Volley Relay

Grade: 6   Equipment: One volleyball for each team

Divide group into teams of eight; each team forms a circle with 7 to 9 foot space between each player. No. 1 starts

the ball by throwing it in a high arch, slightly above the head of No. 2 who receives the ball and hits it to No. 3. Each player may play the ball as many times as is necessary to get it into a favorable position for passing. If a player drops the ball, he retrieves it, takes his position and throws it to the next player. Groups that are more advanced in skills may put the ball in play by setting up to themselves then hitting the ball to the next player. The team that gets the ball back to No. 1 first, wins. *Fouls:* Holding and throwing except in cases mentioned.

Zigzag Volley

Grade: 6

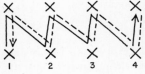

Team may be divided equally into parallel lines facing each other. The ball is volleyed back and forth down the line and back. The team that gets the ball back to the starter first, wins.

4. BASKETBALL RELAYS

Basket Shooting Relay

Grades: 5 to 6   Equipment: Basketballs for each team   Distance: 15 to 20 feet from goal

On signal, the first player runs to shooting position and tries to make a basket. He shoots until a basket is made and runs back to the line and gives the next player the ball. Team finishing first wins.

Variation: Dribble the ball into position and try for a basket and pass the ball back to next in line. Run to foot of line. Determine pass to be used before relay starts. It may be overhead, side, two arm, shoulders, etc. See Basketball skills.

Post Ball

Grades: 4 to 6   Equipment: Two volleyballs, one post or base   Distance: 30 to 40 feet

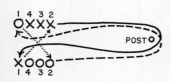

Only two teams should use one post. On signal the first player runs around the post, to the foot of the opposing team's line and throws the ball to No. 2 on his team, who repeats the action of No. 1 and throws the ball to No. 3. The last player who reaches the end of the opposing line, raises the ball high above his head to indicate that his team has finished.

Basketball Pass Relay

Grades: 3 to 6
Zigzag Pass
Players 10 feet apart
Shuttle Pass
Distance: 10 to 15 feet

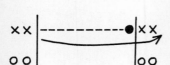

Player may take one step before passing, runs to end of opposite line, moving to the right. Stipulate type of pass.

Arch Goal Ball Relay

Grades: 4 to 5   Equipment: One basketball for each team   Distance: 15 to 20 feet

On signal, the first player passes the ball over his head to the player behind him, and so on down the line. When the last player receives the ball, he runs forward past the line and attempts to shoot for a goal, using a chest or shoulder throw. He is allowed 3 trials. Whether he is successful or not, he takes his position at the head of the line and passes the ball overhead. To determine the winning team, score one point for finishing first and two points for each goal. Deduct one point for each foul.

5. SOFT BALL RELAYS

Post or Baseball Relay

Grade: 4 to 6   Equipment: Baseball or bean bag   Distance: 10 to
12 feet

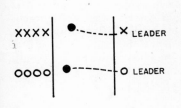

Choose a leader for each team. Leaders stand about 10 to 12 feet in front of
teams in parallel lines. On signal, the
leader throws the ball to the first player
using the underhand throw. The first
player catches the ball, throws it back
to the leader and immediately squats
in line. The leader throws to the second in line, etc. Game continues until
all players are squatting. The winning
team finishes first with the fewest errors.
Errors: Failure to catch ball, dropping
ball.

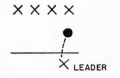

Variation: *Pass and Squat.* Grades 4 to
6. This relay is played in the same
manner except for the formation. Players line up side by side.

Cross Over Relay

Grades: 4 to 5   Equipment: Softball for each team   Distance: Determined by the skill of the players, 15
to 20 feet

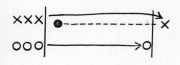

Give a ball to the first player on each
team. On signal No. 1 runs to the goal
line, turns and throws the ball to next
player in line and steps back. No. 2
catches the ball and repeats the action
of No. 1 and steps in front of No. 1.
The team that finishes first with the
fewest fouls wins.

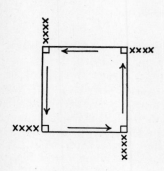

Round the Bases

Grades: 3 to 6   Players: 10 to 36, two to four teams

Two teams: One team lines up at second base, the other team lines up at home plate. If there are enough teams, line up behind all bases. On signal, No. 1 starts around the four bases, touching off No. 2 at the base he started from. Side finishing first wins. Fouls: Running over 3 feet outside base line; failure to touch each base.

OBSTACLE RELAYS

Human Hurdle or Spoke Relay

Grades: 5 to 6

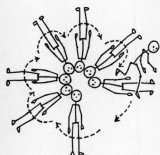

Each team forms a circle and all lie on floor with heads touching in the center. One player is designated as starter. On signal, he jumps up and hurdles (clockwise) each player and when he reaches his place, he touches off the next player and takes his original place on the floor.

Human Obstacle

Grade: 5   Distance: 20 to 30 feet

Place 4 children between starting and turning lines, spaced several feet apart. No. 1 stands upright, No. 2 stands in stride position, No. 3 stoops in leap frog position, No. 4 stands upright. The first player runs around No. 1, crawls through the legs of No. 2, leaps over No. 3, runs around No. 4 and returns in a straight line to his team.

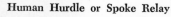

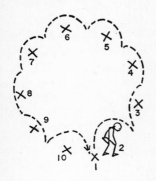

Leap Frog Relay
Grades: 4 to 5

Each team forms a circle and bends over in leap frog position, facing the same direction. Player designated as the starter, leaps over each player, returns to original position and touches off the player in front of him.

Serpentine
Grade: 4 for each team   Equipment: Indian clubs   Distance: 20 to 40 feet

Place clubs about 2 feet apart, starting 2 feet from the turning line. Player zigzags between clubs and runs straight back to line.

Stool Hurdle
Equipment: 3 stools   Distance: 20 feet

Place stools 5 feet apart. Player straddle hops the first, does a flat footed jump over the second and leaps over the third, runs to turning line and returns in a straight line to his team.

NOVELTY RELAYS
(Suitable for special days and parties.)

Balloon or Feather Relay
Grades: 4 to 6   Equipment: Balloon or feather for each team   Distance: 10 to 15 feet

Blows balloon or feather to turning line and back. If it falls to floor must be picked up at that point and put in air again before proceeding.

Box Relay

Grades: 1 to 6   Distance: 10 to 20 feet   Equipment: 2 shoe boxes

Players divide into two teams. Each leader runs to the turning line and back wearing two shoe boxes. If any player steps out of a box he must begin again from the starting line.

Bronco Relay

Grades: 1 to 6

Lines number off by twos to form couples. First couple in each line straddles a broom stick and races to the turning line and back. Second couple takes the stick and repeats action of couple 1, etc.

Paper Bag Relay

Equipment: Paper bag for all participants

Blow up bag at starting line, run across turning line, pop bag and return.

Pilot Relay

Grades: 3 to 6   Distance: 30 to 50 feet

No. 1 faces turning line and grasps hands of 2 and 3 who face in opposite directions. No. 1 runs forward to turning line and 2 and 3 run backwards. On the return, No. 1 runs backwards and 2 and 3 run forward.

Sack Relay

Grades: 1 to 6 Equipment: Sack of burlap or duck Distance: 20 to 50 feet

Players jump with sack pulled up well above the hips.

Spoon and Ping Pong Ball Relay

Grades: 2 to 6 Distance: 20 feet
Equipment: Tablespoon and ping pong ball for each team

Balance ball in spoon and walk rapidly to turning line and back. If the ball rolls off, it may be replaced with the free hand of the player and returned to the place where it rolled off. The relay is more interesting and difficult if the ball is picked up without aid from the free hand.

Sweep Up Relay

Equipment: 5 ping pong balls, a broom and dust pan for each team Distance: 15 to 20 feet

Five ping pong balls are placed directly in front of the starting line. On signal the first player sweeps the balls into the dust pan with a whisk broom and races to the turning point and back, dumping the balls gently to floor so they will not scatter. Second player repeats action of first, etc.

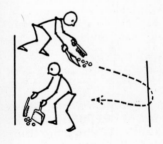

Three Legged Relay

Grades: 2 to 6 Distance: 20 to 40 feet

Double line. Tie inside legs of couple together, run to turning line and back.

Tooth Pick and Ring Relay

Grades: 3 to 6   Equipment: Tooth pick for each team member and a ring for each team (small celluloid curtain ring is light and suitable)   Distance: 15 to 20 feet

No. 1 puts tooth pick in mouth and places ring on tooth pick, runs to turning line and back and transfers ring to tooth pick in mouth of No. 2.

Paul Revere Relay

Grades: 3 to 6   Distance: 20 to 30 feet

This is a shuttle relay. After each team selects a rider the players number off, the even numbers standing on one side and the odd numbers on the opposite side. On signal the rider mounts the back of No. 1 who carries him to No. 2 where the rider, without touching the ground, exchanges mounts and No. 2 carries him to No. 3. Continue until the last man carries the rider across the finish line. If a rider falls off he must mount again at the point of the fall. If he falls off in changing mounts, he must again get on his original mount before making the change.

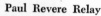

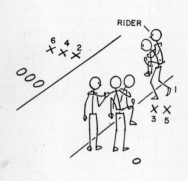

Suggested Readings

Bancroft, Jessie, *Games* (Revised), New York, The Macmillan Company, 1937.

Cleveland Public Schools, *Physical Education Course of Study*, Cleveland, Ohio, Upper Elementary Division, Board of Education, 1946.

Geri, Frank H., *Illustrated Game Manual*, Seattle, Washington, Ernie Rose, 215 Seneca Street, 1950.

Hindman, Darwin A., *Handbook of Active Games*, New York, Prentice-Hall Inc., 1951.

Mason, Bernard S. and Mitchell, Elmer D., *Active Games and Contests*, New York, A. S. Barnes and Company, 1939.

State Department of Education, *A Program of Physical Education for The Elementary Schools of Tennessee*, Revised Edition, Nashville, 1950.

War Department Technical Manual, *Informal Games for Soldiers*, TM21–221, Washington, D.C., United States Government Printing Office, 1943.

Chapter 9

Skills and Lead-up Games to

Team Sports

Skills required in team games taught from the first grade through the sixth grade will gradually increase proficiency in relays, lead-up games, modified team games, as well as formal drill or practice. The desire to play team games, often manifested in the third and fourth grades, can be fulfilled in the fifth grade where interest has become sustained, instead of sporadic, and the participants have reached a level of understanding and skill necessary to thorough enjoyment of games involving group cooperation and complicated rules. When primary level children start asking for team games, let it be remembered that there is no substitute for skill when the child is ready for progressive instruction.

In the primary grades one can teach games that introduce simple skills with the ball, such as catching, throwing, kicking, dodging. These give a general background of mechanics that carry over into all types of games where a ball is used.

Suggested Games Listed According to Degree of Difficulty

Call Ball

Ball Toss

Ball Puss

Stride Ball

Hot Ball

Circle or Line Dodge Ball

Square Ball

Suggested ball technique games include:

BALL PUSS

Gym or playground   Grades: 2 to 3   Players: 9 to 10

1. Each player stands on a base while "It" is in center with ball.
2. At signal all change places and "It" tries to hit someone with the ball.
3. A player who is hit becomes "It."

129

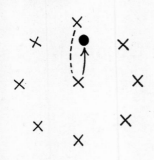

BALL TOSS

Playground, playroom or gymnasium
Grades: 1 to 2   Players: 8 to 12
Formation: Circle   Large ball

1. Ball is thrown around circle.
2. Player in center throws to each player in circle who returns ball to thrower.
3. Concentrate on throwing and catching and as skill improves, increase speed.

BOUNDARY BALL

Gymnasium, playground   Volleyball or soccerball   Players: 20 to 40   Grades: 3 to 4

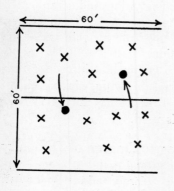

1. Draw two parallel lines 60 feet long and 60 feet apart. Draw a center line.
2. Divide players evenly and place teams in opposite ends of the field facing center.
3. The line back of each team is that team's goal.
4. Give each team a ball. At a given signal each tries to throw the ball so as to cross the other team's goal.
5. The ball must bounce or roll across the goal.
6. Players move freely in their own end of the field trying to keep opponents ball from crossing the goal.
7. Team which gets the ball across goal first wins.

CALL BALL

Playground or gymnasium   8″ rubber ball or volleyball   Grades: 1 to 2   Players: 8 to 12
Formation: Line or circle

1. One player is *Thrower*.
2. Thrower calls name of a player and tosses ball in the air.
3. Player whose name is called attempts

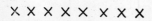

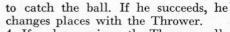

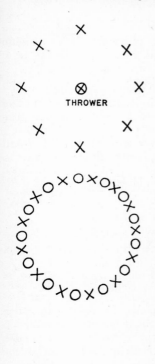

THROWER

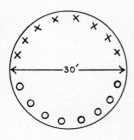

to catch the ball. If he succeeds, he changes places with the Thrower.

4. If a player misses, the Thrower calls names until the ball is caught.

5. In a new and unacquainted group number off and call a number or call colors of clothing.

CIRCLE KICK BALL

Gymnasium or playground
Grades: 2 to 5   Players: 18 to 30
Formation: Circle   Number off by twos to form teams

1. Each player attempts to kick ball between the legs of two opposing players. Score one point for a successful kick.

2. If a player kicks the ball over the heads of the opposing team, the opponents score one.

CIRCLE KICK BALL

Gymnasium or playground
Grades: 2 to 5   Players: 16 to 24
Formation: Circle   Two teams, two captains   Rubber volleyball

1. Ball is put in play by kicking toward opponent.

2. While the ball is in play all players must stay in their half of the circles, except the captains who may move out of position to kick balls which have stopped out of reach of their team mates.

3. One point is scored for a team each time: Player kicks ball through opponents half circle; player kicks ball out over shoulders.

Opponent kicks ball out on his own side. Opponent plays ball with hands (except girls using hands to protect face or chest).

4. Player who receives the ball when it goes out puts it into play again.

5. This game may allow heading as skill permits.

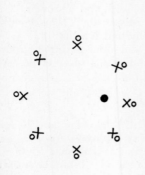

CIRCLE CLUB BOWLS

Playground, gymnasium   Indian
clubs, softball, volleyball   Grades:
2 to 3   Players: 12 to 24
Formation: Circle

1. Form a circle. Place a club back of
each player who stands in stride position.
2. Each player tries to throw the ball
through the legs of another player.
3. Player whose club is knocked down
is out of the game.

CORNER SPRY

Playroom or gymnasium   8″ rubber ball   Players: 30 to 40
Formation: Line relay with 3 feet of
space between each player

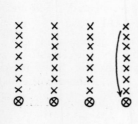

1. Divide the class into four teams with
a captain at the head of each team.
2. The captain throws the ball to each
player who returns it. As soon as the
last player catches the ball the captain
calls, "Corner spry" and runs to the
head of the line and the last player becomes captain. The first team that gets
back to its original position wins the
game.

HOT BALL

Gymnasium, playground, playroom
Any kind of ball   Grades: 2 to 3
Players: 12 to 20   Formation: Cir-
cle or double line

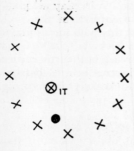

1. Players pass ball as rapidly as possible around circle. Players who drop
ball must drop out of game.
2. Variation 1—"It" in center of circle
may try to touch the ball as it is passed
from one player to the next. If he succeeds, he changes place with the player
who had the ball when it was touched.

3. Variation 2—Group forms double lines facing each other. On signal balls are passed to the end of the line and back. The line finishing first wins.

LINE DODGE BALL

Gymnasium, playroom, playground
Volleyball   Grades: 2 to 3
Players: 12 to 24

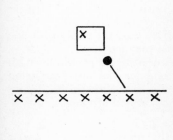

1. Two lines are drawn about 20 feet apart. Halfway between lines a box about 4 feet square is drawn.
2. One player stands in the box. Half the players stand on one line and half on the other.
3. Players on both lines take turns throwing and trying to hit the center player below the waist.
4. The center player may dodge but must never have both feet out of the box at any time. If hit, the center player changes places with the one who threw the ball.

PALM THE BALL

Gymnasium, playground   Softball.
tennis ball or small rubber ball
Players: 12 to 18   Formation: Circle

1. Players stand in circle with hands at back, palms up, forming a cup.
2. "It" places the ball in a player's hands.
3. Player receiving ball turns and runs in opposite direction and each tries to get back to the vacant place first.

SQUARE BALL

Gymnasium, playground   Volleyball or 8″ rubber ball   Grades: 2,
3, 4   Players: 16

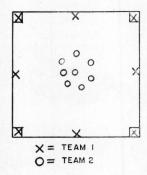

X = TEAM 1
O = TEAM 2

1. Team 1 takes places on bases, team 2
in center of square.
2. Players on bases begin passing ball
around the square.
3. Unexpectedly, a player on base tries
to hit an inside player with the ball.
4. If the center player is missed the
ball continues around the square. If
the player is hit, team 1 runs around
the bases until the player hit picks
up the ball and calls, "Halt."
5. Player with the ball tries to hit one
of the halted players.
6. Game: Score one for each player hit
and score one for the opposing team
for each miss. Set game at 10. Teams
change places at end of game.

STRIDE BALL

Gymnasium, playground   Soccer
or volleyball   Grades: 2 to 4
Players: 12 to 16   Formation:
Circle

1. Players stand in circle with legs in
stride position.
2. "It" stands in the circle and tries to
throw or bat ball between the legs of
other players.
3. If the ball is out of reach a player
may retrieve it but must return to the
circle before he puts it back into play.
4. If the ball goes through a player's
legs three times he must drop out of the
game.

Class Organization

Division of Teams

Some teachers divide classes into teams and keep the same teams
through the entirety of a sports unit. This procedure saves time
and offers the participants the opportunity to become thoroughly

familiar with team mates and the way they play. Others divide teams each week. The latter method has the advantage of exposing the participants to more and different playing situations, hence develops alertness and versatility to meet the unexpected. A teacher must judge which method best meets the situation and needs in that particular school but it is recommended that teams be divided with an equalization of skill. Selected teams may wear distinguishing colors or pinnies given to them by their squad leaders. Skill segregation makes for dull competition. Then, too, a child with poor motor ability or skill weakness often improves more rapidly while playing with others more highly skilled.

Choice of Leaders

Leaders or team captains should be chosen because of their sportsmanship and knowledge of the game. Weekly rotation of captains is advisable in order to develop leadership and acceptance of responsibility within the whole group.

Student officials must not only be grounded in the rules of the game but also must remain fair and impartial in their decisions. Daily rotation of officials permits each equal playing time. Student officials will require frequent advice from the teacher; this help should be exact and consistent. Surprisingly enough, fifth and sixth graders can become quite technical in their insistence that games be played according to the rules. Emotionally some become more touchy about inconsistencies than do high school students.

Teaching Skills

There are three commonly used methods for teaching skills: (1) the part method, (2) the whole method, and (3) the part-whole method. The first consists of teaching each skill through formal drill until a fair degree of proficiency has been reached. In the second the teacher briefs the children on the rudiments of the game, demonstrates the fundamental skills, places the players on the field or court and starts the game, stopping it when necessary to correct errors in form or strategy. In the third, one combines the elements of the first and second method.

Children in elementary grades, as a rule, take a dim view of formal practice. Since they are primarily interested in the game itself, drill should be held to the minimum. Each skill should be explained briefly, demonstrated, then tried individually in a race,

relay or lead-up game. Relays are particularly effective in motivating the learning process, for competition serves as a means of
stimulating and holding interest while skills are being mastered.

Fundamental Skills Related to Team Games
SOCCER SKILLS

SIDE

FRONT

Dribble

Tap ball with the inside of the right
and left foot alternately, keeping the
ball close to the feet and always under
control. Beginners are prone to kick the
ball then run to catch up.

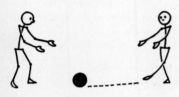

Passing

Take weight on right foot and swing
left leg back and forward hitting the
ball with the inside of the left foot. To
pass forward left reverse action hitting
ball with inside of right foot.

Kicking

Swing leg back and contact ball at
instep. Keep the toe pointed down.

Trapping

Slow balls may be stopped with a
raised foot, toes up. As contact is made,
the toes are lowered to secure the ball.
Fast balls are trapped with the leg. If
the ball is on the right, take a small
step sideways to the left and at the same
time roll the right instep in toward the
ground and trap the ball with the knee
and the inside of the calf.

Heading

Get under ball, lower the head slightly, stiffen the neck and meet the ball with an upward and forward movement to control direction. This skill is too advanced for the majority of elementary children.

CIRCLE KICK SOCCER

Playground, gymnasium   Players: 16 to 20   Grades: 3 to 4 Equipment: Soccerball   Formation: Single circle, hands joined

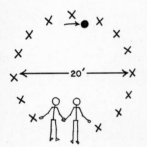

1. Ball is rolled into center of circle and players pass the ball around the inside of the circle.
2. Players trap, block and pass with feet and legs, but keep hands joined.
3. If the ball goes outside the circle, the players between whom it passed are eliminated from the game.
4. When all but five are eliminated, the game is over.

BASE FOOTBALL

Playground   Players: 10 to 20 Grades: 1 to 6   Equipment: Football, bases

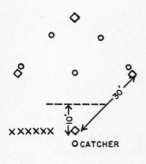

1. Kicker punts (kicks from hands) and tries to make all bases without getting put out.
2. May run until ball is held by catcher at home plate or is played to base at which he is running.
3. Score one point if runner completes circuit.
4. Kicker out if: a. Ball doesn't go over 10' line. b. Ball caught on fly. c. Touched by ball when in hands of opposing team.
5. Player may stay on base and advance on next kick.
6. Kicking team has 3 outs, then changes places.

KICK BALL

Playground   Players: 10 to 24
Grades: 2 to 6   Equipment: Baseball, diamond, bases 30′ apart, soccerball or basketball

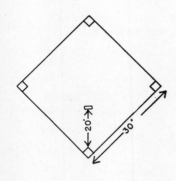

1. Seven innings make a game.
2. Pitcher rolls ball to batter who kicks it into the field.
3. The general rules of baseball apply, with the following exceptions: a. The base runner may be tagged out or "thrown out." b. A runner must be tagged with the ball held in the hand. c. "Thrown out" means the base is tagged with the ball or touched by some part of body of baseman or fielder while the ball is in his hands, before the runner reaches base.
4. There may be from 5 to 12 on the team.
5. Use soccerball or basketball.
6. Pitcher's box 15′ to 20′ from home plate.

KICK FOR DISTANCE

Playground   Players: Any number   Grades: 3 to 6   Equipment: Football, soccerball

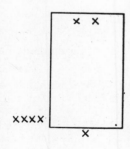

1. Line up behind kicking line—two players stand at end of field to recover kicks.
2. Each player given definite number of tries.
3. Longest kick recorded—player with longest kick winner.

KICKOVER BALL

Playground, gymnasium   Players: 12 to 24   Grades: 3 up   Equipment: Soccerball

1. Players are divided into two teams and placed in parallel lines facing each other. Teams alternate putting ball in play.

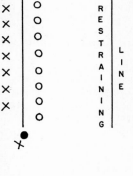

2. A space is left between the feet of the teams. By superior kicking, one team tries to kick the ball over the heads of the other team.

3. After the ball is kicked over one team's head, the two end players jump up and try to retrieve the ball and run over a restraining line.

4. The team with the most points wins. Game may continue until all get a chance to retrieve the ball.

LINE SOCCER

Playground: 30′ x 30′ field   Players: Two teams, 8 to 12 players each   Grade: 4   Equipment: Soccerball

1. Teams number off and take positions.

2. On signal the soccerball is rolled in from the sideline and the No. 1's on each team run out and try to dribble and kick the ball over the opponent's goal line.

3. Guards and linesmen try to stop the ball with feet or hands. If hands are used, the ball must not be held or moved.

4. Score two points for kicking the ball across the opponent's goal line. Score one point for a successful free kick.

5. When one player kicks the ball out of bounds, it is given to the other player in the center of the field.

6. A free kick is awarded for: runner using hands, pushing, blocking, or holding.

7. Free kick: Ball is placed in center of field and player tries to kick it over the opponent's goal line. Neither linesman nor the opposing player must interfere with the kick. Free kick must not pass over the heads of linesmen.

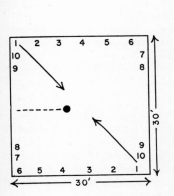

BASEBALL SKILLS
Catching

Cup relaxed hands, closing firmly when contact is made and give with the ball. Balls above the waist are caught with fingers up, thumbs together; balls below the waist are caught with hands down, little fingers together.

Throwing

Underhand. Hold ball in the hand palm up, weight on the right foot. Swing arm backward then forward keeping arm close to body. Simultaneously step forward with the left foot and release the ball at hip level and follow through. This is a legal pitch.

Overhand. Hold ball in hand with palm down with fingers spread easily around the ball. Draw arm backward with elbow bent; swing arm forward using hand, wrist, elbow and shoulder to deliver ball as weight is shifted to the left foot and follow through with entire arm and body.

Batting

Stand facing plate with body parallel to the flight of the ball. Hold the bat in both hands close to the end with right hand on top. Weight is evenly divided on comfortably spread feet, bat is held over the plate, back and at shoulder level. The distance from the box to the plate in softball is short so it is important to get set to hit every ball. As the pitcher releases the ball, put weight on right foot shifting to left as the bat is swung parallel to the ground. Drop bat and step off on the right foot for the run to first base.

Fielding

Stand with feet spread to allow movement in any direction. Ground balls often bounce, so fielder steps forward with fingers down and fields the ball off of his toes.

Base Running

Weight is on the left foot as the pitcher starts the throw. Step off on right foot as the pitcher releases the ball or batter gets a hit. Run close to the base line and touch each base.

BAT BALL

Playground, gymnasium   Players: 10, 24   Grades: 3, 4, 5   Equipment: Volleyball or 8″ rubber ball

1. Divide into two teams, one in field, one at bat.
2. Batter strikes ball with hand or fist. If his hit is successful, he runs to the base, tags it and returns to home plate.
3. A fielder tries to hit the runner. He may only take two steps and can pass the ball to team mates.
4. A player is out when: a. A fly is caught. b. He is hit by a ball. c. He does not tag the base. d. He does not hit the ball beyond the scratch line.
Game may be timed or played by innings. Score 2 points for each completed run and 1 point for a foul made by fielder.

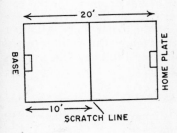

BEATBALL

Playground, gymnasium   Players: 2 teams   Grades 2, 3   Equipment: Volleyball

1. Play on playground ball diamond.
2. Batter throws ball into field and runs the bases, keeping going until he reaches home or is put out.
3. Fielders field ball and throw it to

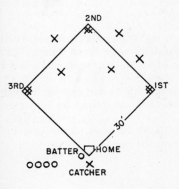

first base; first baseman throws it to second, and on around bases.

4. If runner reaches home before ball does, he scores one point. Otherwise, out.

Variation. Hand beatball: Same except pitcher pitches ball and the batter bats it with open hand.

Variation. Bowl beatball: Same except pitcher rolls ball and batter kicks it.

DIAMOND OR BOX BALL

Playing field   Players: Two teams
of equal size   Grades: 3 to 6
Equipment: Volleyball or soft rubber ball

1. "Box" or square made by 3 bases and home base for lower grades. Baseball diamond may be used for upper grades.

2. The pitcher throws the ball so that it bounces once before crossing home plate. The batter strikes the ball with his open hand, or clenched fist, out into the field. The ball must first strike within the box or diamond for the batter to be safe. If the ball strikes outside the diamond the batter is out. All other baseball rules apply. One point is scored for each successful runner. Nine innings makes a game.

HAND BASEBALL

Baseball diamond   Players: 2
teams, 9 on each   Grades: 3, 4, 5
Equipment: Volleyball or soft rubber ball

1. Pitcher delivers ball to batter with underhand throw, 15′ from home plate.

2. Batter hits the ball with open hand or fist.

3. A runner may be put out by hitting him with a ball any time he is not on base.

4. Game: Nine innings. Score one for each completed run.

LINE BOWLING

Playroom, gymnasium Players: 8, 12 Grades: 4, 5 Equipment: 3 Indian clubs 6″ to 8″ ball

1. Two parallel lines, 20′ apart, with boxes at opposite ends from the court.
2. Alternate teams try to knock down the pins from their respective boxes.
3. The bowling player on team "A" replaces the pins in a triangle, 12″ apart, and goes to the foot of his line.
4. Team "B" player retrieves the ball and bowls from his box.

BASEBALL OVERTAKE CONTEST

Baseball diamond Players: 8, 12 Grades: 3, 4, 5 Equipment: Softball

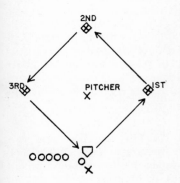

1. All positions of the infield are occupied except shortstop. Pitcher holds softball.
2. Runner stands on home base and at signal runs the bases.
3. At same time, pitcher throws the ball to catcher on home base and from there it is thrown around the bases.
4. One point is scored for each base the runner reaches ahead of the ball.
5. After all the running team have run, the teams change positions.
6. Runner throws ball to any player on the opposite team. The fielder throws ball to catcher, etc.

PROGRESSIVE BAT BALL

Gymnasium or playground Players: 10 player to a team—any number to 150 Grades: 4, 5, 6 Equipment: Volleyball

1. Teams line up in rows directly behind one another (3 to 4 yards apart) with two arms lengths between each player, with their backs to the "back line."

2. The team farthest from the "back line" turns and faces the rest.

3. A player tosses a ball and bats it with his hand, then runs to the "back line." The ball must go within the square and the other players attempt to hit the runner before he reaches the line.

4. The runner is out if the ball is caught in the air or if it hits him. If the runner reaches the "back line" safely, he must return to his team on the next play. Players must maintain their positions and advance the ball by passing only.

5. A batted ball striking outside the square is a foul and the batter is out.

6. One point is scored for each player who reaches the "back line" and returns to his team.

7. Three outs retires a team which then moves to the back line and the next team in line moves into play.

LONG BASE

Playground   Players: 14, 20
Grades: 1 to 6   Equipment: Bat and softball

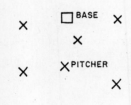

1. Divide into 2 teams.

2. Pitcher throws ball to batter who bats.

3. Runner runs to long base and remains if he arrives before ball.

4. Next runner does same and runner No. 1 comes in.

5. Fielders catch ball and try to put either one out.

6. Runner may make home run if has time.

7. Out if doesn't hit in 3 times.

8. When team has 3 outs they change places.

TARGET

Playground, gymnasium   Players: 8, 12   Grades: 1 to 6   Equipment: Target, soccerball or volleyball

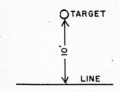

1. Target suspended on wall, fence, tree, 10' away from thrower.
2. Thrower attempts to hit bull's eye with soccer or volleyball.
3. Each has 3 successive turns and best of three scores is counted.

RACE AROUND THE BASES

Playground   Players: 12, 24
Grades: 2, 3, 4

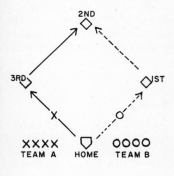

1. Two players start from home plate.
2. One player runs to first, second, third and back to home. The second player runs to third, second, first and home.
3. Player that reaches home plate first wins.
4. If a player fails to touch a base, he must go back and do so.

THROW IT AND RUN

Playground, gymnasium   Players: 10, 18   Grades: 3, 4   Equipment: Softball or volleyball

1. Thrower scores run by throwing softball (or rubber volleyball) out into playing field, running to first base and back to home plate.
2. If a fielder catches fly ball or returns ball to catcher before thrower returns home, thrower is out.
3. Team scoring most runs wins.

VOLLEY BALL SKILLS

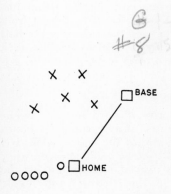

Service

The underhand serve is the simplest to teach, easiest to learn, and most practical for use in placement of the ball. Stand facing opposite court with ball in left hand. Weight is on the right foot

as right arm swings backward to shoulder height. Shift weight to left foot as right arm swings forward, knocking the ball out of the left hand. Follow through with the whole body as the ball leaves the right hand. The ball may be struck with the open palm, palm side of the closed fist, or thumb and forefinger side of the closed fist. The assist is generally used in elementary grades.

Receiving the Ball

Take a stance with knees slightly flexed. If the ball is high, flex elbows with hands up, take a small step forward, and meet the ball with fingers relaxed. If the ball is low, flex knees more deeply, step forward, and meet the ball with fingers down and palms forward. Children should be taught from the start to keep their eyes on the ball and be ready to receive a volley, or a pass, from a team mate.

Passing the Ball

Try to give upward impetus to the ball and direct it by turning the hands and body toward the desired objective. A high ball can be handled more easily and gives a good background for the teaching of the "set-up" and juggle (girls) which is taught in junior high school.

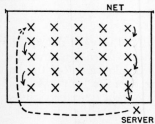

Rotation

Snake or "S" type rotation is used because of its simplicity and the fact that generally thirty to forty play on each side.

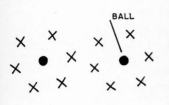

KEEP IT UP

Playground   Players: Entire class
Grades: 2, 3, and up

1. Divide into as many groups as there are volley and basketballs.
2. Pitch the ball up in each group and see which group can keep the ball up the longest without it touching the floor.
3. If you have to use basketballs, be sure to alternate the basketball among the groups.

FIST FUNGO

Playground, gymnasium   Players: 12, 16   Grades: 3, 4   Equipment: Volleyball   Formation: Scattered

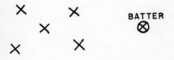

1. Batter faces scattered players and bats ball toward them with open hand or fist.
2. A fielder who catches the ball exchanges with the batter.
3. A player who fields the ball but does not catch it on the fly, tries to hit the batter. The batter may not move his feet.
4. If the batter is hit, he exchanges places with the fielder. If he is not hit, he has another turn.

SHOWER BALL

Volleyball court   Players: 20, 50
Grades: 2 to 6   Equipment: Net and 1 ball for every 10 players

1. Ball may be batted or tossed over the net. Only one player on each side may handle the ball, and it cannot be held over 3 seconds.
2. A player may only take one step with the ball.
3. Points are given for violations and each time the ball touches the ground.

CAGE BALL

Playing field: 30' to 80' according to age groups   Players: 10 to 50
Grades: 2 to 6   Equipment: Large ball and volleyball net

3	X	X	X
2	X	X	X
1	X	X	X

1. The net is placed at 8', and the area is marked into 3 playing divisions.
2. Each player must stay within his assigned area.
3. The server stands back of the line and tosses or bats the ball to a player who assists it over the net.
4. Players rotate for service, and only the serving team can score.
5. When the ball is not assisted on service, dropped, goes into net, or out of bounds, it goes to the opposing team.

NEWCOMB

Playing field: Tennis court or volleyball court   Players: Any number to form 2 teams   Grades: 4, 5 6
Equipment: Volleyball or soccerball and net

1. The ball is thrown back and forth over the net, and each team attempts to keep it from touching the ground on their side.
2. Any number of players may handle a ball on one side, but it must not be held over 3 seconds.
3. A point is scored when the ball touches the ground or goes out of bounds.

BASKETBALL SKILLS

Stance

Stand with feet apart, knees slightly bent to permit shifts in all directions.

Passing

Concentrate on accuracy, passing with just enough momentum so that the ball may be caught easily. Step in the direction of the pass in order to back up team mates.

Overhead

Two Arm. Arms above head, elbows slightly bent. Propel ball straight forward.

One Arm. Same as above except ball is balanced on one hand.

Chest

Ball is held to chest with elbows bent. Push ball forward and upward, as arms are extended, and release when arms are straight.

Side-Arm

Balance ball on hand, arm back, weight on the foot on the same side. Transfer weight to other foot as ball is thrown.

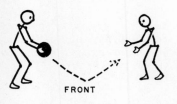

FRONT

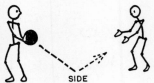

SIDE

Bounce

Arms in position as for chest pass. Keep ball low as high bounces are easily intercepted. Ball is held to side, one arm across chest, both elbows bent. Throw ball as arms are extended.

Roll Pass

Allow children who have not advanced far in skills to roll the ball on the floor as in bowling.

Catching

Receive high balls with fingers up, low balls with fingers down. Relax hands and give with the ball. Always keep your eye on the ball.

Shooting Baskets

Arch. Hold ball slightly to the front about chin level, with fingers up, elbows bent. Look at the basket, straighten arms and push the ball in a high arch.

Lay-Up Shot. Player receives ball under or close to basket, jumps into air and tries to lay the ball so that it will enter just over the rim of the basket.

Dribble

Body in crouch position, head up so that the player can look over the court. Bounce the ball low by flexing the wrist back and hitting the ball with the fingers. Elementary grade children do not develop a high degree of skill in dribbling as they lower their heads to watch the ball.

Foul Shots

Arch. Same as high arch shot only knees are flexed more and toes must not cross the foul line.

Scoop. Small children find it easier to shoot a foul shot by catching the ball with fingers down and throwing it underhanded in a high arch.

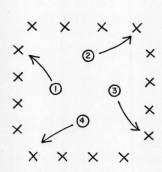

CATCH, THROW AND SIT

Playground, gymnasium, playroom
Players: 12, 16   Grade: 3
Equipment: Softball, football, or volley ball

1. Divide group into teams of from 8 to 12. Line up against walls of gym or in a hollow square.
2. Captain faces his team and must keep one foot in a three foot circle.
3. Captain stands 15′ from team.
4. At signal, he throws ball to first player on right, who catches it, throws it back and then sits down. This is repeated down the line.
5. If any player or captain fails to catch the ball, he must recover it and return to position before throwing it.
6. Team wins which has all players seated first.

KEEP AWAY

Playground   Players: 8 to 32
Grades: 1, 2, 3, and up   Equipment: Baseball or basketball

1. Draw court of four rectangles about 6′ x 10′.
2. Place 2 pupils in each rectangle. The alternate rectangles are partners and try to keep the ball away from the other two.
3. When a player steps on or out of the line, the ball goes to the opposite team.
4. This can be played either with baseball or basketball.

TWENTY-ONE

Basketball Court   Players: 2 to 12
Grades: 4, 5, 6   Equipment: Basketball

1. Players take a long shot (15′ to 20′) at the basket, and a short shot.
2. Long shot scores 2 points and short shot 1 point.

3. Players take turns and the first to score 21 points wins.

4. Variation: Players may shoot from the foul line, retrieve the ball and take a short shot. Small, light ball may be used for primary children.

SIDE LINE BASKETBALL

One half regulation basketball court
Players: Two teams, 6 to 8 per team
Grades: 5, 6   Equipment: Basketball

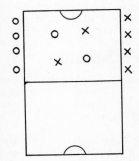

1. Two members of each team play on the floor and players line up on side.

2. Regulation basketball rules are followed except the ball may be passed to team mates on the side lines.

3. Both teams play the same basket.

4. The defensive team becomes offensive by throwing the ball to a player on the side lines.

5. The center line is out of bounds, and stepping over any line gives the ball to the opposing team on their side line.

6. Ball may be put into play by center toss up, or by giving the ball on the side lines to the team scored against.

7. Players on sidelines rotate with players on floor.

8. Score 2 points for each basket made and 1 point for free throw after a foul.

KEYHOLE BASKETBALL

Area around basket   Players: 2 to 10   Grades: 4, 5, 6   Equipment: Basketball

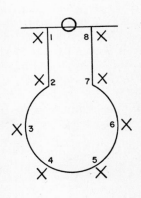

1. Chalk eight marks around basket.

2. No. 1 player shoots from the first mark.

3. If he makes the basket, he moves on and shoots from the No. 2 mark, and on around until he misses.

4. The other players shoot in turn and advance counterclockwise.

5. The first player who reaches his original position wins.

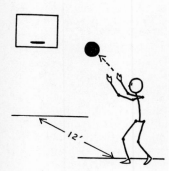

FREEZE OUT

Basketball court   Players: 8 to 10
to a basket   Grades: 5, 6
Equipment: Basketball

1. Players scatter out and take turns at shooting for the basket.
2. The first player shoots a long shot, then a short shot. If he misses the first but sinks the short shot, the next player must make a long shot that would cover the short shot, or a short shot. If he does not succeed, he is frozen out of the game.
3. Each player in turn must try to make the same shots as the preceding player.
4. The last player to remain in the game wins.

NINE COURT BASKETBALL

Basketball Court: divide court into 9
equal areas   Players: Two teams
of 9 each   Grades: 5, 6
Equipment: Basketball

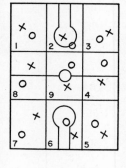

1. Played as basketball except each player is assigned an area and must stay within that boundary.
2. Players advance the ball toward their goal by passing and may dribble one time. Only forwards may shoot at the goal.
3. Ball is put in play by a center toss up.
4. Unguarded free shot, worth one point, is awarded for fouls, as blocking, holding, etc.
5. Ball is taken out of bounds for infractions as crossing line, traveling, etc.

Suggested Readings

Bauer, Lois, M. and Reed, Barbara A., *Dance and Play Activities for the Elementary Grades*, Vol. II., New York, Chartwell House, Inc., 1951.

Cleveland Public Schools, *Physical Education Course of Study*, Cleveland, Ohio, Upper Elementary Division, Board of Education, 1946.

Dallas, Public Schools, *Outline Course of Study*, *Physical Education and Health Instruction*, Grades One through Eight, Dallas, Texas, Board of Education, 1947.

Geri, Frank H., *Illustrated Game Manual*, Seattle, Washington, Ernie Rose, 215 Seneca Street, 1950.

Hindman, Darwin A., *Handbook of Active Games*, New York, Prentice-Hall, Inc., 1951.

LaSalle, *Guidance of Children Through Physical Education*, New York, A. S. Barnes, 1946.

Mason, Bernard S. and Mitchell, Elmer D., *Active Games and Contests*, New York, A. S. Barnes and Co., 1939.

Neilson, N. P. and Van Hagen, Winifred, *Physical Education for Elementary Schools*, New York, A. S. Barnes and Co., 1932.

Chapter 10

Rhythms and Dance

Rhythm has been described as ordered movement that runs through all beauty. It is seen in a lace pattern with design repeated on different levels or in architecture where beams, arches and windows balance in harmony. In nature itself one observes plant life following a prescribed rhythm in symmetry and growth. All body movements tend to be rhythmical. Watch for rhythm in the following:

Cobbler soling a shoe.

Metalsmith raising a bowl.

Pitcher winding up and delivering a baseball.

Tumbler executing a roll or a flip.

Housewife using a mop, broom, or vacuum cleaner.

Child transferring sand from pile to bucket.

Rhythm in the dance is unlike rhythm found in sports or daily chores in that it serves no utilitarian purpose but is simply expressive movements made with or without music. In teaching children one starts with the familiar and progresses as skill and perception increase.[1]

Rhythms

HOW TO INTRODUCE RHYTHMS

1. Time

Have children recite and clap in rhythm familiar nursery rhymes as: Pat-a-cake, Little Bo Peep.—Nursery Rhymes—Frank Luther, Decca Records, CU 100, CU 101, and 75522-3. Clap to known songs such as Yankee Doodle. From the third grade on the rhythm pattern and underlying beat can be explained; the groups can clap the two parts, then do it in rounds. Most children above the first grade know a number of radio commercials and enjoy clapping out the rhythm.

[1] Murray, Ruth Lovell, *Dance in Elementary Education*, New York, Harper Brothers, 1953.

Example 1.

Ha - lo everybody ha - lo
Ha - lo is the shampoo that glorifies the hair, etc.

Example 2.

Row, row,/ row your/ boat
Gently/ down the/ stream
Mer ri ly,/ mer ri ly,/ mer ri ly,/ mer ri ly/
Life is/ but a/ dream.

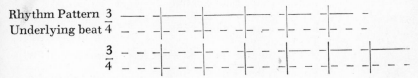

Rhythm Pattern 3
Underlying beat 4

3
4

2. Bouncing Balls

   a. Bounce balls to music.

   b. Bounce balls to each other in couple or circle formation.

   c. Children act as balls and bounce around the floor as music indicates.

   d. Form couples, one child is the ball, the other the bouncer. Bounce to music alternating as ball and bouncer.

   e. Combinations of bounces to music.

   f. Rhythm combinations by Ruth Evans—Record 203–204.

3. Jumping Rope

This may be introduced as a self-testing activity or offered along with rhythms since it requires skill and timing. In any case it is a must in any elementary program. Long ropes of 12 to 16 feet are more practical but additional individual ropes can be used to good advantage, if the budget will stand the extra expense. Class instruction should be given in progression as follows:

Rope is swung back and forth in pendulum fashion. Child jumps from one side to the other.

Child stands by rope and jumps as it describes a large full circle.

Front door—Child learns to run in as rope comes toward jumper.

Back door—Child learns to run in as rope goes away.

Hot pepper—fast jump.

Jump rope ditties—The most popular ditties chanted by today's children as they skip rope are included below. These ditties are made up by the children and apparently understood by the young fry though the connotation in some may seem vague to adults. Sometimes the words dictate certain movements while others simply give each jumper a fair turn at the rope.

DITTIES

1. Had a little radio
   Put it in free
   Only station I could get
   Was W-B-Z. (*Hot pepper until jumper misses*)

2. Bubble gum, bubble gum,
   Chew and blow,
   Bubble gum, bubble gum,
   Scrape your toe.
   Bubble gum, bubble gum,
   Tastes so sweet
   Get that bubble gum off your feet. (*Runs out*)

3. Fudge, fudge, call the judge
   Mamma has a new baby.
   Wrappit in tissue paper (*motions*)
   Send it down the elevator (*squat*)
   Second floor, first floor
   And out the back door. (*Runs out back door*)

4. Ice cream soda
   Delaware punch
   Tell me the name
   Of your honey bunch.
   Alphabet a, b, c, etc.,
   (*When jumper misses she names a boy
   to take her place whose name begins
   with the letter on which she missed*)

5. Blue bells, cockle shells
   Evie, Ivy, Over. (*Count 1, 2, 3, etc., until misses*)

6. Cinderella dressed yellow
   Went upstairs to kiss her fellow
   How many kisses did she get? (*Count 1,
   2, 3 until misses*)

   Cinderella dressed in green
   Went upstairs to eat ice cream
   How many spoonfuls did she eat? (*Count jumps 1, 2, 3*)

   Cinderella dressed in black
   Went upstairs and sat on a tack
   How many stitches did it take? (*Count jumps 1, 2, 3*)

7. One, two, buckle my shoe
   Three, four, shut the door
   Five, six, pick up sticks
   Seven, eight, lay them straight

Nine, ten, big fat hen
Eleven, twelve, bake her well. (*Count 1, 2, 3*)

8. Down in the meadow
Where the green grass grows
There sat Mary (*name of jumper*)
As sweet as a rose.
She sang and she sang
And she sang so sweet
Along came Joe (*boy friend*)
And kissed her on the cheek.
How many kisses did she get? (*Count*)

9. Teddie Bear, Teddie Bear
Turn around
Teddie Bear, Teddie Bear
Touch the ground
Teddie Bear, Teddie Bear
Go upstairs (*jumps toward head of rope*)
Teddie Bear, Teddie Bear
Say your prayers
Teddie Bear, Teddie Bear
Turn out the light
Teddie Bear, Teddie Bear
Say good night.

10. Mable, Mable
Set the table
And don't forget
the Red Hot Pepper.

11. *Twenty-four Robbers.*
Not last night but the night before
Twenty-four robbers came knocking at my door.
I ran out and they ran in
And this is the song they sang to me.
Spanish dancer, do a split
Spanish dancer, do a high kick
Spanish dancer, turn around
Spanish dancer, touch the ground
Spanish dancer, do the kangaroo (*squat and jump*)
Spanish dancer, skit, skat, skidoo!

12. Shirley Temple (or Charlie McCarthy) went to France
To teach the children how to dance
A heel and a toe and around you go,
A heel and a toe and around I go,
Salute to the Captain,
Bow to the King,
Turn your back on the Ugly Ole Queen.
(*Run out back door*)

13. *Nonsense.*
   Buster Brown went to town
   With his britches up-side down.
   Out rolled a nickel
   He bought a pickle
   The pickle was sour
   He bought some flour
   The flour was yellow
   He bought him a fellow
   The fellow was mean
   He bought a bean
   The bean was hard
   He bought a card
   And on the card
   It said, Red Hot Pepper.

Fundamental Movements

Even movements are walking, running, hopping, and leaping. Uneven movements are skipping, sliding, and galloping. Each movement should be defined and demonstrated without and with the drum beat. If the space is large the whole class may execute the movements in unison. Where the space is limited, as in a play-room, take the class by couples, lines, or waves. The use of records adds interest. Book sources for all the following dances can be found at the end of this chapter. Record references, listed alphabetically, are also to be found at the end of this chapter.

LOCOMOTOR MOVEMENTS

1. Even movements—walk, run, jump, hop, and leap.
2. Uneven movements—skip, slide, and gallop.
3. Define and demonstrate each:

   a. *Walk*—shifting of weight from one foot to the other at a moderate rate of speed.
   b. *Run*—same as walk but faster and remaining in air longer between shifting of weight.
   c. *Hop*—leave floor on one foot and return to floor on same foot.
   d. *Jump*—leave floor from both feet and return on both feet.
   e. *Leap*—same as walk and run, only more height and in air longer.
   f. *Skip*—combination of walk (or run) and hop-step, hop on right foot, step, hop on left foot.
   g. *Slide*—step to side on left foot, slide right foot to left.

Step lf., close rt. When time is accelerated, a tiny hop accompanies the step-slide.

h. *Gallop*—leap on left foot, step with right, bringing it beside left. Leap, step, etc.

Formations and floor patterns can be introduced at this time that will lend interest and variety to the simplest locomotor movements. On the primary level, children are inclined to lump themselves in a knot as a bunch of sheep and it will be necessary at times to chalk formations on the floor such as:

WEDGE CIRCLE OBLIQUE ARC SQUARE

ACCOMPANIMENT

1. Hand clapping (refer to A. on how to introduce rhythms).
2. Drums.
   a. Manufactured—A small snare-type drum open on one side and played with a large lamb's wool hammer is fairly inexpensive and will last a long time, if properly cared for. The closed leather drum made in India or China is played with a small, hard hammer. This type of drum requires careful handling, is expensive, but does have a good, decisive tone.
   b. Homemade drums.
      (1) American Indian—Buck skin stretched tightly and tacked to a hollowed out piece of wood as a tree limb, stump, or mixing bowl.
      (2) Cheese box—Remove lid, stretch tightly, and attach with tacks or staples a piece of unbleached muslin or domestic. Wet the muslin and allow to dry thoroughly. Decorate box and

muslin and apply one or two coats of white shellac.

(3) Oatmeal box or similar round container of paper. A two pound coffee can may be used but the sound is not as pleasing. Cut two circles of leather or inner tube. With a leather punch place holes 1 inch apart. Lace top and bottom together with leather or plastic thongs or strips cut from an old inner tube. This type of drum is not durable but is easily made and gives out a resonant tone when played with the hand.

3. Hard sticks or paddles
   a. Round doweling or 1x1 sticks, 12 inches long of hard wood as maple, oak or teak wood.
   b. Paddles of any wood cut out a half of an inch thick give a sharp sound.

4. Vocal accompaniment
   a. Half of the class recites a poem and the other half follows cadence or suggested thought.

Example[1]

    This is the way the lady rides,
    Gentle and slow, gentle and slow
    This is the way the lady rides
    All on a pleasant morning. (*Slow easy run*)
    This is the way a gentleman rides. (*High stepping spirited* horses)
    This is the way the farmer rides. (*Clumsy gait and gallop of* farm horses)

  b. Singing—Song indicates movement

Example. With Your Hands

    With your hands go clap, clap, clap;
    Now with your feet go tap, tap, tap;
    Join your fingers in a ring with me
    And jump in the circle one, two, three.

[1] Salt, Benton, Fox, G. I., *Teaching Physical Education in Elementary Schools*, A. S. Barnes, New York, 1942, pp. 215–216.

Formation. Single circle

Children face toward inside of circle and execute action indicated in the song. On the last line all join hands and move clockwise with the movement in the words of the song which may be a hop, skip, run, gallop, etc.

5. Piano
   a. The piano is excellent for accompaniment because the teacher can accent each beat, stop at any time, and take up again at the same place. The use of the piano requires special talent, aside from the ability to play, as instruction and demonstration must be interwoven with the accompaniment, requiring a great deal of change from piano to floor. It is ideal in schools where an accompanist is available.
6. Record player
   a. The record player has become standard equipment in most schools and the supply of available records is becoming more complete each year. The most satisfactory machine has a speed regulator and will play 33, 48, and 78 R.P.M. records.
   b. Best use of records
      (1) Buy records that carry six to eight rhymes, singing games, or dances. Albums seem expensive but are actually economical because of the number of recordings on each record. The playing time on a standard 78 record is too long for elementary grade children.
      (2) Play record and clap rhythms lightly, accenting change of phrasing with a heavy clap.
      (3) Dance with prescribed steps. Listen to music. Do first step without music, then with music. Master and proceed to second step. Do first and second, etc.

Progressive Presentation
MIMETICS

Mimetics can be presented from the first through the sixth grades. A child loses self-consciousness quickly in interpreting the suggested subject. At first the movements will be actual imitations of the toy, machine, or animal. Later the movements can become more subtle and suggestive rather than purely imitative. Mimetics serve as a smooth lead up to creative dance. An accompaniment is not always necessary for mimetics but will be suggested where there is a need for music in each of the following activities.

1. Mechanical[1]
   Bicycle—Series I, Ruth Evans

[1, 2] Record Reference A.

    See-Saw—Series I, Ruth Evans
    Airplane—Series I, Ruth Evans
           Rhythms for Children—Vic. 20162
    Jumping Jack—Series II, Ruth Evans
    Fire Engine—No music—pantomime—sirens, driving through the streets, unwinding the hose, etc.
    Train—Series I, Ruth Evans
    Dolls—Dance of Chinese Dolls, RCA Victor 22163-A
    Tops—Series I, Ruth Evans
    Clocks—Series II, Ruth Evans
    Elevator—Series II, Ruth Evans
    Swing—Series I, Ruth Evans

2. Animals[2]
    Horse—Series I, Ruth Evans
    Bear—No music—pantomime—walk in slovenly, rolling gait, looking for honey.
    Elephant—Series I, Ruth Evans
    Kangaroo—No music—pantomime—hop
    Deer—No music—pantomime—being chased by hunters and hounds
    Squirrel—No music—pantomime—short jerky movements, hiding nuts

3. Insects
    Butterfly—Butterfly Dance—Indian Rhythms, RCA Victor 22174, Ponies and Butterflies—RCA Victor 22079
    Bee—The Flight of the Bumblebee
    Cricket—No music—pantomime—lively jumping movements, rubbing arms together
    Firefly—No music—pantomime—quick flitting movements, interspersed with pauses

4. Miscellaneous
    Bird—Rhythms for Children—20401
    Witch[1]—Series I Ruth Evans
    Giant—In the Hall of the Mountain King—Victor 11835 The Giants—Victor 20743
    Elf[2]—Gnomes and Dwarfs—Victor 19882

CREATIVE DANCE

Creative dance is feeling expressed in movement. It is an activity which releases seeds of creative ability that grow with great abandon when sown at an early age. The child on the primary level is full of energy and free of inhibitions. This provides an opportunity to develop innate creative ability at a productive age.

[1, 2] Record Reference A, Vol. I.

Every child intensely feels his surrounding environment and is acutely conscious of change or new additions. Each child would naturally react in a different way to these stimuli, this is as it should be, but such is not the case when creative dance is introduced. There will always be the more aggressive leader who sets a pattern that will be followed sheep-like by other less imaginative children. Participation may be accepted as a goal but is an inadequate one. Aping should be discouraged from the first and differences pointed out to develop pride in the originality of individual expression.

Whether the exercise involves abstract feeling or a story or theme, a picture should be painted by the teacher to fire the imagination.

1. *Story or theme*—The use of a story or theme offers excellent transition from mimetics and story acting to creative rhythm.
    Story example—Little Red Riding Hood
                  The Three Bears
    Theme example—Circus Day
                  Clown
                  Marionettes—RCA Victor 22163
               Parade
                  Horses
                  Elephants
                  Dancing Bears

2. *Free feeling*—Examples
    a. Walk in the leaves—The first frosts have painted the leaves with many colors and they lie in a heavy carpet on the ground. The leaves are dry and crackle underfoot; a kick sends them sailing into the air.
    b. Wind in the trees—The wind sighs in the tall pines as they sway back and forth. The limbs of the large oaks sway more gently while the leaves of the elm, aspen, and cottonwood quaver and chatter at an excited pace.
    c. Fire—The freshly built fire crackles and the flames leap high, gradually dying down to coals, then embers.
    d. Growing things—The planted seed swells sprouts and pushes through the ground to take on leaves, buds and flowers.
    e. Feeling for color—Using the primary level for observation, the following reactions were recorded.[1] (Construction paper was used for colors)
    Red—exciting, pugnacious, challenging.
    Blue—calm in light shade, intriguing in intense shade.
    Green—soothing, restful, lazy.

[1] Foster, Mildred, Original Unit on Creative Dance taught at Margaret B. Henderson Elementary School, Dallas, Texas, 1950.

Yellow—happy, delightful, uplifting.

Black—depressing, still, quiet.

If these exercises seem too abstract, the color may be tied in with tangible things such as:

Red—bull fighter's cape, football jersey, rubber ball, shoes.

Blue—sky, water, eyes, blue bird, glass.

Green—grass, trees, moss, fish.

Yellow—sun, light, canary bird, fire, gems.

3. *Importance of Imagination*

Imagination is innate in all children. It flowers richly in some but must be extracted with consummate skill from others. An idea presented may bring an alert look, a sparkle in the eye, or it may find the dead look of flat unconcern. An idea must fit the known field of experience or ground must be spaded previously to prepare the soil for growth. Fundamental activities, such as chasing, fleeing, dodging and reaching, will find acceptance in all children. Known games succeed, this is also true of rhythms. A child who has been raised on the prairie will not be able to feel the wind in the pines, while he has a definite feel for a whining wind that blows sand into dunes of ever-changing patterns or rolls tumble weeds crazily across vast, open spaces. The child from the north will hold visions of the soft fall of snow, feather light, the drifts, the eerie cry of the blizzard. Smudge pots often darken the skies of California and Florida, but more familiar is the smell of orange blossoms, the waxy white of the trees, the fruit-laden abundance of a warm climate. There is the beach with scampering waves, the sun by day, the moon by night painting the ripples; the hard cold winter of northern days and nights, frozen with a hard pristine sparkle; the stream that runs through great canyons and moves later at a sedate pace by flat, shallow banks. The sun shines on maple, aspen, fir, cottonwood, spruce and pine; on corn, cotton, tobacco and wheat our land over. These things children see, and can express if the teachers guide and help release their feelings.

Singing Games

There is a variance of opinion as to the best method of presenting singing games and dances. Some teach children to listen for phrasing; some describe a step in rhythm with the music as step, close step; still others count as for the waltz, one, two, three. Few teachers will be blessed with classes that can progress, to a child, with the first method. A combination of all three reaches the monotone and the child with two left feet.

Jolly Is the Miller

Record—Victor 20214; Columbia A3078 Album; Victor 45-5065A (English)

Jolly is the miller who lives by the mill,
The wheel goes around with a right good will,
One hand in the hopper and the other in the sack,
The right skips forward and the left skips back.

Formation. Double circle, facing clockwise, inside hands joined. One child in the center of the circle.

Action. All skip forward while singing the first three lines. On the last line those in the outer circle step forward and those in the inner circle step backward, changing partners. The child in the center tries to get a partner, leaving one odd player in the center.

Did You Ever See a Lassie

Record—Victor 21618B (German)

Did you ever see a lassie, a lassie, a lassie,
Did you ever see a lassie do this way and that?
Do this way and that way,
Do this way and that way,
Did you ever see a lassie do this way and that?

Formation. Single circle facing clockwise. One child in center.

Action. All skip around circle singing until they reach the words "Do this way." The child in the center performs as: jumping in place, skips, etc. All face center and follow the leader. Repeat the game with a new leader. Substitute "laddie" for "lassie" when a boy is in the center.

The Farmer in the Dell

Record—Victor 21618B (English)

1. The farmer in the dell,
   The farmer in the dell,
   Heigh-o! the dairy-o!
   The farmer in the dell.

2. The farmer takes a wife,
   The farmer takes a wife,
   Heigh-o! the dairy-o!
   The farmer takes a wife.

3. The wife takes a child,
   The wife takes a child.
   Heigh-o! the dairy-o!
   The wife takes a child.

4. The child takes a nurse, etc.
5. The nurse takes a cat, etc.
6. The cat takes a rat, etc.
7. The rat takes a cheese, etc.
8. The cheese stands alone, etc.

Formation. Single circle, facing in, one child in the center represents the farmer.

Action. Verse 1. All stand in place and sing.
Verse 2. Farmer chooses a child from the circle as his wife.
Verse 3. The wife chooses a child.
Verse 4. The child chooses a nurse.
Verse 5–7. Continue as above.
Verse 8. On the last verse the children clap hands and jump

up and down. At the end of the verse, all return to the circle except the cheese who becomes the farmer in the new game.

Captain Jinks

Record—Victor 20639 (American)

    A. I'm Captain Jinks of the Horse Marines,
       I feed my horse good corn and beans,
    B. I swing the ladies in their teens,
       For that's the style in the army!
    C. I teach the ladies how to dance, how to dance,
       How to dance, I teach the ladies how to dance,
       For that's the style in the army!
    D. Salute your partner, turn to the right,
       And swing your neighbor with all your might,
       Then promenade with the lady right,
       For that's the style in the army!

Formation. Single circle, girl in front of boy, facing clockwise.
Action. Verse 1. All march forward.
        Verse 2. Partners do two-handed swing skipping clockwise.
        Verse 3. Partners join inside hands and skip forward.
        Verse 4. Face partner, boy bows while girl curtsies (boy may salute) and moves to his right to swing his neighbor two times around and promenades his new partner (boy stays on outside of circle.)

Way Down in the Paw Paw Patch

Record—Victor 45-5066B (American)

    1. Where, oh where is dear little (Betty)?
      Where, oh where is dear little . . . . ?
      Where, oh where is dear little . . . . ?
      'Way down yonder in the paw paw patch.

    2. Come on boys and let's go find her
      Come on boys and let's go find her,
      Come on boys and let's go find her,
      'Way down yonder in the paw paw patch.

    3. Pickin' up paw paws, puttin' them in a basket,
      Pickin' up paw paws, puttin' them in a basket
      Pickin' up paw paws, puttin' them in a basket
      'Way down yonder in the paw paw patch.

Formation. Five or six couples form a double line—
        Boys: X X X X X X
        Girls: O O O O O O
The first name of the girl is sung as each new lead couple takes their place.
Action. Verse 1. First girl turns to her right and skips clockwise around the entire group.

Verse 2. Girl encircles group again and line of boys follow her and come back to original place.

Verse 3. Partners join hands and skip clockwise. When the head couple reaches the foot of the line, they hold joined hands high to make an arch and the other couples skip under it. The second couple is now the head couple. The game is repeated, singing out the name of the new girl until all couples have been at the head of the line. On the last verse, the children act out the motion of putting paw paws in a basket.

Here We Go Over the Mountain Two by Two[1]

1. Here we go over the mountain, two by two
   Here we go over the mountain, two by two
   Here we go over the mountain, two by two
   Rise up, Sugar, rise.

2. Show us a lively motion, two by two
   Show us a lively motion, two by two
   Show us a lively motion, two by two
   Rise up, Sugar, rise.

3. That's a very lively motion, two by two
   That's a very lively motion, two by two
   That's a very lively motion, two by two
   Rise up, Sugar, rise.

Formation. Single circle of partners, facing in. One couple stands in the center.

Action. Verse 1. Children sing and walk counterclockwise while the center couple figures some movement.

Verse 2. The center couple executes movements they have chosen.

Verse 3. Entire group imitates action demonstrated by couple in center. The center couple chooses a couple to take their place and the game is repeated.

Hokey Pokey

Record—Capitol 1496 (American)

1. You put your right hand in,
   You take your right hand out,
   You put your right hand in,
   And you shake it all about,
   You do the Hokey Pokey and turn yourself about,
   That's what it's all about—Yeah!

2. You put your left hand in, etc.

3-10. You put your right and left elbow, shoulder and hip, head, and whole body.

[1] Book Reference 2.

11. You do the Hokey Pokey,
    You do the Hokey Pokey,
    You do the Hokey Pokey,
    That's what it's all about.

This singing game is a modernized version of Looby Loo and finds favor in primary through adult groups.

Formation. Single circle facing in.

Action. Players follow calls performing action indicated.

Verses. When the song calls to do the "Hokey Pokey" the elbows are bent, the hands are up, palms out and are wig-wagged backward and forward in front of the face. The player takes a quick turn clockwise and claps out the rhythm of the song, thrusting the right hand toward the center of the circle at the conclusion.

Last Verse. Hands are held high and waved in a trembling motion. Players kneel, slap the floor with both hands, rise and shout as the music finishes.

Rig-a-Jig

Record—Disc 5038; Childhood Rhythms, Series VI, Record 602.

As I was walking down the street,
Heigh-o, heigh-o, heigh-o, heigh-o
A little friend I chanced to meet
Heigh-o, heigh-o, heigh-o.
Chorus
Rig-a-jig-jig, and away we go
Away we go, away we go,
Rig-a-jig-jig, and away we go
Heigh-o, heigh-o, heigh-o.

Formation. Single circle facing center. One player stands inside circle.

Action. The child in the center walks around the inside of circle until the words "A little friend" are sung. He chooses a partner and skips around circle. As the chorus is repeated, each child inside the circle chooses a partner until all have been chosen.

Bluebird[1] (American)

Bluebird, bluebird, in and out my windows,
Bluebird, bluebird, in and out my windows,
Oh! Johnny, I am tired.
Chorus
Take a little boy and tap him on the shoulders,
Take a little boy and tap him on the shoulders,
Oh! Johnny, I am tired.

Formation. Single circle facing center with hands joined and held high to make arches. One child, the Bluebird, stands in the center of the circle.

[1] Book Reference 23, music found on page 50.

Action. LINES 1 AND 2. Bluebird walks around circle weaving in and out under the arches.

       LINE 3.   Bluebird stops behind boy.

       CHORUS.   Bluebird places hands on shoulders of child and taps lightly through chorus.

The dance is repeated with the boy becoming the leader and the girl follows behind with hands on his shoulders. Continue the game until all are chosen. Substitute "Jenny" for Johnny when girls are chosen.

Jingle Bells

Any recording of this tune with a lively rhythm. (American)
Grades. 3 to 6
Formation. Double circle facing counterclockwise.

PART I.

Dashing thru the snow	With hands in skating position, partners slide forward four slides with right foot leading.
In a one-horse open sleigh	Leading with left foot, repeat above.
O'er the field we go Laughing all the way Bells on bob-tail ring Making spirits bright, What fun it is to ride and sing A sleighing song tonight!	Continue this "skating step" alternately leading with right foot and left foot.

PART II.

Jingle bells! Jingle bells! Jingle all the way!	Partners face and clap in rhythm to words.
Oh! What fun it is to ride In a one-horse open sleigh.	Partners link right arms and skip about each other eight skips making two complete circles.

PART II. (Repeated)

Jingle bells! Jingle bells! Jingle all the way!	Partners face and clap.
Oh! What fun it is to ride	Link left arms and skip four skips.
In a one horse open sleigh!	Boy moves forward to next girl.

Repeat all.

SINGING GAMES FOR OTHER SEASONS[1]

1. My Valentine (page 27)
2. Our Big Turkey (page 10)
3. Pumpkin Man and Brownie (page 32)
4. Did You Ever See Dear Santa? (page 12)
5. This Is the Way (page 4)

SAFETY AND OTHER SINGING GAMES

Singing games may be created by the children to make them more aware of what is expected of them in the school community. These games can pertain to citizenship, safety, special events or good manners and can be adapted to well known melodies or, with the help of the music teacher, written to tunes of their own.

Examples

1. *Swing* (Set to original tune)

> I swing high a bit, and low a bit.
> But when I swing, I always sit.
> Swinging sideways, and swinging double.
> Is not for me, it means trouble.
> Up, up I go into the sun,
> Swinging safely makes swinging fun.

2. *Trapeze* (Sung to Rock-A-Bye Baby)
Formation. Single circle, facing clockwise.

I am a monkey,	Children walk swinging arms.
I swing so free,	
You may see bars,	Stretch arms high.
It's really a tree,	
I hang by my knees,	Squat with hands on floor.
I cut di do-es,	Jump around.
I look when I drop,	Take big jump toward center of circle and land lightly on toes.
And land on my toes.	

3. *Lunch Room* (Sung to Old Mac Donald Had a Farm)

> We wait for the bell to sound,
> To the lunch room we are bound,
> In a line so straight with tray and plate,
> We move and never crowd.
> The food is good,
> The milk is fine,
> We slowly chew,
> And take our time.

[1] Book Reference 2.

Our plates are clean, our tables too,
Did you, did you, did you?

Formation. Single circle facing forward.

Action. Children sing and march making the motions of taking a tray, eating food and cleaning off their tables. On the last line, they stop, turn and point to three children in the circle.

Square Dance

Folk dancing has been enjoyed by limited groups in the larger cities of the United States for a long period of time. The repertoire of these groups was composed chiefly of international[1] dances. The past ten or fifteen years have seen a revival of square dancing which has enthusiastically swept the whole country, cities, small towns, and hamlets alike. The eagerness of these groups has given a tremendous boost to all folk dancing, for they gradually added to their "know-how" couple and group dances from all countries.

Square dancing patter and calls vary in different parts of the country and even in towns in the same state. However, the fundamental formations and steps are the same.

A teacher may start square dancing in the third or fourth grades using circle or round dances. In the fifth or sixth grades the children should be able to execute a number of simple round, square, and longways dances.

TEACHING SUGGESTIONS

1. Choose a square dance record that is moderately slow and do your own calls. Records with calls move too fast for children to follow.

2. Call in modulated voice keeping the words of the call in time with the music and spaced to give the dancers time to follow instructions. Beginners will require more time to execute any call, but teach them from the start to LISTEN to the calls. Keep the patter simple to avoid confusion.

3. Teach the shuffle step emphasizing smoothness and grace and discouraging any tendency to bounce, skip, or hop. The proper performance of this one step makes the difference in square dancing between a thing of fluid beauty or a comical, grotesque caricature of a jumping jack.

4. Keep the square symmetrical and snug so that the dancers can progress easily from one call to the next. Children are in-

[1] Book Reference 14, p. 1.

clined to spread out into a ragged circle; this causes them to break the rhythm and run to the next figure that is called.

5. Practice each call until the children know *where* they are going.

6. Be patient and accept enthusiastic participation as your goal rather than letter perfect execution.

TEACHING PROGRESSIONS

The Circle[1]

Form a single circle alternating boys and girls. The boy's partner is on his right, his corner on his left. The following terms and figures may be taught in the circle:

Honor Your Partner. Boy bows from the waist with his right arm in front and left arm in back (avoid stomach clutching and head ducking). Girl does a simple curtsey by placing one foot behind the other and flexing knees slightly. She may hold her skirts at the side.

Honor Your Corner. Same as above to corner.

Circle Left. All join hands and move forward around the circle.

Circle Right. Move to right as above.

Promenade

Couples move counterclockwise around the circle with the girl on the boy's right. The boy has the girl's right hand in his right hand and her left hand in his left hand, his right arm crossed over girl's left arm.

Grand Right and Left

Partners face, touch right hands and pass on to the next, touching left hands, and on around the circle, weaving in and out until partners meet again. The boys move counterclockwise, the girls clockwise. It may be necessary to have the children hold on to partner's hands until they can touch the left hands, release, hold left hands, etc.

Swings

Two Handed Swing. Partners face, clasp both hands and swing around. This swing is recommended for children up to the sixth grade.

[1] Book Reference 31, pp. 43–55, Record Source D.

Elbow Swing. Hook right or left elbows and swing around once. Use alternately with two handed swing.

Waist Swing. Boy takes girl in social dance position and swings her around to the right, stepping left, right, left, etc. Usually a waist swing calls for two turns.

Allemande Left. Boy and corner face, join left hands, walk around each other and return to home position. Practice this figure a few times and add the Allemande left to the grand right and left and end up with the promenade home.

The Square[1]

Break the large circle into small circles of eight each which constitutes a set. Teach the sets to "square up." Each couple in the set forms one side of the square which should be large enough to allow free movement and tight enough to prevent running back to home position. First couples have their backs to the Caller or music. Proceeding counterclockwise are couples two, three and four. First and third are called "head couples" and second and fourth are called "side couples." A couple's starting position is "home." Have the couples identify themselves by raising their hands. Review all fundamentals learned in the circle and you are ready to teach a dance.

Red River Valley[2]

There are a number of good recordings of this tune.
Grades 4, 5, 6
This simple version is a favorite among the youngsters of the Southwest. Many groups sing as they dance, which helps them know what steps to do next. Different versions may be found in the listed references.

Formation. Squares of eight.

The first couple lead down the Valley,
And you circle to the left and to the right.

First couple moves to Couple No. 2 and all form a circle. Move to left, move to right.

Then you swing with the girl in the Valley,

Each boy swings his opposite girl one and a half times around. Each boy swings his

---

[1] Book Reference 13, pp. 5, 6, and Book Reference 33 p. 3.
[2] Book References 13, 16, 33.

And now you swing with your Red River Girl.

partner one and a half times around. Couple No. 2 should be in home position and Couple No. 1 in the center of the square.

Then lead right on down the Valley,
And you circle to the left and to the right.
Then you swing with the girl in the Valley,
And now you swing with your Red River Girl.

Couple No. 1 moves on to Couple No. 3 and repeats action of first verse.

Then lead right on down the Valley,
And you circle to the left and to the right.
Then you swing with the girl in the Valley,
And now you swing with your Red River Girl.

Couple No. 1 moves on to Couple No. 4 and repeats action of first verse.

Repeat all with Couples 2, 3 and 4 leading out.

The square dance has four parts: (1) an introduction or opener, (2) the main figure, the trimmings, (3) fill-ins or mixers and (4) the ending. Numerous examples of patter for all dances may be found in the references listed at the end of the chapter.[1] There is no doubt that the Allemande left, and grand right and left, takes on color when called as, "On your corner with the old left hand, why in the world don't you right and left grand," but it is suggested that calls at this level be kept simple with just enough variation to avoid monotony.

Examples of Introductions
Honor your partner, the lady by your side (*corner*)
All join hands and circle wide (*move to left*)
Break and swing and promenade home.

All eight balance, all eight swing,
Now promenade around the ring.

[1] Book References 13, 14, 31, 33.

Examples of Endings

> Bow to your partner, bow to your corner,
> Bow to your opposite, and there you stand.

> Promenade (add girl's names) two by two,
> Take her home like you always do.

Take a Little Peek[1]

Grade 6

Formation. Squares of eight.

First couple, balance and swing,	Holding inside hands couple faces, takes two steps away from each other, then waist swings.
Out to the couple on the right, and take a little peek.	Couple 1 moves to Couple 2, divides and peek at each other around Couple 2.
Back to the center and swing your sweet.	Couple 1 swings once around with a waist swing in center of square. Peeks again.
Out to the side and peek once more.	
Back to the center and swing all four.	Couple 1 waist swings in the center while Couple 2 does same in home position.
Circle four in the middle of the floor.	No. 1 boy picks up Couple 2 and all join hands and circle to the left.
Do-si-do, and a little more do,	Do-si-do—left to partner and swing, right to corner and swing.
Grab your partner, on to the next, and take a little peek.	Take partner and move on to Couple 3. Couple returns to home position.
Back to the center and swing your sweet.	Repeat action above. Repeat entire call with Couples 2, 3 and 4 leading out.

Cowboy Loop[2]

Grade 6

Formation. Squares of eight.

First couple, balance and swing.	Two steps backward, bow and swing.

[1] Book Reference 33, p. 23.
[2] Book Reference 32, p. 31.

Out to the couple on the right,

Lead out to Couple 2. Boy joins hands with girl in Couple 2.

And circle four in the middle of the floor.

Form a circle and move clockwise.

Two hold up, and four trail through.

No. 1 boy drops his corner's hand and leads the line under the joined and raised hands of Couple 3 who walk forward as the line passes under the arch.

Turn right around and go back through.

Couple 3 drops hands, pivots, forms an arch with other hands. No. 1 boy turns his line and leads it back under the arch. Couple 3 walks down the line, as it passes under the arch, back to home position.

Tie that knot like the cowboys do.

The line has passed under the arch. No. 1 boy moves to the right and leads the entire line under an arch formed by Couple 2. Couple 3 waist swings in home position.

Circle six and all get fixed.

No. 1 boy picks up couple 3 and all circle to the left.

Now, two hold up, and six trail through.

Couple 4 forms the arch.

Turn right around and go back through.

Repeat action above.

Tie that knot like the cowboys do.

Repeat action above.

Circle eight and all get straight.

All circle to the left.

Round and round and round you go.

Continue circling.

Break that ring with a do-si-do.

Left to partner, swing once around, swing corner once around with the right hand, come back to partner.

And promenade home.

Promenade counterclockwise back to home position.

Repeat: Couples 2, 3 and 4 lead out.

Additional Suggested Dances and Sources.

1. All Hands Across (Ref. 13, p. 54, 31, p. 200)
2. Sisters Form a Ring (Ref. 14, p. 30, 33, p. 19)
3. Wagon Wheel (Ref. 14, p. 41, 33, p. 44)
4. Texas Star (Ref. 13, p. 59, 14, p. 59, 33, p. 33)

Longways Formation

There are two types of longways formations used in dances. The type of Figure 1 is formed by a double line with partners facing forward. This formation is used in the party game, "Way Down in the Paw Paw Patch." The type of Figure 2 is used in the "Virginia Reel" which remains one of the most popular of American folk dances among all age groups. It serves as an excellent introduction to square dancing as a number of the basic movements are learned. Third and fourth graders prefer the skip as the basic step but fifth and sixth graders show a preference for the shuffle step which is less strenuous and more dignified.

Fig. 1		Fig. 2	
O	X	O→X	
O	X	O X	
O	X	O X	
O	X	O X	
O	X	O ˎX	
O	X	O→X	

Head of Set
O—girls
X—boys

Virginia Reel

Formation. Six to eight couples longways, partners facing.

Action. In the first six steps the head boy and girl move forward to the center to execute the movement and move backward to places. The head girl and foot boy repeat the same action by moving to the center of the set and returning to their places.

STEP 1. Boys bow to corners, girls curtsy to corners	Measure: 1–4
Head boy and head girl move to center, bow and return to places	
Head girl and foot boy repeat action	Measure: 5–8
STEP 2. Hook right arms and swing around once clockwise	Measure: 1–4
Repeat	Measure: 5–8
STEP 3. Hook left arms and swing around once clockwise	Measure: 9–12
Repeat	Measure: 13–16
STEP 4. Join both hands and turn clockwise	Measure: 9–12

Repeat   Measure: 13–16

STEP 5. Dos-a-dos, passing right
shoulders   Measure: 17–20

Repeat   Measure: 21–24

STEP 6. Dos-a-dos, passing left shoul-
ders   Measure: 25–28

Repeat   Measure: 29–32

STEP 7. Head couple faces, joins
hands and moves sideward to the foot
of the set with four slides and returns to
the head of the set with four slides   Measure: 1–4

STEP 8. Head couple hooks right elbows and turns one and a half around
until the boy is facing the girls' line
and the girl is facing the boys' line. The
boy hooks left elbows with the second
girl as the girl hooks left elbows with
the second boy. They swing half way
around counterclockwise and meet back
in the center, hook right elbows and
turn half clockwise. This is repeated
down the line with the head couple
turning each dancer with a left arm and
turning each other with the right arm.
When they have turned the last dancer
at the foot of line, they turn one and a
half times around, join both hands and
slide back to the head of the set.   Measure: 5–16

(If there are more than six couples the
twelve measures may not provide sufficient music to complete the action. Repeat if necessary.)

STEP 9. All face head of set, head   Cast
boy turns outward and leads the line to-   off
ward the foot of the set with a slow   Music
shuffle. At the same time the head girl
turns outward and leads the girls to the
foot of the set with the same step.

STEP 10. Head couple joins hands high
to form an arch and all couples pass
through. The second couple is now the
head couple and the dance is repeated
until all couples have been at the head
of the set.

Variation. Some groups who like more action stand farther apart and all dance the first six steps, first dancing with their partners then with their corners.

COUPLE DANCES

Jesse Polka

Record—Beer Barrel Polka, RCA Victor: 25-1009-B, (American-Bohemian) Any good polka.   *Grade 6*

Formation. Couples in varsovienne position. Boy and girl on same foot.

STEP 1. Touch left heel forward and take weight on left foot. Count 1 and   Measure: 1

STEP 2. Touch right toe back. Count 2. Step beside left foot without taking weight, and touch right heel forward and step back, count 3, taking weight on right foot, and   Measure: 2–3

STEP 3. Touch left heel forward, lift left foot, cross toe in front of right foot (cut) and   Measure: 4

STEP 4. Four two-steps, beginning left.   Measure: 5–8

Repeat the entire dance.

Cotton-Eyed Joe

Record—Columbia 37658—Foot N' Fiddle, Sept., 1947 (American-Texas)   *Grade 6*

Formation. Partners in social dance position. Boy begins on left foot, girl on right.

STEP 1. Touch heel to front, touch toe to back by right foot—step, together —step (two-step). Repeat in reverse direction.

STEP 2. Turn away from partner, to boy's left, to girl's right, with three two-steps. Complete circle and face partner with three stamps.

STEP 3. Four slides to boy's left. Repeat in reverse direction.

STEP 4. Four two-steps in social dance position. Repeat all.

This vigorous Texas frontier dance

usually follows the description in steps one, two and four. In step three, one finds many variations, two of which are:

1. Boy and girl go in opposite directions, clapping and sliding for four counts, returning to original position in four counts.

2. Push or paddle step to boy's left for four counts, and to boy's right for four counts.

Veleta

Record—Michael Herman (American British)   *Grade 6*

Open Position

STEP 1. Partners join inside hands. Starting with outside foot, boy's left, girl's right, take two waltz steps forward.   Measure: 2

Face partner, change hands and do two draw steps to left.   Measure: 2

Repeat in opposite direction.   Measure: 4

Closed Position

Start backward, boy on left foot, girl follows on right. Do two waltz steps.   Measure: 2

Two draw steps, boy with left foot, girl with right.   Measure: 2

Four waltz steps.   Measure: 4

Repeat entire dance.

Mixers

Teachers, who are working with children who have had rhythmic training from the first grade up, will encounter little trouble in directing or teaching mixed groups. However, where groups are new to each other or shy, it is well to warm up with a Grand March, a group dance or a mixer to get everyone acquainted and relaxed. A child should not be allowed to "sit out" too often. If there is an odd dancer, make a game of the mixer and let the boy or girl try to get a partner as a change is made. The children should be allowed to choose their own dance partners at intervals but if they get in a rut, partners should be juggled with a mixer. Mixers are fun and an excellent method of juggling partners in shy groups.

Maine Mixer

Record—Gloworm, Imperial 1044 (American)   *Grades 4, 5, 6*

Formation. Double circle facing right (counterclockwise). Join hands with girl or boy's right. Group sings or chants instructions until mixer is learned.

Everybody goes to town

You pick 'em up, you lay 'em down	Eight steps right.
Back away and say adieu	Take one step away, face partner and wave.
And balance to the right of you.	Boy and Girl balance to opposites to their right. This is their new partner.
Dos-a dos and watch her smile	New partners circle back to back and return to original place.
Step right up and swing her awhile	Boy swings girl with waist swing.
Give that girl an extra swing	Boy twirls girl and takes promenade position.
And promenade around the ring.	

Mexican Mixer

Record—La Bios de Coral, Imperial 119 (American)   *Grades 5, 6*

Formation. Couples in social dance position form a circle, boys facing counterclockwise, girls facing clockwise.

STEP 1. Do grapevine to inside of circle. Boy steps back of left foot with right, to the outside with the left foot, forward right and swings the left leg out. Girl does same, starting on left foot.

Repeat same to outside of circle.

Step left back, right side, left forward, right swing.

STEP 2. With a wrist hold, couple turns to right with four step-hops— right, left, right, left.

STEP 3. Boy claps while girl moves away to right (step1) with a step right, left, right, swing, four step-hops turning with hands on hips.

Repeat moving left to partner.

Girl claps and boy does same, girl
moving to inside of circle and back. As
he does the step-hops, he turns to his
left (counterclockwise) and moves on to
the next girl.

International Dances

Increasingly educators are teaching children that other countries are not foreign if one knows enough about them. In any
metropolitan city a teacher has a wealth of material in one class
whereby world fellowship could be taught with live authenticity.
The mores, habits and folklore of a people cease to be strange
when explanations throw light on their origin.

Folk dancing is one phase of education for international understanding that should not be tampered with if one desires a true
picture of a people. A way of life, the very character of a people
is expressed in its folk music and dance. Hence, if we use these
dances they should be taught as near the original as possible,
giving the student a rich background in the country, costume and
reason for the dance. The Czechs take on new stature when one has
seen the *Beseda*. A Slav is a person to be admired once the intricate
and subtle steps of a *Kolo* have been mastered. The child, who
has been taught the *Ländler*, will rarely mention Hitler when the
word "German" appears because he will recall a noisy, lusty, fun
loving people who like to "stomp" out a good tune. Likewise,
Stalin will fade into his proper proportion when the beautiful
strains of *Alexandrovski* remind one that Russians love beauty in
movement. The close knit barrier of race falls limply as one joins
in a circle to dance the friendly *Cherkessia* which is both joyous
and sad with its undercurrent of the tragic Jewish past. Folk
dancing can be an invaluable adjunct to the teacher who is trying
to present world geography in an honest way.

There are other facets to folk dancing. Coordination and skill
can be developed that carry over into all dancing, particularly
social dancing. Children need to learn how to do social dancing
as much as they need to know almost any other subject taught in
schools. Folk dance develops in one the ability to move to rhythm,
to coordinate hands and arms with feet and legs. Often our most
polished social dancers of the high school level have been the best
dancers in a fourth grade folk dance class.

The European and American folk dances that appear in published form have been acknowledged in this book. The sources of a number of American dances are unknown, for a dance will pop up in one community and a visiting folk dance devotee who is present will take it back to his own group with slight changes. Credit has been given to known individuals who have introduced dances to folk dancing groups. In many folk dances the music practically calls the steps. In describing these simpler dances where the music phrasing speaks for itself counts and measure have been excluded.

Kalvelis

Record—Sonart Folk Dance Album I—Folkraft 1051A (Lithuanian-Blacksmith)   *Grades 5, 6*

Formation. About eight couples form single circle facing counterclockwise.

STEP 1. All polka (without hop) eight steps right.	Measure: 1–8
All polka (without hop) eight steps left.	Measure: 1–8
CHORUS. Clap own hands, partner's right, own hands, partner's left. Double hand grasp and skip to left four times, skip to right four times.	Measure: 9–16
Repeat.	Measure: 9–16
STEP 2. Girls do four polka steps into circle, turn and four polka steps back to place. Boys do same.	Measure: 1–8 Measure: 1–8 Measure: 9–16
CHORUS—twice	
STEP 3. Girls weave around circle going back of the first dancer and in front of the next, etc., sixteen polka steps. Boys do same.	Measure: 1–16 Measure: 1–16
CHORUS.	
STEP 4. All do grand right and left.	Measure: 1–16
CHORUS—twice	Measure: 1–16
STEP 5. All join hands and polka eight times right as in Step 1.	Measure: 1–8
Polka eight times left.	Measure: 1–8

Tantoli

Simple Version—Crampton, The Folk Dance Book—Record—(Scandinavian)   *Grades 3, 4*

Formation. Couples in double circle facing counterclockwise with inside hands joined and free hands on hips.

STEP 1. With outside foot, place heel to floor forward, and toe on floor backward. Polka step hopping on inside foot. Repeat three times, beginning on inside foot, outside, and inside.

Measure: 1

Measure: 2
Measure: 3–8

STEP 2. Partners face, join hands at shoulder level and turn clockwise with sixteen step hops, boy starting on left foot, girl on right.

Measure: 8

(This step has been called the "Windmill" as the arms are lowered toward the foot that the hop is taken on and raised on the opposite side.)
Repeat dance.

Tantoli

Advanced Version—Folk Dancer, July–August, 1946—(Swedish)
Scandinavian Album—Victor   *Grades 5, 6*

Formation. Double circle facing counterclockwise, boy places arm around girl's waist, girl has left hand on boy's right shoulder. Free hands on hips.

FIGURE 1. Couples move forward with two step hops on outside foot (boy's left, girl's right). Couples turn clockwise with two hop steps.
Repeat three times.

Measure: 1
Measure: 2
Measure: 3–8

FIGURE 2. Moving counterclockwise, take one Schottische step forward: Boy's step: left, right, left, hop on left. Girl's step: right, left, right, hop on right. Couples take one Schottische step backward, beginning on inside foot. Couples turn twice around in place (clockwise) with four step hops. Face in slightly. Repeat measures 9–12.

Measure: 9

Measure: 10

Measure: 11–12
Measure: 13–16

FIGURE 3. Facing counterclockwise, couples do heel-toe Polka as described in simple version, without hop. Boy's step: heel of outside foot (left) forward, toe backward. Step left, close right, step left. Girl does same, starting on right foot.

Measure: 1
Measure: 2

Repeat measures 1–2 beginning on inside foot.

Repeat measures 1–4.

Lean backward as heel is forward, and lean forward as toe is backward. Chorus: "Windmill" step described as simple version. Sixteen hop steps, alternately raising and lowering arms. Boy begins on left foot, girl on right.

Measure: 3–4
Measure: 5–8

Measure: 9–16

FIGURE 4. Couples form a double circle facing each other, boy on the inside of circle, girl on outside, hands on hips. Both move counterclockwise with four side steps.

Side step: Boy takes a step to the side, swinging the foot in an arc, brings the right foot to the left.

Repeat three times, and on the third time, he steps on the left foot with a stamp and swings the right leg across. Girl does the same, starting on right foot.

Repeat measure 1–2 in opposite direction, moving clockwise.

Repeat measures 1–4.

Repeat chorus, in open position as in Figure 3.

Measure: 1–2

Measure: 3–4
Measure: 5–8

Measure: 9–16

FIGURE 5. Face counterclockwise as in Figure 1 and take one Schottische step forward beginning on outside foot. Boy, left, right, left, hop. Girl, right, left, right, hop. One Schottische step backward, beginning on inside foot.

Bend knee (outside) and brush foot forward and backward on floor twice.

Carry foot back and tap toe on the floor three times.

Repeat measures 1–4.

Repeat chorus as in Figure 3.

Measure: 1
Measure: 2

Measure: 3

Measure: 4
Measure: 5–8
Measure: 9–16

Csebogar

Record—Victor 20992 (Hungarian)   *Grades 2, 3*

Formation. Partners form single circle facing in, girl on boy's right, hands joined.

STEP 1. All move clockwise with eight slides.

Measure: 1–4

STEP 2. All move counterclockwise with eight slides.

Measure: 5–8

STEP 3. Hands still joined, and held high, take four skips toward center of circle.

Measure: 9–10

Lower hands, skip backward to original places.

Measure: 11–12

STEP 4. Partners face and place right arm around partner's waist and raise left arm high, with elbow straight. Skip eight times turning clockwise.

Measure: 13–16

(Variation. Upper grades may use eight paddle steps, or the Hungarian. Turn twice, around with a hop right, step left, step right.)

STEP 5. All face partners, join both hands and step sideways toward center of circle, closing with opposite foot in four slow slides, or draws.

Measure: 17–20

Repeat to outside of circle.

Measure: 21–24

STEP 6. Repeat action of Step 5 with two draw steps.

Measure: 25–28

STEP 7. Repeat Step 4.

Measure: 29–32

Gustaf's Skoal

Record—Victor 20988 (Swedish) "Skoal" means formal greeting
Grades 2, 3

Formation. Square—Four couples.

1. Head couples—3 steps forward and bow on 4th count.

Measure: 1–2

2. Head couples—3 steps backward and feet together on 4th count.

Measure: 3–4

3. Side couples do same.

Measure: 5–8

4. Repeat all.

Measure: 1–8

5. Side couples join inside hands and form arch. Head couples skip toward each other, take new partners. Skip through arch, girls go to right, boys to left. Leave new partners and return to original positions meeting own partners.

Measure: 9–12

6. All clap hands, join both hands with partner and make one complete turn.

Measure: 13–16

7. Side couples repeat step 5 with
head couples forming arch. All repeat
step 6.   Measure: 9–16

Danish Dance of Greeting

Record—Victor, 17158   *Grades 1, 2*

Formation. Single circle dancers facing the center with hands on hips.

Action.

STEP 1. Clap hands twice; turn to
partner and bow. Clap hands twice,
turn and bow to neighbor.   Measure: 1–2

STEP 2. Stamp right, stamp left; turn
in place four running steps.   Measure: 3–4
Repeat measures 1 and 2.   Measure: 1–4

STEP 3. All join hands and take six-
teen running steps to right.   Measure: 5–8
Repeat to left. Repeat entire dance.   Measure: 9–16

Chimes of Dunkirk

Record—World of Fun Series, M 105 (French, Flemish, Belgian)
Grades 1, 2

Formation. Double circle of partners facing each other, boys with
back to center of circle.

Action.

STEP 1. Clap three times, pause.   Measure: 4

STEP 2. Partners join both hands and
walk around circle in eight counts.   Measure: 5–8

STEP 3. Partners join right hands and
balance. Repeat.   Measure: 9–12

STEP 4. Partners walk around each
other once and boy moves on to his left
to the next girl.   Measure: 13–16

Ace of Diamonds

Record—Victor 20989; World of Fun Series, M 102 (Danish)
Grades 2, 3

Formation. Double circle, partners facing, boys with back to center
of circle.

Action.

STEP 1. Partners clap hands once,
stamp foot once, hook right arms and
swing around once.   Measure: 1–4
Repeat using left arm.   Measure: 5–8

STEP 2. Girl puts hands on hips and moves backward toward center of circle with a step, hop. Step left, hop left; step right, hop right. Repeat. Boy follows with arms crossed on chest; step right, hop right, step right, hop right. Repeat. Return in reverse.

Measure: 8–16

STEP 3. Polka—skating position, going counterclockwise.

Measure: 1–16

Troika

Record—Kismet S112 (Russian)   *Grades 5, 6*

Formation. Groups of three facing counterclockwise. Center dancer is a boy, outside dancers girls. Hands are joined, free hands on hips.

FIGURE I

STEP 1. Four running steps forward diagonally to right.

Measure: 1

STEP 2. Repeat diagonally to left.

Measure: 2

STEP 3. Eight running steps forward around circle.

Measure: 3–4

STEP 4. Hands still joined the girl on the boy's right runs under arch, made by boy and girl on left, in eight steps. Other two run in place.

Measure: 5–6

STEP 5. Girl on left runs under arch and back to place in eight steps.

Measure: 7–8

FIGURE II

STEP 1. Each group of three joins hands in a circle and runs to left (clockwise) for twelve steps, beginning on left foot.

Measure: 9–11

STEP 2. Stamp in place—left, right, left. Repeat steps 1 and 2 running to right (counterclockwise).

Measure: 12

Measure: 13–16

Release hands and repeat entire dance with same partners. Partners may change in measure 16. Girls raise outside hands to make an arch, release boy and he runs with four steps to next group while girls stamp in place.

Measure: 16

Green Sleeves

Record[1] (English)   *Grades 3, 4, 5, 6*
[1] Record Reference H, J, K.

Formation. Double circle in sets of two couples, numbered 1 and 2, facing counterclockwise, girls on right.

STEP 1. Holding hands, walk forward sixteen steps.

STEP 2. Form a star in sets. Man No. 1 gives hand to girl No. 2 and man No. 2 to girl No. 1. Walk clockwise eight steps, change to left hands and walk back to place counterclockwise.

STEP 3. Couple No. 1 join hands and back under arch made by couple No. 2 who walk forward four steps, then walk backward while No. 1 makes the arch. Repeat.

Repeat entire dance.

Tropanka

Folk Dancer Record—Disc Album 635 (Bulgarian stamping dance) *Grades 3, 4, 5, 6*

Formation. Single circle, little fingers joined.

Stamping step—cross foot over in front in ballet position with heel turned out.

STEP 1. Beginnnig on right foot, take five running steps to right and stamp twice with left foot. Turn and run to left five steps and stamp twice with right foot.	Measure: 1–2 Measure: 2–4
Repeat first four measures.	Measure: 1–4
STEP 2. Facing center, all step on right foot, hop on right foot and swing left foot in front. Step, hop, swing, starting on left foot.	Measure: 5
Step on right foot, cross left foot over and stamp twice.	Measure: 6
Repeat measures 5 and 6, starting on left foot.	Measure: 7–8
Repeat measures.	Measure: 5–8
STEP 3. Moving toward center of circle, all starting on right foot, step, hop right, step, hop left. Step right and stamp twice with left foot. (Arms raised high shout "Hey!")	Measure: 5
	Measure: 6

Repeat action of measures 5 and 6, dancing backward, starting with left foot. Gradually lower arms.

Repeat measures 9 through 16 as in measures 1 through 8.

Cherkessia

Sonart Folk Dance Album M8 (Jewish)   *Grades 5, 6*

Formation. Single circle, hands joined

Teaching Suggestions. There should be quite a bit of bending backward and forward and swing of joined hands as the dance progresses. On the verse the circle moves to the right, on the chorus the circle moves to the left.

Action.

CHORUS.   The dance begins with the chorus and is repeated after each figure.

Circle moves to the left. All step forward and stamp with the right foot in front of the left (ct. 1), step with the left foot behind right (ct. 2), step back on right foot (ct. 1) and bring left foot beside the right foot (ct. 2).   Measure: 1–2

Repeat first two measures three times.   Measure: 3–8

Bend forward on steps to the front and lean backward on steps to the back.

FIGURE 1. Circle moves to the right with sixteen steps. All step to the side on the right foot, extending the left leg to the side (ct. 1), place left foot behind the right and bend both knees slightly (ct. 2).   Measure: 9

Repeat seven times.   Measure: 10–16

CHORUS   Measure: 1–8

FIGURE 2. Step hop—all turn to right and step on the right foot with the left leg (bent at knee) extended backward, hop on the right foot (ct. 1). Same on the left foot (ct. 2).   Measure: 9–10

Repeat measures 9 and 10 for remainder of music.   Measure: 11–16

CHORUS   Measure: 1–8

FIGURE 3. Feet are held close together. All move toes to the right (ct. 1), all move both heel to the right (ct. 2). Repeat.   Measure: 9–16

CHORUS   Measure: 1–8

FIGURE 4. All kick alternately feet
forward 16 times, beginning right.   Measure: 9–16

CHORUS   Measure: 1–8

FIGURE 5. All kick alternately feet
backward 16 times. Lean forward.   Measure: 9–16

CHORUS   Measure: 1–8

FIGURE 6. All turn to the right and
move forward in the circle with 16 shuffle steps done in a semi-crouch position.
The shuffle is a step right, close left,
step right, etc. End dance by raising
joined hands high in the air.   Measure: 9–16

Broom Dance

Victor Record—20448 (German)   *Grades 2, 3*

Formation. Couples form double circle facing counterclockwise. One
child is left in the center of the circle with a broom.

Action.

PART 1. Couples march around the
room to the music and the child in the
center gives the broom to someone in
the circle and takes his place. This one
gives the broom to another quickly and
takes his place and so on for 8 meas-
ures.   Measure: 1–8

PART 2. The child who has the broom
at the end of the eighth measure must
dance with the broom in the center of
the circle while the couples skip around
singing Tra, la, la through 8 measures
and the dance begins again with the
center dancer passing the broom on.   Measure: 9–16

The verse and music may be found in
the listed reference.

The Crested Hen

(Danish)[1]   *Grades 2, 3*

Formation. Sets of three, one boy with a girl on either side.

STEP. The hop-step is done through
the entire dance. Step on left foot on
count one, hop on left foot, swing right

[1] N. P. Neilson and Winifred Van Hagen, *Physical Education for
Elementary Schools*, A. S. Barnes and Company, New York, 1929.

foot in front of it on count two, keeping
the knee bent. Reverse and step-hop on
right foot, swing left foot to front.

FIGURE 1. All sets of threes join
hands to form circles. Moving to left
(clockwise) stamp left foot and do eight
step-hops. Dancers lean back as they
circle.   Measure: 1–8

Repeat measures 1 to 8, moving counterclockwise with eight step-hops.   Measure: 1–8

FIGURE 2. Girls release hands and
place free hands on hips. Boy never releases the hands. Girl at the left of boy
dances (step-hops) in front of him and
under the arch made by raised hands of
the boy and the girl on the right.   Measure: 9–12

Repeat same action with girl on the
right, passing through arch.   Measure: 13–16

Patito, Patito

Music and dance arranged by Berta Almaguer, Recreation Department, San Antonio, Texas. (Mexican Nursery Rhyme)   *Grades 1, 2*

> Patito, patito, color de café,
> (Little duck, little duck, color of brown)
>
> Si tu no me quieres,
> (If you do not love me)
>
> Y luego de que?
> (So what?)
>
> Ya no me presumes,
> (Don't be presuming)
>
> Que alcavo yo sé,
> (For in the end I know)
>
> Que tu es un patito,
> (You are a little duck)
>
> Color de café.
> (Color of brown)

PATITO, PATITO

Formation. OX OX OX OX—Partners in single line with boy and girl alternating, facing off stage, boys behind girls.

STEP 1A. *Push Step*—Weight is taken mainly on the left foot as it is pushed forward in flat, tiny steps. Step left (and) step right forward (count 1)	Measure: 1
Step left (and) step right backward (count 2)	Measure: 2
Repeat measures 1 and 2 through part A.	Measure: 3–16
STEP 1B. Point right heel toward partner. Point left heel toward neighbor.	Measure: 17–18 Measure: 19–20
Paddle step turn clockwise toward partner—weight on left foot and push with right foot.	Measure: 21–24
Repeat measures 17–24	Measure: 25–32
STEP 2A. Hook right elbows and push step turning right.	Measure: 1–8
Hook left elbows and push step turning left.	Measure: 9–16
STEP 2B. Partners are back to back with hands on hips. Point right heel diagonally forward and look over right shoulder at partner. Point left heel forward and look over left shoulder.	Measure: 17–18 Measure: 19–20
Change places by turning back to back with paddle step.	Measure: 21–24
Repeat measures 17–24 ending side by side.	Measure: 25–32
STEP 3A. Change places with partner using Step 1. Boy passes back of girl.	Measure: 1–8

Repeat measures 1–4 changing back to
original place.   Measure: 9–16

STEP 3B. All turn back to audience,
point right heel forward and look over
right shoulder.   Measure: 17–18
Point left heel diagonally forward
and look over left shoulder.   Measure: 19–20
Turn in place with paddle step. Re-   Measure: 21–24
peat measures 1–8.   Measure: 25–32

STEP 4A. Dancers change places. Half
the line turning to the right, half to the
left. Use push step as in Step 1.   Measure: 1–16

STEP 4B. Face audience and do cross
waltz step forward—swing right leg
over left, step right step left, step right.   Measure: 17–18
Repeat—swinging left leg over. Turn   Measure: 19–20
clockwise with paddle step. Repeat   Measure: 21–24
measures 17–24.   Measure: 25–32

STEP 5A. Dancers leave floor with
push step as in Step 1.   Measure: 1–16

Raatikko

Folk Dancer Record—Scandinavian: 1123 (Finnish Polka—Old
Maid's Dance)   *Grades 5, 6*

Formation. Couple, social dance position.

STEP 1. Eight polka steps, turning
clockwise.

STEP 2. Four draw steps. Boy has girl
by one arm pulling and girl moves re-
luctantly toward rock.

STEP 3. Eight slide steps away from
rock.

STEP 4. Repeat steps 2 and 3.
Repeat all.

Background. On the coast of Finland, one finds a large rock close to
the beach. The story goes that, if a boy succeeds in pulling a girl behind the rock, she will be an old maid.

Gie Gordon's

Beltona Record—BL-2455 (Scotch—The Gay Gordons)
Grades 5, 6

Formation. Couples in varsouvienne position.

Action.

STEP 1. Both start on left foot. Take four walking steps forward. Reverse and take four walking steps backward, but continue in the same line of direction. Repeat.

STEP 2. Boy holds girl's right hand high with his right hand and polkas forward as girl does four polkas (clockwise) turning under boy's arm.

STEP 3. In social dance position, do four polka steps turning clockwise.

Repeat entire dance.

Finger Polka

Standard Record—2001A (Lithuanian)   *Grades 3, 4, 5, 6*

Formation. Couples form double circle, facing counterclockwise, boys on inside of circle.

Action.

STEP 1. Eight polka steps in open position (hold inside hands, starting hop on outside foot, etc., back to back and face to face).

STEP 2. Eight polka steps in closed position turning clockwise.

STEP 3. Drop hands and face partner. Stamp three times, clap own hands three times. Repeat. Shake right finger at partner, make turn on own left, slapping right hand against partner's right hand as turn is taken. Stamp three times.

Repeat entire dance.

Road to the Isles[1]

Record—Imperial 1005A (Scotch)   *Grades 5, 6*

Formation. Couples in varsouvienne position.

STEP 1. Point left toe forward and hold. Grapevine step moving to right. Step left foot back of right foot, step right to side, step left foot in front of right foot and hold.

Measure: 1

Measure: 2–3

Point right toe forward and hold, and   Measure: 4

[1] Reference 16.

grapevine to left stepping right, left,
right and hold.   Measure: 5–6
  Point left toe forward and hold.   Measure: 7
  Point left toe backwards in deep dip
and hold.   Measure: 8

STEP 2. Schottische forward diagonally to left, beginning on left foot—
left, right, left, hop.   Measure: 9–10
  Schottische forward diagonally to
right, beginning on right foot—right,
left, right, hop. On hop, in measure 12,
half turn to right facing in opposite di-
rection, keeping hands joined.   Measure: 11–12
  Schottische, beginning on left foot.
On hop, take half turn to left facing
original direction.   Measure: 13–14
  In place, step right, left, right, hold.   Measure: 15–16

Bleking

  Record—Victor 20989 (Swedish)   *Grades 2, 3, 4*

Formation. Partners face with both hands joined.

STEP 1. Bleking (Blē-king): Jump
lightly to left foot placing right heel to
floor—count 1.
  See-saw arms by extending right arm
forward with elbow straight and left
arm backward with elbow bent. Reverse
arms and jump lightly on right foot,
placing left heel to floor—count 2   Measure: 1
  Repeat Bleking step three times in
quick time—count 1 and 2.   Measure: 2
  Repeat measures 1–2 three times.   Measure: 3–8

STEP 2. Extend arms sideward and
turn in clockwise directions with sixteen step-hops, alternately raising and
lowering arms and kicking free leg to
the side of the hops.   Measure: 9–16
  Repeat entire dance.

Social Dancing

  Children who have advanced progressively through fundamental rhythms, singing games, creative, folk, and square dancing
find themselves ready in the sixth grade for social dancing. Since
this is the type of dancing the majority will be doing as they grow
older it is well to at least expose them to the simple fundamentals

before they enter Junior High School. Basic steps learned in group and couple dances pave the way to this more restrained type of movement; the desire to emulate adult patterns serves as a neat motivating force. The children will get some practice at parties in their own homes but it is suggested that at school affairs the social dancing be interspersed with folk dances as mixers, couple and group dances. In this way the future Fred Astaires, Gene Kelleys, and Arthur Murrays get an opportunity to "let off steam" and are less likely to become tense in this new field of experience.

Basic fundamentals as to body position, leading, following, turning, the fox trot and the waltz adequately introduce sixth graders to social dancing. Teachers who desire additional information will find it worthwhile to read the listed references.[1]

TEACHING SUGGESTIONS

Body Position

WRONG   WRONG

RIGHT

The boy's arm is around the girl's waist, fingers together and palm toward the body. His left arm is extended to the side at a comfortable height and he holds the girl's right hand lightly with his palm down. The girl rests her hand lightly on the boy's right shoulder or arm, depending upon his height. Both face with toes pointed directly forward. Stand a comfortable distance apart to allow freedom of movement and hold the body erect with heads up.

Leading

The boy leads by pressure with the right hand, arm and the upper part of the body. His lead should be firm and indicate positively to his partner what he intends to do. The girl must anticipate the next step or change of direction by being alert and following the indicated directions. The boy generally steps off on

[1] Book References 1, 14 and 19.

his left foot and the girl follows on her right. A good leader mixes his steps, going forward, backward and sideward so that the girl does not have to go backwards all the time.

Basic Steps

Dance Walk. Walk forward and backward in time with the music, keeping the feet in contact with the floor and close together, swinging the legs from the hip with knees relaxed. Stress the importance of moving smoothly as if the bodies were "lighter than air." (Note: Young boys are prone to duck their heads and in an earnest manner plow the west forty with a flat-footed "clomp" or to bob up and down energetically with bent knees forcing their partners to do likewise.)

Two-Step

Step forward left and take weight.	Ct. 1
Bring right foot to left and take weight right.	Ct. 2
Step left and take weight.	**Ct. 3**
Pause with the weight still on the left and move right foot forward.	Ct. 4
Finish the step forward and take weight on right.	Ct. 1
Bring left foot to right and take weight.	Ct. 2
Step right and take weight.	Ct. 3
Pause with weight on right and move left foot slowly forward.	Ct. 4
Continue alternating left and right. This step is executed in the same manner forward, backward and sideward.	Ct. 4
Direction: Step, together, step, and, step, together, step, and.	

Fox Trot

The Fox Trot is danced to 4/4 time and is the step most used in social dancing. Lack of body control at this level eliminates the dip, rock and hesitation for the average pupil. It is well to concentrate on combinations of the dance walk, two-step and turns. The turn presents quite a problem to the beginning leader who generally progresses in a wide arc or finds himself facing a wall and awkwardly backs away. Turns to the right seem to come more easily to both boys and girls and since the pivot turn is generally done to the right it may be taught first.

Pivot Turn. Boy steps backward on the left foot, pivots to R as he steps forward on the right foot.	Ct. 1
	Ct. 2

Two-step turn.

Step left sideward	Ct. 1
Bring right foot to left	Ct. 2
Step left forward, take quarter turn to left	Cts. 3–4
Step right sideward	Ct. 1
Bring left foot to right	Ct. 2
Step right backward, take quarter turn to left	Cts. 3–4
Repeat above to make complete turn.	

The leader will develop step patterns that form, in time, his own individual style but in the beginning, it is helpful to teach a few set routines that can be learned by the entire group.

Simple Patterns

Dance Walk

1. Forward fast—Step L (ct. 1), R (ct. 2), L (ct. 3), R (ct. 4)
   Forward slow—Step L (cts. 1–2), R (cts. 3–4)

2. Forward step L (ct. 1), R (ct. 2), L (ct. 3), Pivot R (ct. 4)

3. Backward step L (ct. 1), R (ct. 2), L (ct. 3), Pivot R (ct. 4)

4. Combinations—Step forward L (ct. 1), R (ct. 2), L (ct. 3), pivot R (ct. 4); step backward L (ct. 1), R (ct. 2), L (ct. 3), pivot R (ct. 4); step forward L, R, L, pivot R, step backward L (cts. 1–2), R (cts. 3–4). Repeat all.

Two-Step

1. Dance as described on page 200, forward, backward and sideward.

2. Dance with two-step turn.

3. Combine with dance walk as: Step forward L (ct. 1), close R to L (ct. 2), step forward L (cts. 3–4), step forward R (cts. 1–2), step forward L (cts. 3–4).

Waltz

The popularity of the waltz has waxed and waned but still remains today in America as an integral part of our dance. The slow tempo waltz is preferred in the United States to the faster Viennese waltz or the more heavily accented waltz of the Germans. Waltz music is played in 3/4 time and there are three beats to each measure. The two-step waltz will not be included here.

True Waltz

Move forward—Step L	Ct. 1
Step R	Ct. 2
Bring L to R, weight on L	Ct. 3
Step R	Ct. 1
Step L	Ct. 2
Bring R to L, weight on R	Ct. 3

Box Waltz

Step L forward	Ct. 1
Step R sideward	Ct. 2
Bring L to R, weight on R	Ct. 3

This step is a good lead-up to teaching turns. On the first beat the dancer steps diagonally forward on the left foot and takes a quarter turn to the left and repeats the box step as described above. If the turn is made each time the left foot goes forward, a complete turn is accomplished in four times.

Teaching Suggestions for the Waltz. Have the children line up across the end of the gymnasium. Take a position in front of the class so that each child can see your feet, turn your back on the group and demonstrate the forward waltz. Lead the class slowly down the floor repeating at first: Step L, step R, close L, step R, step L, close R and later: step, step, close, step, step, close. Practice until the pattern is set, stressing the weight transfer on the third count which permits the step left, then right. Now play a slow waltz and repeat the above directions to music. Teach the backward and box waltz in the same manner. When the children have mastered these steps *alone* let them practice the same routine with partners.

Dancing Terminology

Allemande Left. Boy and corner face, join left hands, walk around each other and back to place.

Allemande Right. Partners join right hands, walk around each other and back to place.

Balance. Step forward left, step forward right beside left, rise slightly on toes. Step backward on right, step back left beside right and rise slightly on toes. In square dance, take two steps backward and bow to partner.

Break. Release hands, used in square dances.

Corner. The girl on the boy's left. The boy on the girl's right.

Dos-a-dos. Boy and girl circle each other passing right shoulder to right shoulder and back to back returning to original position.

Do-si-do. Boy faces partner, both join left hands and walk around (counterclockwise) until each is facing their corner, join right hands with their corner and walk around (clockwise) to original positions.

Draw Step. Step to side on left foot and draw right foot to left, shifting weight to the right foot.

Elbow Swing. Hook right or left elbows and swing around once.

Foot Couples. Last couples in a longways set.

Fox Trot. See page 200.

Gallop. See page 161.

Grand Right and Left. Partners face, touch right hands and pass on by to the next touching left hands and on around the circle until partners meet again. The boys move counterclockwise, the girls clockwise. In square dancing, an Allemande left usually precedes the Grand Right and Left and partners Promenade home when they meet.

Grapevine. Step left to side, step right behind left, step left to side, step right in front of left.

Head Couples. First and third couples in a set.

Home Position. Original position of each dancer in the set.

Marching. Walking in a military or dignified manner with even steps.

Paddle Step. Weight is on the left foot. Pivot on left, turning clockwise, stepping around with the right.

Polka. Weight is on the left foot. Hop on left, step on right, bring left to right and transfer weight to right foot. Hop on right, etc. (very often in folk dancing the hop is left off). Hop, step, close, step.

Positions

Closed Position. (Ballroom or social dance position.) Partners face, boy has his right arm around girl's waist; girl has left hand on boy's right shoulder. Boy holds girl's left hand in his right hand at about shoulder level, elbow slightly bent.

Open Position. Partners are side by side facing the same direction. Boy has his right arm around girl's waist and the girl has her left hand on the boy's right shoulder. The free hands may, as the dance demands, hang loosely or be placed on the hips.

Skater's Position. See Promenade.

Varsouvienne Position. Partners face in same direction, girl slightly to front of boy. Boy holds girl's left hand in his left hand at shoulder level and extends his right arm across the girl's shoulders and holds her right hand in his right hand.

Schottische. Step left, step right, step left, hop left—run, run, run, hop, or one, two, three, hop.

Shuffle. A flowing one step with feet in contact with the floor. This is the principal step in square dancing and when done properly gives the impression that the dancer is moving without any apparent effort.

Side Couples. Couples two and four in a set.

Slide. See pages 160–161.

Step-hop. Step on left, hop on left, step on right, hop on right.

Step-swing. Step on left, swinging right leg forward in front of left. Step right and swing left leg over.

Two-step. Step forward left, bring right to left, step forward left. Step forward right, bring left to right, step forward right. Teach: Step, close, step.

Waltz. Step forward left, on count one, step forward right, on count two, close left to right on count three. Step right, step left, close right to left.

Book References

1. Ballwebber, Edith, *Group Instruction in Social Dance*, New York, A. S. Barnes, 1938.

2. Barnett, Cecille Jean, *Games, Rhythms, Dances,* 22 W. Monroe St., Chicago, Illinois, Arrow Business Service, 1950.

3. Beliajus, Finadar V., *Dance and Be Merry,* Vol I, Chicago, Illinois, Clayton F. Sunny Company, 1940.

4. Bryans, Helen L. and Madsen, John, *Scandinavian Dances,* Vol. I and II, Toronto, Canada, Clarke Irwin and Company Limited, 1942.

5. Burchenal, Elizabeth, *American Country Dances,* 1918; *Folk Dances and Singing Games,* New York, Sheet music: G. C. Schrimer Music Co., 1932.

6. California Folk Dance Federation, *Folk Dances from Far and Near,* Berkeley, California, The California Book Company Ltd., Four Volumes, 1945, 46, 47, 48.

7. Colby, Gertrude R., *Natural Rhythms and Dances,* New York, A. S. Barnes, 1930.

8. Crampton, C. Ward, *The Folk Dance Book,* New York, A. S. Barnes, 1937.

9. Duggan, Anne, Schlottman, Jeanette and Rutledge, Abbie, *Folk Dance Library,* Four Volumes, New York, A. S. Barnes, 1948.

10. Durlacher, Ed, *Honor Your Partner,* New York, Berin-Adair Company, 1949.

11. Eisenberg, Helen and Larry, *And Promenade All,* 2403 Branch Street, Nashville, Tennessee, 1947.

12. Ford, Mr. and Mrs. Henry, *Good Morning,* Dearborn, Michigan, Dearborn Publishing Co., 1943.

13. Greggerson, H. F. Jr., *Herb's Blue Bonnet Calls,* El Paso, Texas, 1946.

14. Harris, Jane A., and Pittman, Anne and Swenson, Marlys, *Dance A While,* Minneapolis, Minnesota, Burgess Publishing Company, 1950.

15. H'Doubler, Margaret N., *Dance: A Creative Art Experience,* New York, Appleton-Century-Crofts Inc., 1940. *Rhythmic Form and Analysis,* Madison, Wisconsin, J. M. Rider Publisher, 1950.

16. Herman, Michael, *Folk Dances For All,* New York, Barnes and Noble Inc., 1947. Publication, *Folk Dancer,* Community Folk Dance Center, P. O. Box 201, Flushing, Long Island, N. Y., Back copies available.

17. Hinman, Mary Wood, *Gymnastics and Folk Dancing,* New York, A. S. Barnes, 1930.

18. Hood, Marguerite V. and Schultz, E. J., *Learning Music Through Rhythm,* New York, Ginn and Company, 1949.

19. Hostetler, Lawrence, *Walk Your Way to Better Dancing,* New York, A. S. Barnes, 1942.

20. Hughes, Dorothy T., *Rhythmic Games and Dances,* New York, American Book Co., 1942.

21. Hunt, B. A. and Wilson, H. R., *Sing and Dance*, Chicago, Hall and McCreary Co., 1945.

22. Lampkin, Lucy, *The Dance in Art*, New York, J. Fischer and Brothers, 1935.

23. LaSalle, Dorothy, *Rhythms and Dances for Elementary Schools*, New York, A. S. Barnes, 1951.

24. Mains, Dorothy Small, *Modern Dance Manual*, Dubuque, Iowa, Wm. C. Brown Co., 1950.

25. Radir, Ruth Anderson, *Modern Dance*, New York, A. S. Barnes, 1944.

26. Rath, Emil, *The Folk Dance in Education*, Minneapolis, Minnesota, Burgess Publishing Company, 1949.

27. Royal Academy of Dancing and Ling Physical Education Association, Seven books in the series: *Dances of Czechoslavakia, Sweden, Netherlands, Austria, Finland, Greece and Switzerland*, 41 E. 50th Street, New York, Chanticleer Press Inc., 1949.

28. Ryan, Grace L., *Dances of Our Pioneers*, New York, A. S. Barnes, 1939.

29. Shafer, Mary Severance, *Dramatic Dances for Small Children*, New York, A. S. Barnes, 1921.

30. Shambaugh, Mary Effie, *Folk Dances for Boys and Girls*, New York, A. S. Barnes, 1938.

31. Shaw, Lloyd, *Cowboy Dances*, 1943. *Round Dance Book*, 1948, Caldwell, Idaho, Caxton Printers Inc., 1942.

32. Shurr, Gertrude and Yocom, Rachael D., *Modern Dance Techniques and Teaching*, New York, A. S. Barnes, 1949.

33. Smith, Raymond, *Square Dance Hand Book and Collection of Square Dances and Mixers*, 1038 Cedar Hill, Dallas, Texas.

34. Warner, Lorraine, *A Kindergarten Book of Folk Songs*, Boston, G. C. Schrimer Music Company, 1922.

35. Whitlock, Virginia B., *Come and Caper*, New York, G. C. Schrimer Music Company, 1932.

Record References

A. *Childhood Rhythms*, Vols. I, II, VI, Ruth Evans, 326 Forest Park Avenue, Springfield, Massachusetts.

B. *Swiss Folk Dances*, Set J-9, Columbia Recording Company, Bridgeport, Connecticut.

C. Playtime Records—These records are nonbreakable, cost twenty-five cents and are found in most drug stores or record shops. Each contains a simple nursery rhyme or singing game.

D. Decca Records—*Ye Old Time Dance Nite, Cowboy Dances*—Called by Lloyd Shaw. Book of instructions included. Decca Album A-524.

E. Durlacher, Ed, *Honor Your Partner*, Square Dance Associates, 102 North Columbus Avenue, Freeport, New Jersey.

F. Folkraft Record Company, *Library of International Dances*, 7 Oliver Street, Newark, New Jersey.

G. Henlee Record Company, *Texas Square Dance Music* (without calls), 2404 Harris Boulevard, Austin, Texas.

H. Herman, Michael, *Folk Dancer Records*, Box 201, Flushing, Long Island, New York.

I. Imperial Records—*Square Dances* (without calls) Jimmy Clossin.
　　　　　　　　　Square Dances (with calls) Lee Bedford Jr.
　　　　　　　　　American Folk Dances, Russian Folk Dances, Baltic Folk Dances.

J. Methodist World of Fun Series, Methodist Publishing House, Nashville, Tennessee, *Singing Games, Folk Dances, Couple Dances,* etc.

K. Radio Corporation of America, RCA Victor Division, Camden, New Jersey. *RCA Victor Record Library for Elementary Schools* which includes: *Music of American Indians* with instruction and suggestions for sixteen dances; *Rhythmic Activities*, 5 volumes for primary and upper grades; *Singing Games.*

L. *Scandinavian Folk Dance Album*, Michael Herman, Box 201, Flushing, Long Island, New York.

M. *Sonart Folk Dance Album M-8*, Sonart Record Corporation, 251 W. 42nd Street, New York. Order from Michael Herman.

N. *Square Dance Albums*—Capitol, Disc, Keystone and others.

O. Ultra Records—*Jewish Folk Dances*, Vol. I, II, New York City, (Also available from Michael Herman, Box 201, Flushing, Long Island, New York.)

Chapter 11

Graded Stunts, Self-testing Activities, and Tumbling

A program which excludes self-testing activities, stunts, and tumbling has missed a golden opportunity in aiding the development of the whole child. The abundant use of large muscles in these activities plus the development of fine coordination, flexibility, balance, and timing round out the muscle building process in a most satisfactory manner. The resultant body control gives a sureness of movement and confidence to the child which cannot be gained through any other aspect of the total physical education program.

Physical and social end results more than justify the inclusion of this activity. The pleasure derived from viewing one's progress gives stature to all, but particularly to the boy or girl who does not take naturally to sports, i.e., the frail or obese child. Individual disciplined control necessary for good performance in class carries over into play and social life.

Elementary school children do not have to be sold on this part of the program if it is scaled to their age and skill level. The majority will look forward with enthusiasm to periods spent learning stunts and tumbling. The cause for the small percentage of holdbacks can be traced generally to family objections, where the word tumbling is used in a general way to include all self-testing activities. Parents have visions of their children hurtling through space with resulting neck and back injuries. This fear is inevitably transferred to the child. Public demonstrations of grade level accomplishments coupled with thorough explanations of each activity will give parents and children alike new appreciation of the program. People support things in which they believe!

Uniforms

Boys and girls enjoy working together in these activities through the fourth grade; consciousness of body is absent, in most groups, through the second grade. However, there are parents who object to mixed classes in this activity. Usually this problem can be eliminated by having the girls wear slacks, jeans, or shorts in class.

Equipment

The size of the budget is always a deciding factor in the purchase of equipment. However, many stunts require only limited space, and little equipment, and can be done inside or outside the school. Wands are inexpensive but a sanded mop or broom handle serves the same purpose. Mats are comparatively expensive equipment but, with proper care, will last for years. Ingenious instructors have used cotton mattresses with good results. These may be purchased at Army-Navy surplus stores or from local mattress factories. The cotton filling will lump in time but washable covers hold the mat firm. Athletic firms make mats of all sizes. A 5' x 7' mat is small enough to be handled by four children and heavy enough to hug the floor. Foam rubber is being used as a filling but hair felt is more commonly used in mats because it offers resistance plus the necessary resiliency.

The heavy canvas mat cover is the least expensive and the most durable. Its drawback is that it soils easily. Some mats are backed with plastic on the floor side. There are all types of detachable covers available in washable cotton, plastic, and rubberized materials. They not only aid in cleanliness but add years to the life of the mat.

If storage is available, it is best to store mats flat. Where mats must be hung from the walls, safety brackets are best, as they push flush against the wall preventing sagging, thus eliminating a safety hazard. *Never* allow a mat to be pulled or dragged across the floor and *never* allow hard-soled shoes on a mat. Canvas-covered mats should be beaten often and cleaned with a vacuum cleaner. Cotton covers should be laundered frequently and plastic covered mats should be washed weekly with a mild soap and rinsed with a cloth wrung out of clear water.

Safety

Safety instruction should be given by the instructor but children become more aware and cooperative when they write and post their own version of precautionary safety measures. A fourth grade group worked out the following list of suggested directions.[1]

FOUR ON A MAT—Do not move mats that are too heavy.

PLACE MATS clear of walls, bars and benches.

LEADERS CHECK mats before and during class to see that they do not separate.

DO NOT walk, jump or play on mats except in class periods when a teacher is present.

LINES should stand a good 12 inches from the mat and ALWAYS move in the same direction.

GET OFF the mat as soon as the stunt is completed.

DO YOUR clothes keep you from moving or get in your way?

ARE YOUR pockets EMPTY?

DO YOU have on sox or tennis shoes?

GIRLS, have you taken off all bobby pins, hair ornaments and jewelry?

Alert teacher spotting is necessary through the elementary grades to anticipate and forestall accidents. Men are physiologically better equipped as spotters but women can work safely with most children on this level if they will observe a few simple suggestions. A spotter should assume a position that permits easy, quick assistance and rapid shifts to avoid hampering the activity and to escape flying arms and legs. The stronger arm (generally the right) should receive the weight of the child and slightly flexed knees allow quick movements in any direction. Kneel on the knee away from the performer. It is not wise to give too much assistance as it is frustrating and robs the child of the feeling of accomplishment. In less difficult stunts the presence of the spotter is all that is necessary to instill confidence. Two pupils standing on either side of each mat can be trained as assistant spotters.

Class Organization and Presentation

Each stunt should be analyzed and all possible risks eliminated by:

1. Explanation and demonstration from start to finish.

[1] Margaret B. Henderson School, Dallas, Texas, 1950–1951.

2. Teacher spotting.

3. Teaching progressive skills to permit easy transition from known to unknown.

4. Being sure in couple stunts that the size of the two pupils are approximately the same.

5. Having classes prepare posters with rules and regulations for procedures with safety and the best learning conditions in mind.

6. Taking into consideration physical limitations. *Watch* for fatigue and do not allow children who exhibit such to continue the activity. Do not allow children recuperating from recent illnesses. to participate. Allow only minimum participation and watch carefully children with chronic sinusitis, bronchitis, asthma, epilepsy, and heart conditions.

Activities which follow have been graded as near as possible to pupil ability level but the teacher must be guided by the skill of the group, for some stunts listed for the first grade would be enjoyed by sixth graders and are not repeated in the list of suggested stunts. It is important that interest be held by introducing enough material each period to challenge the more proficient and by organizing the class in squads to allow frequent individual turns at trying. In large groups of the lower elementary level simple stunts may be done in double lines on either side of the mats. Only one child should be allowed to a mat when more advanced stunts are taught for the first time.

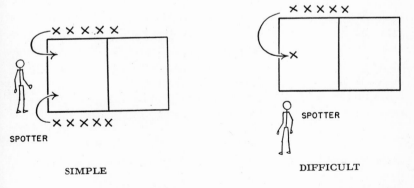

SIMPLE   DIFFICULT

After a number of variety of stunts have been taught, each child may be allowed to call the stunt to be executed.

Try to develop a group feeling of pride in good execution and discourage laughter or critical remarks directed toward poor performers. Place praise and attention on the ones who *try* as well as on those who show excellent form.

It is wise to keep the activity on the ability level of the group as adventurous youngsters will try to do stunts they have observed that are too difficult for their background of experience.

Suggested Lesson Plan

Class: third grade, third month of instruction
Period: 30 minutes   Number: 20 to 40

ENTIRE CLASS (Spaced about floor to permit free movement)

Sit-Ups
Turk Stand

INDIVIDUAL STUNTS

Monkey Run
Crab Walk
Seal Crawl
Rabbit Hop
Measuring Worm

COUPLE STUNTS

Wheelbarrow
Rocker

TUMBLING

Cartwheel
Forward Roll (Standing Position)
Backward Roll

Graded Stunts

Grade 1

Elephant Walk
Monkey Run
Rabbit Hop
Frog Hop
Duck Walk

Tight Rope Walking
Chicken Walk
Seal Crawl
Lame Puppy Walk
Human Ball

Weather Vane
Log Roll
Sit-Ups
Somersault
Bear Walk

Grade 2

Turk Stand
Egg Roll
Crab Walk
Jumping Jack
Inch Worm

Spanker
Backward Kick
Bent Knee Hop
Knee Lift
Kangaroo Hop

Step Over the Wand
Jump and Slap Heels
Forward Roll
Backward Roll
Cartwheel

Grade 3

Free Standing
Full Squat
Wicket Walk
Balance Stand

Mule Kick
Bear Dance
Dip
Frog Dance

Egg Sit
Thread the Needle
Knee or Stump Walk

Couple Stunts

	Grade		Grade		Grade
Bouncing Ball	1	Chinese Get Up	4–6	Cock Fight	2–6
Wring the		Rocker	4–6	Rooster Fight	1–6
Dishrag	1–3	Churn the Butter	3–6	Hand Wrestle	2
Row Boat	1	Wheelbarrow	1	Pull Across	3–5
Rooster Fight	2–6				

Graded Self-Testing Activities
INDIVIDUAL STUNTS

Grade 4

Stiff Leg Bend	Under the Bridge	Upswing
Stiff Knee Pick Up	Long Stretch	Upspring
Folded Leg Walk	Jump and Reach	Human Rocker
Bells or Clicks	Knee Dip	Jump Foot
Knuckle Down	Cut the Wand	Coffee Grinder
Knee Mark	Backward Jump	
Stoop and Throw	Palm Spring	

Grades 5-6

Grasp the Toe	Forearm Head Stand	Hand Stand
Fish Hawk Dive	Jump Over the Stick	Double Forward Roll
Tripod	Corkscrew	Through the Stick
Head Stand	Crane Dive	Dive Over One

Grade 6

Head Spring	Shoulder Mount	Shoulder Stand
Hand Spring	Rising Sun	

COUPLE AND GROUP STUNTS

Grades 4, 5, 6

Leap Frog	Bull Dog Pull	Toe Wrestle
Skin the Snake	Hog Tying	Elephant Walk
Wand and Toe	Walking Chair	Eskimo Roll
Wrestle	Merry-Go-Round	Back to Back Roll
Indian Wrestle	Pull Across	

Description of Stunts[1]

BACKWARD JUMP—4

Stand on mat with toes at the edge, heels toward center. Jump backwards as far as possible swinging arms forcibly. Land lightly.

[1] The grade for which stunt is best suited is shown at the right.

BACKWARD KICK—2

Jump in place on both feet four times. On fourth jump, kick both heels backward. Land lightly on toes.

BALANCE STAND—3

Stand on either foot, bend body forward to right angle with body, supporting free leg slightly bent from knee, head up, arms to side horizontal.

BEAR DANCE—3

Squat on one heel, other foot extended forward. Draw extended foot under body and shoot other foot out to front. Arms are folded across chest.

BEAR WALK—1

Place hands on floor with arms and knees straight. Body sways from side to side as a lumbering bear would walk.

BELLS—4

Hop on left foot, extend right leg to side and bring left heel to click with right heel.

BENT KNEE HOP—2

Child squats and takes a tuck position (arms and hands wrapped around knees). Walk on balls of feet.

COFFEE GRINDER—4-6

Child places one hand on floor, other in upright position. He straightens his legs and arms and walks around using the hand on the floor as a pivot.

CORKSCREW—6

Stand with feet 15 inches apart. Place piece of paper at toe of right foot. Swing left arm across body and go between legs to pick up paper.

CRAB WALK—3

Hands and feet on floor, face up, back straight. Walk backward, using right arm and right leg, then left arm and left leg.

CRANE DIVE OR NOSE DIVE—5

Toe a line. Place a piece of folded paper, at least 6 inches high, 6 inches in front of feet. Bend forward, raising one leg to rear and pick up paper.

CUT THE WAND—4

Hold a wand about 3 feet long vertically in front of the body, grasping one end and resting the other end on the floor in front of the feet. Release the wand and lift right leg over and catch before it falls.

DIP—2-6

Place crumpled paper 12 inches in front of body. Kneel with hands behind back, bend and pick up paper with teeth.

DOG RUN—1-3

Place hands on floor in front of body. Knees and arms lightly bent. Imitate a dog walking and running.

DUCK WALK—1-6

Squat position with knees wide, hands under arm pits. Swing feet wide to the side with each step and flap wings. First graders love to bring the arms to the back and make a tail by placing the hands together.

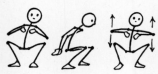

EGG ROLL—2-6

Cross legs and kneel. Wrap arms across chest. Roll using arms and knees to start.

EGG SIT—2-6

Sit on floor with knees bent close to chest. Grasp ankles, rock back and extend legs.

FISH HAWK DIVE—5

Kneel on one knee with the other leg entirely off the ground. Bend forward and pick up an object which is directly in front of the resting knee.

FOLDED LEG WALK—4-6

Sit on mat. Take left foot and place it as high as possible against the right thigh. Cross right leg over the left and place high on the left thigh. Fold arms or extend to side for balance. Rise to kneeling position and walk across mat on knees.

FREE STANDING—3

Lie on back on mat with arms folded across chest. Come to standing position without unfolding arms or using elbows.

FROG DANCE—3-6

Squat, keep back straight, and fold arms across chest. Hop on left foot and extend right leg to side. Hop again on left foot and draw the right leg under body and extend left leg to side.

FROG HOP—2-6

Squat position, arms between legs, hands on floor. Take short hops by placing hands ahead of feet and bring feet up to hands.

FULL SQUAT—3

Clasp wrist with right hand behind the body. Keep back straight and bend knees deeply and touch floor with fingers. Knees are spread wide.

GRASP THE TOE—5

Stand on one foot, grasp the other foot at the arch with two hands. Bend forward and at the same time lift the foot attempting to touch the toe to the forehead.

HUMAN BALL—1-6

Sit on mat with knees up and feet together. Reach arms under inside of legs and lock fingers over ankles. Roll over.

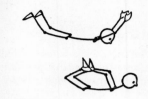

HUMAN ROCKER—4-6

Lie face down, bend knees, arch back and grasp right foot with right hand and left foot with left hand. Rock forward on chest and back on thighs. Rock in open position, holding arms and legs together tightly.

INCH WORM—2-6

Lean prone position. Keep hands stationary and walk feet to hands and walk back with hands to starting position keeping legs straight.

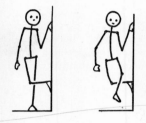

JUMP FOOT—4-6

Stand with one foot against wall, about 12 inches from floor and in front of inside leg. Spring from inside foot and jump over leg.

JUMPING JACK—2-6

Take a squat position, arms across chest. Spring to erect position weight on heels, back straight, arms horizontally to sides.

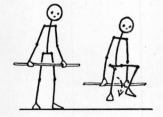

JUMP OVER THE STICK—5

Hold wand in horizontal position in front of body, palms down. Swing wand forward and back, jumping over wand.

JUMP AND REACH—4

Stand facing wall. Without lifting heels reach high with both hands and mark with chalk highest point reached. Stand with side to wall. Start from crouch position, jump and mark point reached with chalk held in nearest hand.

JUMP AND SLAP HEELS—2-6

Jump into air, bring heels up to side. Slap heels.

KANGAROO HOP—2-6

Squat with arms folded over chest. Spring into air and come back to squat position with knees flexed to prevent jar.

KNEE DIP—3-6

Stand on one foot and grasp the other foot behind the back with opposite hand. Bend down with arm outstretched for balance, touch knee lightly to floor and return to standing position.

KNEE LIFT—2

Stand with feet apart and hands extended forward at hip level. Jump up and try to touch the knees to the palms. Repeat, raising hands higher.

KNEE MARK—4-6

Kneel on both knees behind a line on the floor. Place one hand behind the back and reach forward with a piece of chalk and mark point reached.

KNEE WALK OR STUMP WALK—4-6

Kneel and grasp ankles or toes with hands. Walk on knees, leaning forward slightly to maintain balance.

KNUCKLE DOWN—4

Place toes on line. Without moving toes from line or using hands, kneel and rise.

LAME PUPPY WALK—1-4

On all fours, raise one foot in air and walk as a dog on three legs.

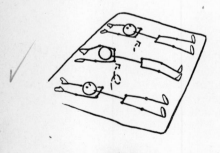

LOG ROLL—1-6

Lie on back with arms extended over head, legs straight, roll slowly over to end of mat. The body must move as "one piece" to keep direction straight.

LONG STRETCH—4-6

Stand with feet together, toeing line. Hold piece of chalk in one hand. Bend knees deeply and place free hand on floor. Walk forward on hands as far as possible without moving toes from line and mark on floor. Walk back to squat position and stand.

MONKEY RUN—1-6

On all fours scamper agilely, imitating monkey. Put down hands, then feet.

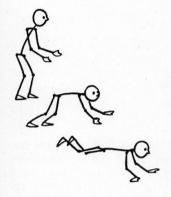

MULE KICK—3-6

Bend forward, place hands on floor, bend knees and kick into air as a mule.

PUSH-UPS—3-6

Get on hands and knees with arms below shoulders and shoulder distance apart. Extend legs backward until hips and knees are straight. Lower body, by bending elbows until nose touches floor. Raise body and repeat.

RABBIT JUMP—1-6

Squat with hands in front of feet. Push with feet and lift hands from floor. Catch weight on hands and bring feet to hands.

SEAL CRAWL—1-3

Prone leaning position with fingers turned to side as flappers. Keep legs together, weight on toes. Drag body along by walking on hands and let hips swing.

SINGLE SQUAT—5-6

Stand on mat, raise arms to side for balance. Raise one leg in front, knee straight. Squat, keeping weight well over supporting leg. Return to standing position without losing balance.

SIT-UPS—1-6

Lie flat on floor with arms extended above head, legs straight and together. Come to sitting position and keep legs tight to floor. Lie down slowly.

SOMERSAULT—1-2

Stand on floor at end of mat with feet astride. Place hands on mat between feet without bending knees. Touch back of head to mat. Body will roll forward and somersault will be completed.

SPANKER—2-6

Take position as for Crab Walk. Raise both feet in the air and slap seat with right hand, then left hand. Advanced: Hop and extend right leg and spank with left hand, hop and extend left leg and spank with right hand.

STEP OVER THE WAND—2-6

Grasp a wand at both ends with the backs of the hands toward the ceiling. Keep wand close to floor, bend forward, and step over the wand first with one foot, then with the other. Stand straight. Back over in same manner. Stand.

STIFF KNEE PICK-UP—1-6

Stand with feet together, bend forward, and pick up article placed 3 inches in front of toes, without bending knees.

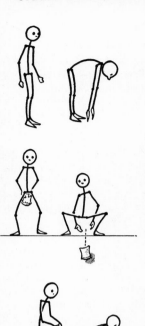

STIFF LEG BEND—1-6

Stand with heels together and arms at side. Bend forward and touch floor with fingertips.

STOOP AND THROW—4-6

Stand in stride position, toeing a line. Hold bean bag behind back with both hands. Bend knees deeply and throw bean bag between legs, using both hands. Keep a record of distance for competition.

THREAD THE NEEDLE—3-5

Clasp the hands in front of body, bend the trunk forward, and step through clasped hands with right foot, then left foot. Return with stepping backward with right, then left foot.

THROUGH THE STICK—4-6

Grasp a wand behind the back, palms forward. Bring wand over head to position in front of body without losing grasp. Swing right leg around right arm and between the hands from front, over stick. Crawl through head first and back over with left foot.

TIGHT ROPE WALKING—1-3

Walk a line drawn on the floor (10 feet long). Use arms to balance.

TURK STAND—1-6

Arms folded across chest. Sit cross-legged on floor. Stand without using hands or changing position of feet.

UNDER THE BRIDGE—4

Stand toeing a line with the feet about 12 inches apart. Have chalk in one hand. Squat and with the hand holding the chalk reach forward between the legs to mark the floor as far forward as possible.

UP-SPRING—4-6

Kneel, ankles extended, toes flat. Swing arms back, then forward vigorously, pushing with the feet at the same time. Bring body to erect position.

UP-SWING—3-6

Kneel with the weight on the balls of the feet. Swing arms back, then forward, coming to standing position.

WEATHER VANE—1-3

Stand with feet apart, hands on shoulders, elbows up. Turn from side to side.

WICKET WALK—3-4

Simple: With knees straight, bend forward touching floor with hands. Walk forward and backward with small steps, keeping legs and arms close together. Advanced: Grasp ankles and walk without bending knees.

Couple Stunts—Primary

BOUNCING BALL—1-2

One child is ball and other the bouncer. Try to achieve feel and rhythm of bouncing ball.

CHURN THE BUTTER—3-6

Back to back, elbows locked, No. 1 bends forward from the hips. No. 2 springs from floor, leans back and lifts feet from floor. Repeat action with No. 2 bending forward.

DOUBLE WALK—2

Couple face and grasp upper arms. No. 2 steps diagonally across insteps of No. 1 who walks forward. No. 2 shifts weight as No. 1 walks.

HAND WRESTLE—2-6

Two children face and join right hands and each raises one foot behind him. On signal each attempts to cause the other to touch either the free hand or foot to floor.

PULL ACROSS—5

Divide class into two equal groups. Draw line on floor and have teams stand on opposite sides of the line. On signal, each child grasps his opponent by the right hand and attempts to pull him across the line. Limit bout to two minutes.

ROCKER—3-6

Partners sit facing each other and extend legs so that each child sits on feet of other child. Grasp upper arms and rock. One leans backward and lifts other child up. Alternate.

ROW BOAT—2

Facing partner, sit cross-legged on mat. Grasp partner's hands. When one child leans back, he will pull the other child forward.

ROOSTER FIGHT—3-6

Couple face with arms folded across chest and weight on one foot. On signal each tries to throw the other off balance by pushing with his arms. First one to lose balance, by putting down a foot, loses.

WHEELBARROW—1-3

No. 1 grasps legs of No. 2 at knees and walks as guiding a wheelbarrow. No. 2 walks on hands and keeps back straight.

WRING THE DISHRAG—1-3

Partners face and join hands. Lower arms on one side and turn away from each other and under the raised arms. Stand back to back. Raise other pair of arms and turn under.

Couple and Group Stunts—Upper Elementary

BULLDOG PULL—5

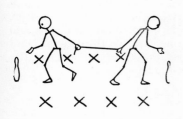

Number of participants: 10 to 20. Equipment: Rope 3 to 5 feet long. Two Indian Clubs. Place rope on floor between two clubs. Divide group into two teams. Line up facing and parallel to rope. Two opponents step forward and grasp ends of rope. On signal each pulls rope and tries to pick up Indian Club. One to two minute bouts. Keep score.

CHINESE GET-UP—4-6

Partners stand back to back with elbows locked. Sink to floor and rise by taking small walking steps and pressing against backs.

COCK FIGHT—5-6

Sit on floor facing partner. Draw up knees close to body and have toes touching partner's toes. Clasp hands in front of knees. Place wand under knees and over arms at elbows. Try with toes to lift partner's feet so he will roll over backward.

ELEPHANT WALK—4-6

Couple face. No. 1 stands in wide stride. No. 2 springs forward and upward around waist of No. 1. No. 2 bends backward and crawls between legs and grasps ankles. No. 1 bends forward and walks with swaying motion.

HOG TYING—5-6

Two face kneeling on hands and knees with a four foot rope each in hands. On signal each tries to tie the opponent's ankles together. Any fair wrestling hold is permissible.

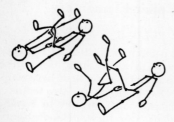

INDIAN LEG WRESTLE—5-6

Two children lie side-by-side, facing opposite directions. Place hips at opponent's waistline. Hook inside legs, hook inside arms. Raise inside legs to count 3 times. On the third count bend knees, hook them and try to force the opponent into a backward roll.

LEAPFROG—4-6

Base takes wide stance, bends forward from the hips, and braces hands on knees. Top runs forward and jumps both feet over base's back. Place hands on base's shoulders and push, extending legs to side. Land on both feet, knees and ankles relaxed.

MERRY-GO-ROUND—5-6

Group of 8 to 10. Form circle and take double wrist lock. 1, 3, 5, 7 sit on floor with knees straight and feet together in the center. On signal 2, 4, 6, 8 take a step outwards and 1, 3, 5, 7 raise hips until body is in inclined position with back straight. 2, 4, 6, 8 walk around circle and the center group are the spokes of a wheel.

SKIN THE SNAKE—6

Forward. All line up directly behind the other in stride position. All bend forward and reach right hand between knees to person behind and reach forward with the left hand and grasp right hand of person in front. Last person in line crawls through and assumes stride position. Next in line follows until all have crawled through.

Backward. Line up as before. Last one in line lies down flat and the rest of the line moves backward. As each person reaches the end he lies down. The last performer to lie down rises and walks forward, straddling the line, and pulls the next performer to feet. Continue until all return to original position.

TOE WRESTLE—5-6

Same as Cock Fight but instead of using a wand the arms are wrapped around knees.

WALKING CHAIR—4-6

Line up behind each other. Hold hips of person in front. All sit back so the legs touch the thighs of the one behind. Each supports own weight. On signal all move forward in step.

Tumbling Stunts Listed as to Difficulty and Grade Level

	Grade		Grade
Forward Roll Progressions	1–6	Handstand	4
Cartwheel	2–6	Dive Over One	4
Backward Roll Progressions	2–6	Hand Spring	5
Tripod	3	Head Spring	5
Headstand	4	Eskimo Roll	6
Forearm Headstand	4	Back-to-Back Roll	6

Description of Tumbling Activities

All of the following stunts require "Spotters."

BACK TO BACK ROLL

Review "Churn the Butter" as a lead-up stunt. Base and top stand back to back, lock elbows, base's on outside of top's. Base stands with one foot forward and one foot backward for better balance, bends knees, gets hips in small of top's back. On signal top springs from mat, brings knees to chest, throws head well back to lean over base. Top, at same time bends forward slightly, pulls up on arms to roll top over back and head.

BACKWARD ROLL PROGRESSIONS

Basic. Start in sitting position. Place hands at shoulders, palms up, thumbs toward neck. Roll back, pushing with the feet, tuck head forward and bring knees close to chest. As hips are vertical to shoulders, push with hands. Land on toes in squat position.

Stand to stand. Start in standing position. Sit, keeping feet as close to body as possible. Roll back, pushing forcibly with hands, and extend legs in a vigorous snap to finish in a standing position.

CARTWHEEL PROGRESSIONS

1. No hip extension. Stand with right side to mat. Bend sideways and place both hands in line on the mat. Push off with feet, first right, then left. Swing legs over arms and push with right hand, then left hand. Finish in crouched position.

2. Alternate, starting from right, then left.

3. Hip extension: Elbows and legs straight, head up, back slightly arched.

4. Click heel in air: As performer reaches vertical position, quickly click heels before lowering one leg.

5. Cartwheel on one hand: Free hand on hip, make push from mat more vigorous. Give this only to those with excellent arm and shoulder development.

DIVE OVER ONE

1. Place obstacle close to edge of mat. May be rolled mat or child in tuck position or kneeling on all fours. Take a short run and when one foot from obstacle, extend arms, duck head and forward roll to standing position.

2. Dive over person kneeling on hands and knees.

3. Dive through spread legs of child doing a head stand.

ESKIMO ROLL

Forward. Base lies on mat, legs raised,

knees flexed. Top stands behind base's shoulders, reaches forward and grasps base's ankles with fingers to outside, thumbs to inside. Base grasps top's ankles in same grip. Top does a forward roll between base's legs, and pulls top to feet. Continue to roll changing positions.

Backward. Same position as above. As top rolls backward base pushes forcibly against top's ankles and against mat with head and shoulders. Stay close together.

FOREARM HEADSTAND

Kneel and place forearms, palms down, on mat. Place forearm between hands. Walk up and kick up one leg, secure balance and raise other leg slowly to vertical position.

FORWARD ROLL PROGRESSIONS

1. Squat to Sit (Somersault): Squat with weight on toes and hands on mat just ahead of toes. Round back by tucking head between knees. Push with hands and feet and roll over to sitting position. Keep body in tight ball to prevent slapping back.

2. Stand to Stand: Execute as in No. 1. Bend forward and place hands on mat. Finish in standing position.

3. Run and take off from one foot.

4. Spring from both feet.

5. Continuous forward rolls.

6. Forward roll with arms folded across chest.

HANDSPRING PROGRESSIONS

1. Over back: Do handstand about 1 foot from base, arch back, drop legs to floor, pushing forcibly with hands.

2. Handspring with assistance of base.

3. Handspring over base's arms.

4. Handspring over two rolled mats.

HANDSTAND

Stand on hands, feet raised straight in air with head and hands making a triangle. Arch back slightly for balance. Walk on hands—Shift weight gently and keep over hands.

HEADSPRING PROGRESSIONS

Place two rolled mats in center of mats. Place head and hands on top. Spring from feet, push hard with head and hands, arch back and snap legs down toward mat. Land in squat position and rise to erect position. Head spring from one rolled mat. More spring and body snap required.

HEAD STAND

Start with tripod position. Gradually raise legs high in rear, keeping legs and ankles together.

TRIPOD

Form a triangle by placing hands on mat, fingers forward and bend elbows to form a shelf. Place right knee above right elbow and left knee above left elbow. Lower one leg at the time or go into a forward roll.

Pyramids

Pyramid building offers excellent training in body control and group adjustment but it also has a dual value in its salesmanship. The simplest of pyramids, if executed in a clean-cut and decisive manner, is showy. Pyramid building is the cherry that tops a sundae. The part below may be more filling and nutritious, and definitely it required more work, but the bright red has eye appeal. Physical educators should not overlook showmanship in selling their program to the public even though they are completely aware that there is no substitute for hard-earned skills, learned with slow, patient, and sometimes monotonous, repetition.

The basic requirements for simple pyramid building are:

1. Strength
2. Balance
3. Timing
4. Knowledge of fundamentals
5. Ability to work as a team

The last requirement explains why this activity is postponed, generally, until the sixth grade. Many fourth graders, who have progressed through a well-planned program, show excellence in performance in individual stunts but are not interested in working as a team. However, the teacher working with small and skilled groups would be justified in introducing this activity at a lower level.

Finished pyramids should meet the requirements of good design, namely, balance, proportion, and interest (varying levels). The structure may start from a line, circle, square, rectangle or triangle, but all units, whether they are composed of two, three or five performers, should give the whole a feeling of continuity. This should not be dependent upon physical contact. In the most commonly used pyramids one finds the high point in the center, but the sides can be higher if symmetry is maintained. In simple elementary pyramids the base looks and is more secure if the ends taper to the floor.

The teacher or a pupil may give the counts or signals vocally, with a whistle, a snapper, or by a sharp clap with the hands. All move to the edge of the mat in a formation arranged to enable first positions to be taken with a minimum of walking.

Count 1: Bases move to positions on mats
Count 2: Tops move to positions
Count 3: All tops mount
Count 4: Tops dismount
Count 5: All return to place

The pyramid is good if:

1. Performers have moved quickly with good posture and precision to positions.
2. Movements have been executed in unison to count.
3. Completed pyramid is maintained until steadiness is attained. (Rhythm of building is impaired if held too long.)

4. Dismounted in positive and orderly manner.

On the following pages are suggested stunts that may be used in typical pyramids. Once the feel has been attained, classes should be encouraged to create their own pyramids.

Stunts Suitable for Pyramid Building

Grade level indicated and listed according to difficulty.

	Grade		Grade
Shoulder Rest	3	Stand on Partner's Knee	5
Triangle	4	Sitting Balance	5
Stand on Partner	5	Angel Balance	5
Horizontal Stand	5	Mercury	5
Thigh Mount	5	Knee-shoulder Stand	6
Sitting Mount	6	Handstand Archway	6
Handstand Supported at Hips	6	Shoulder Stand on Base's Feet	6
Handstand on Partner's Knees	6	Standing Mount (if children had a continuous self-testing program)	6

Description of Stunts for Pyramid Building

ANGEL BALANCE

Base lies on floor with legs raised, knees slightly bent and places feet diagonally alongside of top's pelvic bones. Grasps hands. Top springs forward and base straightens legs. Base lowers arms, and top arches back, and raises arms as in a swan dive.

HANDSTAND ARCHWAY

No. 2 is base. On signal, Nos. 1 and 3 do handstand and base catches at ankles.

HANDSTAND SUPPORTED AT HIPS

Base lies down, places feet across lower abdomen of top who puts hands to floor. Base places hands on top's shoulders. Top springs and base extends legs and supports base's hips with feet.

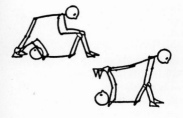

HORIZONTAL STAND

Base grasps top's ankles, with thumbs on inside of legs. As top springs and shifts weight to hands, base straightens arms.

KNEE-SHOULDER STAND

Handstand on knees of base with shoulder support.

MERCURY

Base clasps hands at back, palms up. Top places right foot on base's hands and springs from left foot. Secures balance and extends arms and free leg, brace supporting leg from knee down on top's back.

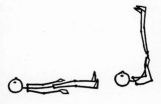

SHOULDER REST

Extend legs straight above head and support hips with hands. Weight on shoulders and elbows.

SHOULDER STAND

(See knee-shoulder stand) Grasp hands. Top does handstand with support of feet at shoulders.

SITTING BALANCE

Base lies on mat, legs in air and slightly bent. Top sits on base's feet, extends arms backward and grasps top's hands. Base straightens legs and releases hands. Top extends arms to side.

SITTING MOUNT

Base stands in stride position, top stands directly behind. Base kneels on one knee and places head between top's legs. Top places legs under base's arms and behind back. Top rises, straightening knees slowly. Stands erect.

STAND ON PARTNER

Stand on lower back with feet placed diagonally or one foot on lower back and one foot on shoulders.

STAND ON PARTNER'S KNEE

Base aids balance by support at knee.

STANDING MOUNT

Top stands directly behind base. Base stands in deep stride position with arms raised up and back. Top grasps base's hands and places right foot on base's thigh, then left foot on left shoulder, right foot on right shoulder. Gradually straightens knees, releases hands and stands tall, arms extended. Base supports top with hands at back of knees.

THIGH MOUNT

No. 2 mounts thigh of No. 1 with right foot and mounts thigh of No. 3. Stands erect and extends arms to side. Nos. 1 and 3 support at waist.

TRIANGLE

Base lifts one of top's legs to shoulder. Top springs and places other leg on base's other shoulder.

Poses for Pyramids
ENDS—SINGLE

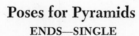

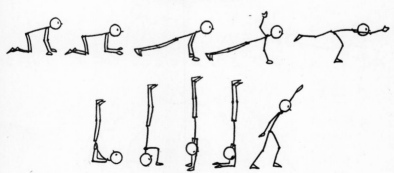

CENTERS—COUPLES AND GROUPS

SIDES

PYRAMIDS

Suggested Readings

Brady, Marna V., *Tumbling for Girls*, Philadelphia, Lea and Febiger, 1936.

Cotteral, Bonnie and Donnie, *The Teaching of Stunts and Tumbling*, New York, A. S. Barnes, 1943.

Horne, Virginia Lee, *Stunts and Tumbling for Girls*, New York, A. S. Barnes, 1943.

La Porte, William and Renner, A. G., *The Tumbler's Manual*, New York, Prentice-Hall, Inc., 1938.

McClow, L. L. and Anderson, D. N., *Gymnastics, Tumbling and Pyramids*, Philadelphia, W. B. Saunders Co., 1934.

Pearl, N. H. and Brown, N. C., *Health By Stunts*, New York, The Macmillan Company, 1926.

Rodgers, Martin, *A Handbook of Stunts*, New York, The Macmillan Company, 1928.

U. S. Navy, *Gymnastics and Tumbling*, Annapolis, Maryland, U. S. Naval Institute, 1944.

Chapter 12

Classroom and Quiet Games

General Techniques

Adverse weather conditions create few problems to the master teacher who has learned to utilize the classroom for active games and contests during stormy, unpleasant days. This emergency period can be one of bedlam for the novice and one of boredom for the pupils. Scheduled playground play need not be cancelled during cold, wet days. Instead, the classroom, corridors, lunchroom, or other space can be used. However, this makeshift period of classroom play should never be substituted for rugged outdoor activity or daily instruction in physical education. Rather it can be an addition to the total program. Although children must learn how to run, skip, jump, and how to use their bodies in other types of the fundamental big muscle movements in order to develop properly, they also need to learn how to play the less active, quiet games which will enable them to use skillfully the smaller muscles of the body. Like adults, children need to know how to have fun with things in their everyday environment—how to entertain themselves rather than be entertained.

Specific objectives to be realized through classroom activities might well include the desire to:

(1) Share with the child interesting "fun to do" activities for classroom and after school play.

(2) Add variety and completeness to the total physical education program.

(3) Develop a sense of fair play and the ability to play with others.

(4) Develop good leadership and fellowship techniques.

(5) Aid in developing good all-round social, physical, and emotional development.

In order to reach these worthy objectives the teacher needs to utilize all available indoor space to the greatest advantage in carrying out a carefully planned program. If she is fortunate enough to have movable chairs in the room, circle tag and it, or other such active games are desirable. If, however, desks and chairs are fastened to the floor, quiet games are more suitable. Knowledge of a wide range of activities and how to modify them to fit into one's own particular situation is imperative.

Rules of conduct should be set up by the children aided by the teacher. Activities chosen by the group should not infringe upon the rights of others in nearby classrooms.

Criteria for Choosing Activities

In selecting games for indoor play the teacher should strive for participation of the whole class. Good questions to keep in mind when selecting activities are:

(1) How many children can safely be active at one time?

(2) How quickly can new players replace ones who have been active?

(3) How much activity will each child actually engage in during the period?

(4) Do the chosen games reach our pupil-teacher objectives?

Safety Precautions

Learning to take chances wisely should be stressed throughout the period. Over protected children often are denied rich learning experiences. This does not imply they should be encouraged to cut their fingers in order to learn the knife is sharp but does connote that many dangers can best be avoided when one learns from a painful experience. Pupil-teacher safety rules are most adhered to, group discovered hazards most avoided.

Suggested safety precautions are:

(1) Avoid running around in small circles or changing directions suddenly.

(2) Establish goal lines away from wall.

(3) Use bean bags or balloons rather than regulation balls, reduce the amount of equipment used.

(4) Limit the number of players to fit into a given space, but be certain that each child gets a turn.

(5) Keep noise at a minimum.

Additions to this list should be made after the teacher gains from the experience of playing with the children in her own room;

she should make a collection of activities most favored by the children and be constantly on the search for new materials.

Equipment

A magic box, which is used only on stormy, dark days, can help turn a dull day into one of great adventure! Checkers, cards, table games, bean balls, ring toss, jacks, miniature bowling pins are among the treasures. Small group or couple play should be encouraged. Or a group of six might choose games they want to play. Each group might be allowed to play their favorite game for the entire period or change with any other willing group at half period time.

A construction box is often found in the rooms of creative experienced teachers. In it are found games made by the pupils on previous rainy days, along with some half-completed ones. Some children made checker boards, others toss boards for fruit jar rubbers. Still others have made miniature table shuffleboard sets on which checkers can be finger snapped up, down, and into given areas. Two boys made a jumping standard by driving nails into two boards and using an old fishing pole to move up and down on the nails to show how high one must jump in order to clear the pole. Two girls and four boys made a balance beam using blocks to steady a railroad tie size board.

These and numerous other pieces of equipment and games can be made in the classroom. Home or class made equipment often is more meaningful to pupils than expensive items furnished by the school. The creative teacher when and if she has a "will" will find the "way" to get equipment for her group. She can even stimulate the class into making many of the things with which they can play.

Suggested minimum equipment includes:
(1) Four ring toss games
(2) Four rubber balls
(3) One treasure box
(4) Card and table games

Game Leadership

Successful game or play leadership requires skill. The leader must know games best suited for her group, how to get play started, when to stop one activity and go on to the next, as well as a wide range of things to play. Mastery of these skills comes from experience providing one has learned from past mistakes. The novice may gain additional experience with church or neighborhood groups in order to become more expert.

Mastery of a best method to gain attention is important. A sudden clapping of hands, playing a piano chord, blowing a whistle are recommended techniques. Although the teacher may ordinarily have control over her group it may be lessened or even lost during this classroom play period. She may find it necessary to stop activities entirely or momentarily in order to regain control. However, the pupils should not be bargained with when they are bad or have been particularly good. The plea, "Please let us play five minutes longer and we will be quieter" or the promise, "Now children, if all of you get your arithmetic lesson we will play ten minutes longer this afternoon" are often significant signs of this type of leadership technique. In the former, the children have found that they can bargain with the teacher. In the latter, the teacher is slipping carrots into the daily diet by promising dessert. Next to compulsion, bargaining is the lowest form of leadership.

An atmosphere of fun should permeate the classroom. If the first game has been wonderful, obtaining class cooperation will be easier when the second one to be played is introduced. If, however, a game that looked like fun when described in the book should fall flat, it is best to change to another rather than insisting "now children this game really *is* fun" when obviously it is not.

Rules and the setting of necessary boundaries should be briefly explained. A description of how to play coupled with actual demonstrations is ideal. If when saying, "Everyone get into a circle," the teacher will join hands with a youngster on either side the pupils will quickly get into this formation. The use of imitation is a standard teaching method, for children are copy-cats. A major portion of their learning comes through what they see and try to do. Educators call this trial and error learning through imitation.

Changing activities at their fun peak adds to their enjoyment. Children often say then, "Oh let's keep on playing, please!" Grown-ups realize that stopping the activity at the climax will cause the children to have greater desire to play the game again because it was such fun. This need for completeness, as psychologists call it, drives us to take up willingly or return joyfully to interrupted tasks or pleasures. Recognition of fun peaks can be developed.

Going from the known to the unknown is an educational principle applicable to game as well as subject matter material, for basically the same principles of teaching underline all learn'ng materials. Each new game period should begin with the most favored game from the previous period. Since we all like to do those things which we can do well, the wise teacher aids children to learn many skills with above average ability. It is wise to learn at least two new activities during the game period as well as review others. It is unwise to insist upon skill perfection at the sacrifice of an unpleasant experience or unfavorable attitude.

Active Circle Games

KICK THE PIN

Grades 4, 5, 6   No. of players: 10 players for each circle.

Equipment. A volley or rubber play ball, an Indian club or milk bottle for each group.

Directions. Each circled group with approximately 6 feet between each player tries to kick the ball so as to knock down the centered pin. All kicking is done from this circle. Each team tries to knock over the pin first. The succeeding team scores one point. Ten points constitute a game.

RING THE BOTTLE NECK

Grades 1, 2, 3   No. of players: 4–6 on each team.

Equipment. Catsup or pop bottle, brass or wooden ring suspended from the end of a two-foot stick with 20 inches of string, both for each group.

Directions. Player holds the stick at end opposite from where the string is fastened, and tries to get the ring over the neck of the bottle. Each player on each team gets one try while the leader counts slowly from 1 to 10. Score one point for each successful attempt. The team scoring 10 points first wins.

BALL BOUNCE

Grades 1, 2, 3   No. of players: 4–6 on each team.

Equipment. A soccer, rubber playground or tennis ball, a chair, and one wastebasket for each player.

Directions. From a distance of 8 feet each player tries to bounce the ball over the chair and into the upturned wastebasket. Each player gets one turn. The team scoring 10 points first wins.

BULL IN THE RING

Grades 2, 3   No. of players: entire class.

Equipment. None.
Directions. Players form a circle around the chosen "bull," who tries to break through. If he gets through, all chase him. His catcher becomes the "bull."

STRIDE BALL

Grades 4, 5   No. of players: 10 players in each circle.

Equipment. One volley, soccer, or basketball.
Directions. "It" stands in a circle. Outside players stand with feet in straddle position. "It" tries to roll the ball outside the circle between the legs of some players. The players try to stop the ball with their hands. If they can, they roll the ball back to center player. When "It" rolls the ball between the legs of a player, the two exchange places.

POISON CIRCLE

Grades 4, 5, 6   No. of players: 8–10 in a circle.

Equipment. Chalk.
Directions. Draw circle 4 feet in diameter. Place players around the ring. The object of the game is to keep out of the poisoned circle by trying to pull others into it. When a player steps in or on the poisoned circle he is out.

CIRCLE CATCH BALL

Grades 4, 5, 6   No. of players: 8–10 in a circle.

Equipment. Volley, soccer or basketball for each group.
Directions. "It" stands inside the circle of players standing 3 feet apart. Players throw the ball around or across the circle to each other while "It" tries to catch the ball. If he succeeds, he trades places with the person who last threw the ball.

FISH AND NET

Grades 2, 3   No. of players: 8–10 in a group.

Equipment. None.
Directions. Divide the group into two teams. Line each up at opposite ends of the room. One group is called "fish" the other, "the net." At the signal "the net," composed of players with linked arms, moves toward the fish and tries to catch them. The fish try to cross the line opposite their own. Caught fish help "the net" encircle others.

SCHOOLROOM TAG

Grades 1, 2, 3   No. of players: entire class.

Equipment. Chalk.
Directions. A circle is drawn about 4 feet across in the front of the room. "It" stands near the circle. The leader names any 3 children to

try to get into the circle without being tagged. The one tagged first becomes "It." If no one is tagged, the first player becomes "It."

RING MASTER

Grades 1, 2, 3   No. of players: entire class.

Equipment. None.

Directions. All players form a circle without holding hands. A ring master stands inside and pretends to flourish a whip. As he turns he calls out the name of some animal and all move around the circle imitating that animal. When the ring master says, "Now all join the circus parade" each imitates any animal he wants to. The teacher or class chooses the one who has done the best imitations.

EXCHANGE TAG

Grades 1, 2, 3   No. of players: entire class.

Equipment. None.

Directions. "It" faces the group and calls out the names of any two players who must exchange seats. "It" tries to tag one of them before he reaches a seat. The tagged player becomes the new "It."

INDIAN RUNNING

Grades 1, 2, 3   No. of players: entire class.

Equipment. None.

Directions. Six are chosen to leave the room. They arrange themselves in any order, return to the room and run around it, then go out again. When they return the children try to name their running line-up. The child who is successful may choose five others to leave with him and the game continues.

PALM BALL

Grades 4, 5, 6   No. of players: entire class divided into small circles.

Equipment. A rubber ball for each circle.

Directions. Circled players cup hands behind their backs. "It" places the ball in someone's hands, who must turn and run in the opposite direction. Each tries to get back to the vacant spot first. The loser becomes "It."

NUMBERED CHAIRS

Grades 4, 5, 6   No. of players: entire class.

Equipment. A chair for each player plus one extra.

Directions. Seat players and place extra chair in a line. Players number off. The space retains the number throughout, though players change. Number one calls "four." Immediately "four" responds with another number. When a player whose number is called does not respond immediately he must go to the end of the line. Thus "nine" becomes "eight," etc. Numbers are called rapidly. The object of the game is to send top players to the end of the line.

Variations. Have players clap hands on knees, then together. Then snap fingers on left hand. Then on right hand in rhythm to 1, 2, 3, 4 count. All players must keep this rhythm up while calling out or responding to a number. Failure to keep the rhythm going will send a player to the end of the line. This game may also be played in a circle.

BIRDS HAVE FEATHERS

Grades 1, 2, 3   No. of players: entire class.

Equipment. None.

Directions. One player is the leader. He and all others flap their arms like birds. He calls out names of something with feathers. If a player flaps his wings on calling out something that does not have feathers he is out. The leader flaps his wings on almost all things to confuse the group and calls as rapidly as possible, "Birds have feathers, bats have feathers, babies have feathers, etc."

Variations. Thumbs up and thumbs down. Cats have fur, trees have leaves.

I AM VERY TALL

Grades 1, 2, 3   No. of players: entire class.

Equipment. A blindfold.

Directions. One player is blindfolded. Then another says, "I am very, very tall, I'm very, very small, sometimes I'm tall, sometimes I'm small. Guess which I am now." He stands or squats. "It" guesses whether the player is standing or stooping. If "It" chooses correctly he chooses someone to take his place.

Variations. The whole group stands or squats. Chosen player holds hands up for "tall" and low for "small."

FIND THE LEADER

Grades 1–6   No. of players: entire class.

Equipment. None.

Directions. Players stand or sit in a circle. A leader is chosen. One player goes out. The group starts clapping and continues until the returned player stands in the center of the circle. The leader changes from clapping to waving his hands, swinging his feet, etc. All others imitate the changed actions by watching someone opposite. The player has three chances to find the leader. If he finds him, he chooses a player to take his place. If he does not find him, he again is "It." A new leader is chosen.

CENTER PITCH

Grades 2, 3   No. of players: 3–5 on a team.

Equipment. 1 bean bag, eraser, or ball for each team.

Directions. Players on each team take single turns throwing the bean bag into a metal wastebasket 8 feet away. Add players' scores. The winner is the team scoring 21 points.

Variations. (1) The players begin and stop pitching the bags at the leader's whistle. The winner is the team scoring the most points in five minutes.

(2) Draw chalk circles at one end of the room. Players throw the bags into the circles.

(3) Draw three circles on a board or cardboard. Each player gets three tosses. Team scoring largest number of points in a given time wins. First circle counts 25, second 15, third 5.

Quiet Circle Games

ELECTRIC SHOCK

Grades 1–3   No. of players: 10–15 in each circle.

Equipment. None.

Directions. Players sit or stand in a circle. "It" stands inside and tries to guess where the shock is. All players hold hands; one player begins the shock by squeezing a players hand on his right or left. The shock may move any direction and at any time a player may send it back the other way. "It" tries to find the position of the shock. The caught player becomes "It."

AIR BALLOON

Grades 1, 2, 3   No. of players: circles of 8–10 players.

Equipment. One balloon for each group.

Directions. Divide the group into equally numbered circles. On count of "3" each group competes with the other to see which one can keep the balloon in the air longest by tapping it. Each player may tap the balloon only once, but may tap it after another player has.

Variations. Music may be played. Each player may tap in rhythm to the music or on one separate rhythmical beat.

POISON BALL

Grades 1, 2, 3   No. of players: circles of 8–10 players.

Equipment. Two rubber balls for each circle.

Directions. Players form into circles, each circle has two balls. When music stops or the whistle blows, players in possession of either ball are poisoned and must leave the group. When the group gets down to four only one ball is used. The last player to stay in the circle is winner.

Variation. Musical chairs.

WHO HAS GONE?

Grades 1, 2   No. of players: entire class.

Equipment. None.

Directions. "It" closes his eyes. One player leaves the room. "It" tries to guess who has gone. If he guesses correctly he and the player who went out change places. If not, the game begins again.

ELECTRIC TAG

Grades 1, 2, 3   No. of players: entire class.

Equipment. None.

Directions. Players sit in rows with their hands in their laps and eyes closed. At a signal the last pupil in each row touches the shoulder of the person in front of him, he touches the next person, etc. The row that has their first pupil to stand wins.

STILL WATER

Grades 1, 2, 3   No. of players: entire class.

Equipment. None.

Directions. "It" faces the rest and picks out the quietest one when he says "still water." On the words, "running water" the pupils can move around and talk. The winner choses the quietest and she becomes "It."

ANGELS DO IT

Grades 1–5   No. of players: entire class.

Equipment. None.

Directions. Pupils place hands behind their necks to look like angel wings. The leader gives the direction, "Touch your nose, angels do it." All players must quickly touch their nose and get back to angel position. The first angel team scores 1 point. Suggested "do its"—touch right foot, left foot, clap twice behind you, stand up, touch wood, whistle a tune.

STAGE COACH

Grades 4, 5, 6   No. of players: entire class.

Equipment. None.

Directions. Players are each given a name of a stage coach part. One starts telling a story of the stage coach mentioning all parts assigned. As the child's part is named he gets up and runs around his chair. When the leader says, "Stage coach" all must change chairs with anyone except the player on his left and right. The leader tries to get a seat. The person left seatless becomes the new story teller.

I PASS THESE SCISSORS TO YOU

Grades 4, 5, 6   No. of players: entire class.

Equipment. A pair of scissors.

Directions. Players are seated in circle formation. The leader passes a pair of scissors. The next player passes them on saying, "I have received them crossed and I pass these scissors to you uncrossed." The crossed and uncrossed refers to the passer's legs or feet, and not to the open or closed scissors being passed as the players think. If the receiver's feet were crossed when the scissors are passed, and crossed as he passes them, he says, "I received them crossed and I pass these scissors to you crossed." The game continues until everyone catches on.

THE GUESSING BLINDMAN

Grades 1, 2, 3   No. of players: entire class.

Equipment. One blindfold, a stick or ruler.

Directions. Players are seated in circle formation. One is blindfolded and turned around three times while all others change seats. The blindman walks forward and touches someone with the stick saying, "Can you guess." The touched player, trying to disguise his voice, repeats this question three times. If the blindman guesses who is speaking he and the discovered player exchange places. Otherwise, he is "It" again.

BUG

Grades 3–6   No. of players: individual or 4–10 on each leave.

Equipment. Make two or more hexagon-shaped tops with the letters B, H, T, E, L, F on six sides, paper, pencils.

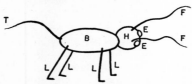

Directions. Each player spins the top. If "B" comes up he draws the body of the bug and spins again. If he gets an "E" he loses his turn, for there is no head into which to fit the eyes. The second best throw, therefore, is an "H" for the head. "T" means tail, "L" means leg, "F" for feeler. Each bug must have two eyes, two feelers, and six legs along with its body, tail, and head before it is a complete bug. When a player tosses something he already has he looses his turn. A player cannot start drawing his bug until he gets a "B" for body. The team or individual drawing a complete bug first wins.

MUFFIN PAN BOWLING

Grades 1, 2, 3   No. of players: 4–6 on each team.

Equipment. One muffin pan, one small rubber ball for each group.

Directions. Set the pan upright against a wall or on a table. Place a board against one edge of the pan to form an incline. Roll the ball up the incline into the compartments. Score one point for each successful attempt. Each player is given 3 trials. The team scoring 10 points first wins.

RING ON A STRING

Grades 1, 2, 3   No. of players: Divide class into circles of 10 players.

Equipment. Ring on a string.

Directions. One stands in the circle. A string with a ring on it is held loosely in both hands by all players in the seated circle. The object of the game is to slip the ring along the string from one player to the next while "It" tries to locate the ring or who has it. If he is successful, he exchanges places with the one under whose hand it was. If unsuccessful he continues as "It."

CATCH THE CANE

Grades 3, 4   No. of players: entire class.

Equipment. Cane or yard stick.

Directions. "It" stands inside the circle. All players, including "It" are given a number. "It" holds the cane upright with one end on the floor. As he calls out a number he lets go of the cane. The player whose number has been called attempts to catch it before it touches the floor. If he fails he becomes "It." If he catches the cane, the first player remains "It."

THE TOY SHOP

Grades 1, 2   No. of players: entire class.

Equipment. None.

Directions. One child is chosen shopkeeper, one the customer, who leaves the room while the others chose which toy they want to be. When the customer returns he asks to buy some toys. If he asks for a ball the player representing a ball bounces up and down, or for an airplane, the player flies around the room, etc. The shopkeeper guides his buying by suggesting and showing certain toys. The customer selects the three best toys.

HOW MANY CAN YOU REMEMBER?
(*Kim's Game*)

Grades 4, 5, 6   No. of players: entire class.

Equipment. A wide variety of objects.

Directions. Place 20 to 30 objects on table. Everyone looks at them 2 to 3 minutes. Then a cover is placed on them. The winner is the person writing down the greatest number of the objects.

Table and Card Games

MAKING SQUARES

Grades 4, 5, 6   No. of players: 2.

Equipment. Five or more up and down rows of dots on a piece of paper.

Directions. Players take turns connecting any two dots with a straight line. No diagonal line may be drawn. Each places his initial in each square his line completes. When all dots have been connected the player having the largest number of initialed squares wins.

JACKS

Grades 1–6   No. of players: 2 or more.

Equipment. Rubber ball and set of jacks for each group.

Directions. All jacks are thrown down. The player picks them up in this fashion: the ball is tossed up, and while it is still in the air he picks up a jack and catches the ball before it hits the floor. He continues this until each jack has been picked up. After the ones he does the twos, threes, etc., until he picks up all jacks. If he is on the threes and is playing with seven jacks he would pick up three the first time and four the next, etc. A player loses his turn if he fails to catch the ball, or pick up the required number of jacks. The winner is the one who has just picked up all jacks.

Variations. (1) Knock on the door: The ball is tossed, the player picks up a jack, knocks on the door with his knuckles, and catches the ball before it touches the ground.

(2) Around the world: The ball is tossed, the player must pick up a jack and with the jack in his hand go around the ball while it is in the air. The ball bounces once before it is caught.

(3) Scrub the floor: Same as above except the pantomime of scrubbing the floor is substituted for going around the ball.

(4) Rock the baby: Same as around the world except the player puts his arms together as if rocking a baby before catching the ball.

Stunts and Games of Skill

HAND TOUCH

Grades 3, 4   No. of players: individual.

Equipment. None.

Directions. Put one hand where the other cannot touch it. After the players try unsuccessfully, have him put the right hand to the left elbow, for this is the secret of the trick.

JUMP THE SHOT

Grades 4, 5, 6   No. of players: 6–8 in each group.

Equipment. A long rope with a shoe tied on it for each group.

Directions. Pupils form a circle around the center player who swings the rope in a circle. He gradually increases the swinging part of the rope until it reaches the knees of the group, and at the same time increases the speed of the swing. All try to jump over the weighted rope as it reaches them. A circle player touched by the rope is eliminated.

CIRCLE SQUAT

Grades 4, 5, 6   No. of players: entire class.

Equipment. None.

Directions. Players run, skip, hop, march, as directed by the leader. All must squat when the leader's whistle blows. Play continues until all but one have been eliminated.

CLOTHES PIN DROP

Grades 4, 5, 6   No. of players: groups of 4–6.

Equipment. Milk bottles and five clothes pins for each group.
Directions. Each player in each line drops 5 clothes pins one at a time in the milk bottle from an upright position. The scores for each player are added together. The winner scores 20 points.

PING PONG BOUNCE

Grades 4, 5, 6   No. of players: groups of 4–6.

Equipment. 3 ping pong balls and a box for each group.
Directions. Each player in each line bounces all of the ping pong balls into the box from a 10 foot line. Team scores are added together. The winner scores 25 points first.

PICK UP

Grades 2–6   No. of players: individual.

Equipment. A coin.
Directions. Stand with back against a wall, heels touching. Try to pick up the coin without moving the heels away from the wall.

CIRCLE TWO

Grades 2–6   No. of players: individual.

Equipment. None.
Directions. Move the arms in large circles of opposite directions, the right hand away from the body, the left toward the body.
Variations. (1) Swing right foot in a circle moving left, then left in a circle moving right.
          (2) Pat the head with one hand and rub the stomach with the other simultaneously.

STAND UP

Grades 2–6   No. of players: individual.

Equipment. None.
Directions. Lie flat on the back, arms to the side, hands flat against the hips. Arise without using the hands. First come to a sitting position, then stand up.
Variations. Lie flat on the back, cross arms on chest. Stand up without uncrossing the arms or using the elbows.

BALANCE WRITING

Grades 4, 5, 6   No. of players: individual.

Equipment. A milk bottle, pad of paper, a pencil.
Directions. Sit down on an upright milk bottle. Cross legs with only the heel of one foot touching the floor. Write your full name on the pad while trying to maintain your balance.

Variations. (1) Light a match.
            (2) Thread a needle.

JUMP THE BROOK

Grades 1, 2, 3   No. of players: divide the class into two groups.

Equipment. Chalk.

Directions. Players line up in two single lines. Each runs and jumps across the brook (chalk marks about 8 inches apart.) If a player misses he must drop out to get his feet dry. Each round the brook is made wider until one is proclaimed champion.

BEAN BAG TOSS

Grades 4, 5, 6   No. of players: groups of four.

Equipment. Plywood with three holes and a bean bag for each group.

Directions. The board has three holes with 5, 10, 15 points values. Players toss the bean bag through the holes and play for total individual or group points.

Variations. (1) Paint a clown's face on the plywood. Score 5 points for hitting the mouth hole, 10 for each eye.

CARD TOSS

Grades 4, 5, 6   No. of players: 4–6 on a team.

Equipment. 10 cards for each group.

Directions. Each pupil tosses 10 cards singly into a propped up hat, or wastebasket 10 feet away. Score one point for each successful toss.

HE CAN DO LITTLE

Grades 4, 5, 6   No. of players: entire class.

Equipment. A cane or stick.

Directions. Players sit in a circle. The leader starts the game by saying, "He can do little who can't do this." He passes the cane to the player to the left who must repeat the action as nearly as possible and then pass the cane on to the player on his left. The leader tells the player whether or not he has done the stunt correctly. The secret is that the tapping is done with the cane in the right hand, is then taken in the left hand and passed on to the next person. The leader may beat out a special rhythm and go through extra flourishes to distract attention.

Active Relays

CHINESE HOP

Grades 4, 5, 6   No. of players: two teams.

Equipment. Ten sticks, candles or ten pins.

Directions. Place sticks in a straight line 1 foot apart. Each player hops on one foot over the sticks without touching any of them. He is disqualified if he touches a stick. After jumping over the last stick the player, still on one foot, picks up that stick and hops back over the other nine. Next he hops over the nine sticks, the eight, etc., each time hopping back down the line of remaining sticks. He continues until all sticks have been picked up. A player is disqualified if he fails to tag the next player to start hopping up his line, if he touches both feet to the ground at any time, or if he touches a stick with his foot. The second player puts down the ten sticks. The third picks them up, etc., until all players have hopped up and down the line.

HORSE AND RIDER
Grades 5, 6 No. of players: 8–10 boys.

Equipment. None.

Directions. Divide the group into equal teams. One player mounts the back of another, legs around his waist and arms around his shoulders. They race to and around line where they exchange positions and race back to the starting line to tag off the next couple.

Variations. The "horse" goes down on all fours. The "rider" straddles his back. They race to the finish line and exchange positions.

HURDLE RACE
Grades 5, 6 No. of players: 10 boys for each team.

Equipment. A rope or broom stick.

Directions. Players 1 and 2 on each team hold a broom stick or rope between them 6 or more inches from the floor. They run down the line with their team mates between them jumping the hurdle as it moves to the end of the line. As soon as they reach the end, number 2 returns to the head of the line and starts down with number 3 in the same manner. Number 3 then runs with number 4 and so on until number 1 is back at the head of the line.

BLACK BOARD RELAY
Grades 4, 5, 6 No. of players: entire class.

Equipment. Black board, chalk.

Directions. Played as any relay except instead of touching the goal, player writes a number on the board in a line. The last player must add all numbers correctly. The team with the first correct answer wins.

TAG THE WALL RELAY
Grades 4, 5, 6 No. of players: entire class.

Equipment. None.

Directions. Seat players in even numbered rows. On a signal, the last player in each row run forward and tags the wall. As soon as this player is past the first seat in the row, everyone moves back one seat, leaving the first seat vacant for the runner. As soon as the runner is seated he raises his hand and the last person seated begins. The line whose players all finish running first wins.

NEWSPAPER RACE

Grades 2–6   No. of players: two equally divided teams.

Equipment. Two newspapers.

Directions. Each contestant is given a newspaper, on which each step of the race must be made. He puts down a sheet and steps on it, puts down another sheet and steps on it, reaches back to get the first sheet and move it forward, and so on until he reaches the goal line, from which he returns in the same fashion and tags off the second player.

SPIDER RACE

Grades 1, 2, 3   No. of players: equally divided teams.

Equipment. None.

Directions. Player number 1 in each line faces the goal. Player number 2 stands with his back turned and they link elbows and race to the goal. Player number 2 runs back facing the end line while player number 1 runs forward. Players 3 and 4 and on down the line repeat the actions.

RAPID FIRE ARTIST

Grades 2–6   No. of players: 2–10 on each team.

Equipment. Pencil or crayon, paper.

Directions. Divide the group into equal teams. Each group sends an "artist" to the leader, who tells him an animal, person, tree, etc. to draw. The "artist" rushes back to his group and begins to draw the likeness of the person, place, or thing given him. As soon as the group recognizes what is drawn the members yell it all together. The group guessing first scores 1 point. 10 points constitute a game. The "artist" cannot talk or give any hints other than drawing as to what he is creating.

NATURE GUESS

Grades 2–6   No. of players: 2–10 on each team.

Equipment. None.

Directions. Divide the group into four teams. Each group sends a different member up each time to the leader who tells him an animal, or person to act out. The first group to guess who or what the person represents scores 1 point. 10 points constitutes a game.

Quiet Guessing Games

GROCERY STORE

Grades 1, 2, 3   No. of players: entire class or divide into teams of 4–10 in a group.

Equipment. None.

Directions. Divide group into equally numbered lines. One player from each line steps forward. The leader calls out any letter. The player who first calls out the name of any grocery article beginning with that letter scores a point for his team. 10 points constitute a game.

Variations. Players call out the name of any animal, a person name, state, etc.

NURSERY RHYMES
Grades 1, 2, 3   No. of players: entire class.

Equipment. None.
Directions. Give each pupil or a group of three a nursery rhyme to act out.
Variations. A poem, a song.

HAND PUPPETS
Grades 1–4   No. of players: entire class.

Equipment. Paper sacks, crayons.
Directions. Each pupil or group of four make hand puppets out of paper sacks and each group puts on a brief show.

MAGIC MUSIC
Grades 2, 3, 4   No. of players: entire class.

Equipment. None.
Directions. One leaves the room while others hide a small object. The player returns and tries to find the hidden treasure by getting his clue from the singing of the group. As he draws nearer the object the singing grows louder, or softer when he moves away. Piano music may be substituted.

WHAT AM I?
Grades 4, 5, 6   No. of players: entire class.

Equipment. Any picture from a magazine and one straight pin for each player.
Directions. Pin a picture on the back of each pupil. Players mingle around trying to find out what the picture is that he is wearing. He may only ask questions calling for a no or yes. answer. When he discovers what he represents, he reports to the leader who pins the picture on his lapel. Pictures of animals, cars, famous people, flowers, etc. may be used.

I SAW
Grades 1, 2, 3   No. of players: two circles.

Equipment. None.
Directions. "It" stands in each circle and each "It" says "On my way to school today I saw—" and imitates what he saw. The others guess what he saw. The one guessing correctly becomes "It." If no one guesses, "It" tells what he was imitating. If his imitation was poor as decided by the group, he must choose a new "It." If the imitation was good, "It" is praised and remains "It."

ALPHABETICAL GEOGRAPHY

les 4, 5, 6   No. of players: entire class.

None.

Ine pupil calls out the name of a state, or city. The next
all out a state or city with the last letter in the name
called. ____ _le: New York, Kansas City, Yucatan, New Hampshire,
etc.

Games from Other Lands

STONE, PAPER, SCISSORS
Japan

Grades 4, 5, 6   No. of players: entire class.

Equipment. None.

Directions. Divide players into two equal lines. Each player faces his
partner with hands behind him. The leader counts "1, 2, 3"; on "3"
each player brings his hands forward with hands in any of the three
positions, depending upon his choice. The stone is represented with
clenched fists; the paper with open hands, palms down; scissors by extending the first two fingers. Because the stone dulls the scissors it
beats them. The scissors beat the paper because it can cut. The paper
beats the stone because it wraps the stone. Points are scored, the team
scoring the most wins.

Variations. (1) All players advance. At "4" one, two, three or four
fingers are held out to represent 1—stone; 2—scissors; 3—paper; 4—
stone.

(2) Man, gun, rabbit, bear.

(3) Man, gun, tiger.

CHICKEN MARKET
Italy

Grades 4, 5, 6   No. of players: entire class.

Equipment. None.

Directions. All players are chickens except the two strongest class
members. One becomes the buyer, the other the seller. All players
squat down and clasp their hands around their knees and are told not
to smile or laugh. The buyer comes to test each chicken by pinching,
chin chucking, or tickling. At last he says, "This one is just right." He
and the seller take hold of the chicken's arms and swing it counting
"1, 2, 3"; as they do so if the chicken laughs he is eliminated. If he does
not laugh he is not sold but remains safe.

HEN AND WILD CAT
Africa

Grades 1, 2, 3   No. of players. entire class.

Equipment. None.

Directions. The "Hen" leads her flock of other players around a chosen "Cat." She warns them of danger and the "Cat" tries to catch any foolish chickens who come too near.

THE TIED MONKEY
Africa

Grades 1, 2, 3   No. of players: entire class.

Equipment. Rope, handkerchief with one end tied into a knot for each player.

Directions. One boy is chosen to be the "monkey." He is tied to a chair. The others try to hit him with their handkerchiefs while he tries to catch them. If successful he changes places with his victim.

CALABASH
Africa

Grades 4, 5, 6   No. of players: three in each group.

Equipment. None.

Directions. Two players lock arms to pen in a third one who stands between them. The middle player is locked in or is "caloshed." He tries to wiggle out while his jailers move their locked arms up and down to keep him in.

SAND BAG BALL
Alaska

Grades 4, 5, 6   No. of players: ten in each circle.

Equipment. One playground volleyball or balloon for each group.

Directions. Players kneel in a circle. The ball is batted in the air and players try to keep it aloft by striking it with one hand. A player is out if he uses both hands, or if he fails to strike the ball and misses. The winner is the last remaining player.

GUESSING GAME (Tlingit Tribe)
Alaska

Grades 3, 4   No. of players: entire class.

Equipment. 20 or more small sticks.

Directions. "It" arranges the sticks in small bunches while others hide their eyes. Each guesses quickly how many sticks are in each bunch. The new "It" is the first to call out the correct numbers.

FROG DANCE
Burma

Grades 4, 5, 6   No. of players: entire class.

Equipment. None.

Directions. Pupils squat in a circle. They hop forward around the ring by throwing out one foot then the other. As each hops he claps his hands (1) in front of his knees, (2) in back, and tries to make others fall over. A player who falls is out. The winner is the one who frog dances longest without falling.

CALL THE CHICKENS HOME
China

Grades 1, 2   No. of players: entire class.

Equipment. A blindfold.

Directions. A blindfolded player stands apart from the "chickens" who run by and touch him after he says, "Tsoo, Tsoo—come and find your mother." Any chickens caught exchanges places with the blind man.

CATCHING FISHES IN THE DARK
China

Grades 1, 2, 3   No. of players: entire class.

Equipment. A blindfold.

Directions. A blindfolded player tries to catch the "fish" who runs past. If one is caught the blindman tries to guess what kind a "fish" the player has chosen to be. If he succeeds, the "fish" and he exchange places, otherwise one "fish" has won freedom.

CATCHING THE FISH'S TAIL
China

Grades 1, 2, 3   No. of players: 10 in each line.

Equipment. None.

Directions. The players grasp arms around the waist of the person ahead so the line becomes compact. The first player is the "head," the last the "tail." The "head" tries to catch hold of the "tail." Any player who breaks hold is eliminated.

SKIN THE SNAKE
China

Grades 4, 5, 6   No. of players: 10 in each line.

Equipment. None.

Directions. Players stand in a single line, each putting his right hand between his legs and holding the left hand of the boy behind him. All walk backward. The last one lies down. The others pass over him and also lie down. The last one gets up first and walks forward outside the line and helps pull the other one up until all are standing again. All players must keep holding hands.

ANIMAL MENAGERIE
England

Grades 1, 2, 3   No. of players: entire class.

Equipment. Chalk, blackboard.

Directions. Each chooses an animal sound he wishes to imitate. The leader writes down all names given on the blackboard and tells a story weaving in each animal. When a pupil hears the name of his animal he imitates the sound. When the leader calls out, "Menagerie" all give their sounds at once.

PEBBLE GAME
Greece

Grades 4, 5, 6   No. of players: entire class.

Equipment. 10 or more pebbles or jacks for each player.
Directions. Place pebbles on back of the hand. When a signal is given turn the hand over and try to catch as many pebbles as possible with the same hand.

PHUGADI
India

Grades 1, 2, 3   No. of players: couples.

Equipment. None.
Directions. Two players face each other with toes touching. They grasp each other by the waist, lean back as far as possible and turn together.

PAINTING COLORED SAND PICTURES
Italy

Grades 4, 5, 6   No. of players: groups of four.

Equipment. Bags of colored sand for each group, white notebook paper.
Directions. Give each group bags of yellow, red, black, blue, and white sand. The white sand is scattered over the paper to form a frame. Next the outline of a bird, person, animal, or object is formed by letting the black sand slowly ooze between the fingers. The remaining colors are used to complete the design. Groups can compete to "paint" the most attractive picture.

SATSUMA KEN
Japan

Grades 2, 3, 4   No. of players: entire class.

Equipment. Blindfold.
Directions. The pupils stretch out the fingers of one or both hands simultaneously. "It," who is blindfolded, tries to guess the total number of extended fingers of all players.

BEAD GUESSING
American Indian

Grades 1, 2, 3   No. of players: entire class.

Equipment. Bead.
Directions. One player holds a bead in one hand behind him. He

stops before one player who tries to guess in which hand the bead is held. At each guess the one holding the bead must bring his hands forward and open them. If the guesser guesses correctly three times, the one holding the bead runs to his seat. If the "guesser" catches him he gets to hold the bead. Each player may guess three times, but unless he guesses correctly all three times the one holding the bead moves on.

CHINESE HOLD UP
China

Grades 3, 4, 5   No. of players: entire class.

Equipment. None.

Directions. Seat players in a circle. One starts the game by holding his hands to both ears. Immediately the players to the right and left of him must hold their ears. The last one to do so is out and starts the game again by pointing to any player. This player grasps his own ears and players on his right and left grasp theirs. The eliminated player starts the game again. The game continues until only two are left.

YEMARI
Japan

Grades 4, 5, 6   No. of players: 6 players in each circle.

Equipment. One tennis or rubber ball for each group.

Directions. Players stand in a circle. One bounces the ball up and back to himself with his open hand. He continues as long as the ball is in reach, but cannot move from the circle. When the ball moves near another player that person keeps it bouncing. The game continues until someone fails to hit the ball and is eliminated. The last remaining player wins.

Suggested Readings

Bancroft, Jessie, *Games for the Playground, Home, School, and Gymnasium,* New York, The Macmillan Company, 1924.

Bauer, Lois and Reed, Barbara, *Dance and Play Activities for the Elementary Grades,* Vols. I and II., New York, Chartwell House, 1951.

Elliott, Elizabeth and Forbush, Maud, *Games for Every Day,* 8th Edition, New York, The Macmillan Company, 1951.

Fraser, Phyllis and Young, Edith, *A Treasury of Games, Quizzes, and Puzzles,* New York, Grosset and Dunlap, 1947.

Geri, Frank, *Illustrated Game Manual,* 215 Seneca Street, Seattle, Washington, Ernie Rose, 1951.

Harbin, E. O., *Fun Encyclopedia,* Nashville, Tennessee, Abingdon-Cokesbury Press, 1950.

Harbin, E. O., *Gay Parties for All Occasions,* Nashville, Tennessee, Abingdon-Cokesbury Press, 1950.

Hindman, Darwin, *Handbook of Active Games,* New York, Prentice-Hall, 1951.

Hunt, Sarah and Cain, Ethel, *Games the World Around,* New York, A. S. Barnes, 1950.

Parent's Magazine, *Family Fun Book,* 52 Vanderbilt Ave., New York, Parent's Magazine Company, 1950.

Chapter 13

Constructed Games

In the average school an inventory of games would include checkers and boards, chinese checker boards, marbles and a few bingo sets. Private schools would rate higher, for student bodies and staffs are smaller, and often there is more money left from the equipment budget to buy new games. Active Parent Teachers Associations in the public schools have felt the need for more equipment and raised money to buy ping pong tables and shuffle board sets. They could, likewise, help establish game libraries. The game library functions as any library. For example, a child who is giving a party could check out a number of games and return them at a designated time. Such a library should include puzzles of metal or wood, magic tricks, manufactured table games as dominoes, checkers, monopoly, and larger constructed games.

Actually, there is no point for having a poverty game program in any school, for children are interested primarily in play and are creative enough to make their own games if given encouragement. The rag bag, the button box, the attic, the garage or the grocery store yields adequate materials for constructing a multitude of games. Building contractors are Santa Clauses for enterprising youngsters who really want to help build permanent games for their schools. Cheese boxes, fish buckets, apple and orange crates, and hundreds of feet of beaver board, sheet rock, moulding, ply board and lumber go each day into junk heaps that would supply the demands of game-hungry children.

There are numerous manufactured games available to schools with money allotted for such purposes. The games described below can be made by the children in the upper elementary grades; they are as inexpensive and expendable as the resourcefulness of teacher and pupils. The actual outlay of money should consist of the purchase of nails, tacks, paint, thinner, and paint brush. Few homes exist where one could not find small amounts of usable enamel that will eventually harden. Paint is essential—the attractiveness of the finished game will depend largely on the eye appeal of bright, clear color.

Pitching Games

BOARD GAMES

Since the bulletin board type game has many uses, it will be as much at home in the classroom as in the playroom. The classroom teacher will find such games most helpful in checking absorption of subject matter which cover states, capitals, terrain, industries, foodstuffs, etc. The inserts can be made in art class. Manila, tag board, wrapping paper or detail paper are satisfactory. The design may be done in water color or tempera paint. Rubber darts are cheap and available at five and ten stores.

Moulding or
1′ x 2′ board
or x 2′ lath
Window glass

36′ x 36′
or
24′ x 36′

BULLETIN BOARD

Frame as for a picture. Back with heavy paste board, beaver board, or wall board. Secure on three sides leaving an opening at the top to permit removal of game inserts.

Maps

Integration of subject matter using a map of the United States is shown in the following game. The room may be divided into two teams by numbering off by seat rows, or by sex, if the boys and girls are equally divided. First three rows are Blue team, second three rows form the Red team. A member of the Red team throws a dart at the map and must name the capital of the state the dart hits. If his identification is correct the Red team scores one point. The Blue team throws next. The team scoring ten points first wins.

Skills and Rules Related to Team and Individual Sports

Knowledge of team games and individual sports may be gained through games which use miniature playing courts or fields and correct game terminology. In all of the following games the players are divided into two teams. It is better to have a legal number of players necessary for the prescribed game and positions designated by the team captains. This procedure familiarizes the students with playing positions, duties of specific players and provides for turns as in the batting order for baseball, etc.

Each player, in turn, is given 8 darts and allowed to throw until a score or out is made. A coin may be tossed to see which team has the first turn. Two players should be chosen as score keepers. Regulation score pads may be used or dittoed or mimeographed sheets modified to suit the indoor game. The abbreviations used should be self-explanatory but modifications of rules are indicated.

BASEBALL[1]

H—Home Run
O—Out
F—Foul Ball
S—Strike

Colors for the divisions are suggested. Any available paint may be used.

[1] Modification of a game by O'Keefe, Patric and Fahley, Helen, *Education Through Physical Activities*, St. Louis, C. V. Mosby Co., 1949, p. 197.

Baseball target diagram:

RED S	GREEN O	RED T
BLUE H	BLUE B	BLUE F
YELLOW D	RED H / YELLOW S	—
F	BLUE O	H
ST	GREEN T	ST

B—Ball   D—Double (2 Base)
F—Foul   T—Triple (3 Base)
H—Home Run   O—Out
S—Single (1 Base)   ST—Strike

FOOTBALL

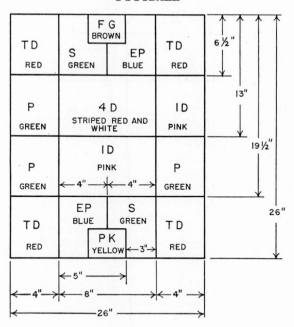

TD—Touchdown—6 points   EP—Extra Point—1 point
FG—Field Goal—3 points   1D—First Down—gets another throw if
PK—Place Kick—3 points   last dart hits this square
S—Safety—2 points   4D—Fourth Down—gives up darts
                               P—Penalty—Gives up darts

BASKETBALL

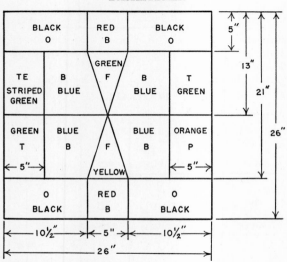

B—Basket—2 points
F—Free Throw—1 point
O—Out of Bounds—loses darts
T—Travel—loses darts
TE—Technical Foul—opposing team gets one throw
P—Personal Foul—opposing team gets two throws

SOCCER

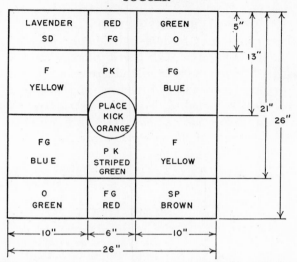

LAVENDER SD	RED FG	GREEN O	5"
F YELLOW	PK	FG BLUE	13"
FG BLUE	PLACE KICK ORANGE / P K STRIPED GREEN	F YELLOW	21" 26"
O GREEN	FG RED	SP BROWN	

←—10"—→←—6"—→←—10"—→

←————26"————→

FG—Field Goal—2 points SD—Successful Dribble—continues to throw
PK—Penalty Kick—1 point SP—Successful Pass—continues to throw
O—Out of Bounds—loses darts F—Foul—opposing team gets darts
Pl K—Place Kick—continues to throw

VOLLEYBALL

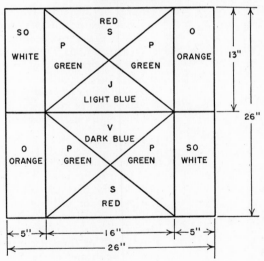

SO WHITE	RED S P GREEN P GREEN J LIGHT BLUE	O ORANGE
O ORANGE	V DARK BLUE P GREEN P GREEN S RED	SO WHITE

←5"→←——16"——→←5"→

←————26"————→

13" 26"

S—Service—gets second throw J—Juggle
P—point one O—Out of Bounds
SO—Side Out V—Volley—second throw

269

TARGET SKILLS

All of these games may be done individually on cork, plyboard, different types of ceiling or wall board. Storage space is an item to be considered. Vacuum darts will adhere easily to glass but will not stick to uneven surfaces. Plyboard must be painstakingly sanded and heavily coated with varnish or shellac. Metal darts will stick in any soft wood or heavy cork, but are taboo in most school systems because of the safety hazards.

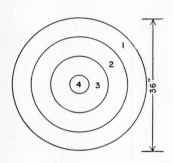

TARGET THROW

Use overhand throw
Inside: Bean bags, rubber or tennis ball
Outside: Tennis or softball

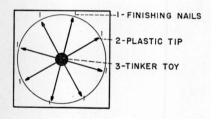

WHEEL OR DIAL WITH NUMBERS

Class is divided into two to four teams and each team numbers off one through ten. A selected leader spins the dial and asks a question. Teams may alternate or the first one who raises his hand after the number is called may answer the question. The questions may be made by the class or teacher on any desired subject. This is also a good party game.

PEG BOARD

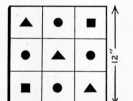

This board has holes for round, square, and triangular pegs. This game is suitable for the first and second grades and is excellent for children with poor manual coordination. Couples may make the play more interesting by counting the length of time it takes to get each peg in its proper place. The boards and pegs can be made in the manual training shop. The board should be painted a light color and the pegs dark red, blue and green.

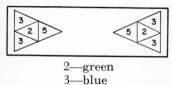

2—green
3—blue
5—red

FINGER SHUFFLEBOARD

Board may be painted on wrapping paper for table use or painted on wall or plyboard. Use checkers or bottle tops for pucks and thump with middle finger. Four may play as for horse shoes and the game point may be set by the players.

There are many pitching games that may be made at little expense. Rings may be tenniquoits of rubber or may be made in class from rope, tubing, or rubber fruit jar rings. Boards may be made to hang on the wall, stand as an easel, or lay on the floor.

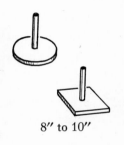

8″ to 10″

HORSE SHOES FOR INSIDE

Set stakes — feet apart according to age level. Use regular rules for pitching horse shoes. Small rope rings, 6 inches in diameter are suitable. The rings are secured with string and scotch or bicycle tape. If tenniquoits are used, lead washers should be imbedded in the bottom of the board for weight.

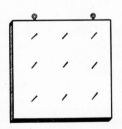

Eye screws
12″ x 12″
Finishing nails slanted
Fruit jar rings

WALL BOARDS

Floor boards that lie flat may be made any desired size from 12″ x 12″ to 36″ x 36″. Nails or dowel stakes are vertical. The size of the ring will be indicated by the size of the board and stakes.

SCHNOZZLE

Beaver board
Molding or lath frame
Dowel pin

Large numbers of children can be entertained in true carnival spirit while developing skill in pitching accuracy. Small rubber balls or bean bags may be pitched into waste baskets, nail kegs, syrup buckets or shallow cheese boxes. The bags or balls can be pitched through holes cut in boards in different shapes as circles, squares, triangles or half circles. Faces or any design may be painted on the board to fit the need. The underhand pitch should be used and the holes should be large enough to permit easy passage of the bag or ball.

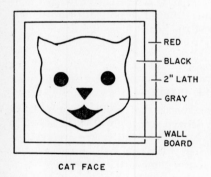

CAT FACE

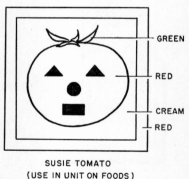

SUSIE TOMATO
(USE IN UNIT ON FOODS)

EASEL

PITCHING

Equipment. 4 rubber balls, 2″ in diameter or 4 bean bags, 5″ square filled with beans, peas, or gravel. Duck is the most durable of fabrics but colored Indian Head domestic is attractive and is available in all colors to tie in with the color scheme of the board.

Rules. The teacher or players can set the game. One point for eyes, two for nose and three for the mouth. It is suggested that the children set and draw their own pitching line and set up penalties for stepping over this line.

Other Suggestions

ALPHABET GAME

Individual letters painted on construction paper may be mounted on detail paper, heavy cardboard, or a very light wall or plyboard. Letters may be sawed out and painted a bright color. Number of sets depends on the size of the class, a different color being used for each team. Word lists are secured for each grade and teacher or pupil calls out the word. Children with the letter rush to the floor and the team that spells the word correctly first wins. Two cards should be made of letters that commonly appear twice in a word.

BOX HOCKEY

Players: 2–4

Equipment. The frame illustrated in the diagram consists of two sides, two ends, and a middle partition. It may or may not have a bottom. Dimensions of the frame are 31/2 feet in width, 7 feet in length, and should be made of 2 inch material. Other equipment needed includes a ball or piece of wood 2 inches in diameter and hockey sticks or any stick 3 feet in length.

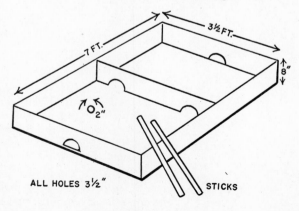

ALL HOLES 3½″   STICKS

Rules. The players stand on opposite sides of the box facing each other. Each player's goal is the hole at the end of the box on his left. The object of the game is to hit the ball through this hole with the stick. To start the game, the ball is placed in the groove at the top of the middle partition. The two players place their hockey sticks on the floor on opposite sides of the partition, raise them, and strike them together above the ball. This is done three times and after the third tap, the ball is hit. If the ball is knocked out of the box, it is put in play by tossing it on the floor of the box opposite the point where it went out. Resume playe after each score with a *face off.* Players may not step inside the box. One point is scored each time a player puts the puck through the hole in the end of the box. Game—5 points.

TIN CAN WALKERS

Cut two holes in each of two large tin cans. Run a string through each hole in each can and tie it together at waist height through both cans.

Use can to walk on.

STILTS

Use two 2 x 4 boards. Nail a foot rest block on each board about 10 inches from the floor. Use the stilts for balancing while walking with them.

BOWLING GAME

Take 10 one-quart cartons, round type, and paint each a different color. Make a half inch slit in top of each and insert ice cream paddles. Color each differently. Number each paddle. Place cartons four, three, two and one in a row like bowling pins. Tennis balls can be used and rolled various distances depending upon the grade. Various scoring methods can be used. Added scores are suggested.

HOOP OBSTACLE COURSE

Set up an obstacle course of boxes, draw parallel lines, etc. Paint a barrel hoop or make one from wire. Each pupil rolls the hoop over the course.

MARBLE DROP BOX

Paint a salt box. Cut a round hole in one end the size of a quarter. Teach pupils how to accurately drop five marbles, one at a time, into the box. The best scorer out of each five tries wins. A cigar box may be used in place of a salt box.

PUT A SPOOK IN A HAUNTED HOUSE

A box is decorated to look like a haunted house. Ghosts are made of white cloth with bean bag heads. Each ghost has a number written on her. If the first grader is able to give the correct number, he may throw the spook in the haunted house.

Santa Claus's sleigh or pack, the Easter Bunny's basket and other seasonal characters with their unique equipment may be used. A Jack-o'-Lantern toss game made from a scooped out pumpkin and played with numbered bean bags is also a good seasonal game.

Suggested Readings

Bancroft, Jessie, *Games* (Revised), New York, The Macmillan Co., 1937.

Champion, Paul, *Games You Can Make and Play*, Milwaukee, The Bruce Publishing Company, 1950.

Lawson, A. H., *Homemade Games*, New York, J. B. Lippincott Co., 1934.

Mason, Bernard and Mitchell, Elmer, *Social Games for Recreation*, New York, A. S. Barnes, 1932.

Morran, Ray, *Table Games—How to Make and Play Them*, New York, A. S. Barnes, 1939.

National Recreation Association, 315 Fourth Avenue, New York:
  No. 332, *Make Your Own Games*
  No. 258, *Outline Guide In Arts and Crafts*
  No. 277, *Homemade Play Apparatus*
  No. 272, *Table Football Game*
  No. 240, *A Folding Table For Table Tennis*
O'Keefe, Patric and Fahey, Helen, *Education Through Physical Activities*, St. Louis, C. V. Mosby Company, 1949.
Pelton, B. W., *How to Build Games and Toys*, New York, D. Van Nostrand Company, 1951.

Chapter 14

Camping and Outing Activities

Now I see the secret of the making of the best persons,
It is to grow in the open air and eat and sleep with the earth.
                                                        WALT WHITMAN

Increasingly camping and outing activities become an integral
part of the total school program. Ideally these activities can best
be stressed from grade 4 through 12, although some may be begun
at any time in the first three grades. Crowded class rooms and
gymnasiums often create a problem, yet every school in America,
whether it be located in a village or teeming city, has access to
wide-open spaces, city parks, or even school grounds where a
camping program might be initiated. Thirty-three cities operate
public school camps on a year-round basis. Over 500 more provide some kind of overnight, day, or weekend camping experiences to their students.[1]

Such camps have been launched primarily as a means of
supplementing and integrating indoor learnings centered around
verbalized theory with outdoor experiences focused around
learning to live in the out-of-doors. At these school camps where
there are no truant officers, no school buildings, no bells, no traditional school subjects taught by ordinary school teachers, no
detention rooms, no failures, youth is gaining experiences that
peak all others in ther educational lives.

Here children are discovering the real meaning of the words
nature, trees, hills, ferns, cooperate, share, contribute. Boys
and girls are living the thrill of seeing, touching, and smelling
the earth and all its magic, and experiencing the joy of hearing
the indescribable music of wind in the pine trees and of rushing
water. For many of these children camping and outing activities

[1] Irwin, Frank, *The Theory of Camping*, New York, A. S. Barnes,
1950, p. 153.

are opening up a world about which they have been told, seen in movies or on television, about which they dreamed, and which they are eager to learn. And here, too, children from rural areas are having the thrilling discovery of learning to play in the out-of-doors with others. City children are learning new skills in a new world of adventure.

What these 533 far-sighted American school systems have done in establishing school camps and outdoor education programs can and should be duplicated. The local community, the state, and the federal government all have vital roles to play in this new educational movement.[1]

Types of Experiences

Camping and outing activities possible for elementary schools include learning to:

1. Live independently of one's family.
2. Adjust and contribute to group life.
3. Care for and select one's own clothing according to the kind needed for changing weather conditions.
4. Make one's own bed and care for it.
5. Set and clear tables, act as host and hostess.
6. Plan group meals confined to a definite budget according to nutritional standards.
7. Make a number of different kinds of fires and cook over them.
8. Use a compass, tell directions from trees, sun, grass.
9. Lay trails.
10. Pace and measure distance.
11. Read maps, construct maps of local areas.
12. Hike long or short distances with the maximum of pleasure and the minimum of fatigue.
13. Know the sky above, the meaning of stars, and their use to man.
14. Understand and know as much as possible for one's age about birds, animals, trees, rocks, insects, and flowers.
15. Recognize harmful plants, trees, insects, animals.
16. Care and use of camp tools including axes, saws, ropes.
17. Enjoy out-of-door sports and games. The school does not

[1] Sharp, Lloyd B., "Basic Planning for School Camps and Outdoor Education," *The American School and University*, 1946.

provide such sports as ice skating, tree climbing, snow shoeing, wood chopping contests, fishing, canoeing, trapping.

18. Make useful articles from native materials—pans from clay, spoons from wood, pan racks from tree branches, hats from reeds.

19. Take an active part in some community project, such as protection from camp soil erosion, building an outdoor theatre, making a new road.

20. Build a number of different kinds of shelters.

21. Use the camp environment to its fullest extent.

22. Practice good health and safety habits.

23. Lashing.

24. Blanket rolling.

Classes in camping should be held out-of-doors for a double period or be the last scheduled in the day. The physical education class is the logical place for the inclusion of camping in the school program. Weekend or afternoon camping trips can easily be incorporated in the program, especially if teachers, as well as the students, are camping minded. Interested parents, local Girl or Boy Scout leaders are usually available as chaperones or assistant leaders.

The key person in the program is the teacher. If she is interested in learning as well as teaching others how to do camping and outing skills, and if she is enthusiastic, she will find ways to include and develop this as an integral part of the total school program. Camping experts in the community can and will offer valuable help, for camping-minded leaders are usually eager to sell outdoor education. Increasingly colleges and universities are requiring camp leadership training courses for major's and minor's in physical education.

The Role of Government

The local community, the state, and federal government all play vital roles in this new movement of outdoor education; each has much to contribute to its growth.

THE COMMUNITY

Through the public school camp or outdoor education program each local community may find a workable solution to the age-old problem of how to bring the community into the school program and vice versa, for the local school administrator will need the utmost cooperation of various community leaders in existing youth-serving agencies to work with him in planning the program. This group should form a committee aided by a school-camp expert to survey the local environment for suitable wooded areas for the program. Desirable land should be purchased, leased, or loaned by someone in the community. Perhaps there are abandoned C. C. C. camps nearby, or unused army barracks, or private or organizational camps available for off-season use. The local city park, some farmer's property, or even the most isolated part of the school grounds can be used for a camp site.

Plans should be made for the payment of the obtained land, for it must be determined whether the funds for the school camp are to come from the existing school budget, or raised by community drives carried on by both adults and youth, or the cost shared by the school and parents, or from gifts from interested citizens, or from the community chest fund. Valuable information concerning the costs of such a program per pupil should be carefully studied.[1] Plans also should include the number and kinds of permanent shelters to be erected. Representative groups from the parents, existing character-building agencies, school administrative and teaching staff, and pupils should make up another basic planning board to set up the objectives of the project, and to determine what existing school subjects which can best be taught out-of-doors from first-hand experience should be included in the program. The actual program made up from the selected subject areas, however, should be planned by the pupils who will attend the camp guided by their teacher, principal, and the school-camp expert. Other experienced camp leaders from the local areas along with the school-camp expert should conduct an in-service training program for the voluntary teaching staff at the camp or before the pupils arrive. Only those children and teachers who want to take part in the program should do so. Those choosing to remain at school should continue classes in the established curriculum. It is recommended that one entire class grade attend the camp with their regular teacher and experienced camp leaders. Other desired staff members should include a dietician, a nurse, and the specialized physical education teacher. Each class group should attend the camp for at least an

[1] Sharp, Lloyd B., "Basic Planning for School Camps and Outdoor Education," *American School and University*, 1946.

overnight period; preferably for a minimum of seven days. Ideally the camp should be operated the year-round and be opened for parents or civic groups during the year for recreational or educational purposes.

Each class group from grade 5 through senior high school should be given, in turn, opportunity to spend at least two weeks at camp during the school year and summer. Provisions might well be made for separate camps for boys and girls, although many opportunities should be provided for both groups to share as well as assume responsibility for the program. Community camps are recommended for smaller cities and rural areas.

School camps are only possible if the public can be told and sold on such a project. Although school administrators tend to believe that the public is a difficult group to whom to sell new ideas, such is not the case *if* the public can see the true value of what they are to buy. Americans traditionally have wanted the best education for their children; unfortunately, too often, they have been misguided or duped as to what is the best education. For the public to embrace a program of outdoor education and school camping will depend upon steady and reliable publicity as well as strong, patient leadership. Progress is made largely through change, which comes as a result of a pressure for something new; after the change is made, adjustment to it is paramount, as is an evaluation of its effectiveness.

The local community might well begin a program of outdoor education on a small scale and conduct it on the school ground or nearby areas. The establishment of the school camp will result from expert leadership, a carefully planned program, a sold public, and much hard work.

THE STATE

The state, whose function it is to provide rich educational opportunities for its citizens, plays a vital role in this new program. It can aid the local community by supplying needed leadership, encouragement, and publicity. The local voice must be heard and echoed by a strong state leader in order to gain the most support. Such a leader might be found in the officers of the Child Welfare Association, the Association of State Directors of Elementary Education, or any other existing powerful group in the State Department of Education. State financial aid might be secured in the form of grants, loans payable on easy terms, land grants, increased state taxations for education, or free use of existing state parts or forest reserves. The state should also pass permissive legislation, such as the 1944 Desmond Bill of the State of New York, giving cities and local communities the legal right to conduct school camps. The state, moreover, should help provide camp leadership training courses for teachers, realizing that if the traditional teacher goes into the program using her traditional teaching methods, the project will crumble. An ideal training course will be conducted in a camp by school camp experts. The program should be built around: (1) a study of the unique contribution camping makes to the growth of children, and (2) basic campcraft skills. The outstanding source of trained school-camp leaders at the present time is National Camps, sponsored by Life Camps, Incorporated. It is under the inspiring leadership of Dr. Lloyd B. Sharp, who more than any single person in America fathered the school camp movement. This camp leadership training center is located near High Point State Park in northern New Jersey. A six weeks summer session at National Camp carries 6 points of graduate credit for the master's or doctor's degree at Teachers College, Columbia University, New York City. New York State Teachers College at Cortland, Western Michigan College of Education, and George Peabody College stand high on the list of eighteen teacher training institutions that are expanding their services to include courses in school camping. Most colleges and universities offer one or more camp leadership courses which are open to interested students.

Since educational progress throughout America is determined by the amount and kind of experimentation that is carried out in each state and local community, each must ever encourage, stimulate, and endorse new experiments which will lead to educational improvement and progress. Since, as the poet reminded, poorly conceived innovations often fail, there is a dire need for much careful planning for school camping and outdoor education on both the state and local levels.

THE FEDERAL GOVERNMENT

Cooperation should be gained on the national level also for the establishment of school camps in the separate states and in local communities. Again powerful national groups should be enlisted to help provide publicity. The N. E. A. and other such educational groups, as well as the Departments of Child Welfare, Agriculture, Forestry, Interior, and Labor all have much to contribute. Low cost use of national parks or forest reserves or financial aid granted to states might be secured. Unused and discarded army camp supplies might be made available to state education departments, who could in turn supply local communities with these materials at nominal fees.

Outstanding leaders in the federal government have in the past given great impetus to the movement in the form of public recog nition, publicity, or endorsement. In this respect, Mrs. Eleanor Roosevelt has contributed valuable aid through public statements, school camp dedications, and newspaper column space. Although the American public does not seem to want federal control of education, even the average citizen is aware that some form of federal financial aid without increased federal control of education is needed to provide better and more equalized educational opportunities in this country. Consequently, the government can best serve school camping and outdoor education by providing and supporting it by some form of financial aid to carry on such a program.

This new educational movement which is snow-balling from the east to west coast and from our northern to southern borders is more than a present-day fad. As a means of providing rich and meaningful educational experiences, such a program has already proved to be an answer to many of our present education ills and problems. Today, far-seeing educators with this new program are helping children to grow as democratic citizens, skilled in basic tool subjects, and more aware of the wonderful world in which they live.

The Program

The program of outdoor education and school camping should be built around: (1) learning to live with others in the out-of-doors, (2) healthful personal and community living, (3) basic campcraft skills, (4) work experiences, and (5) conservation projects. Subject areas which have been found to be best taught, in part, in the out-of-doors through first-hand experiences are physical education, health education, science and nature, dramatics, music, arts and crafts, mathematics, local history, geography, English, as well as government or civics.

Program activities for 1949–50 at the Tyler Texas Public School Camp included:[1]

Intra-group evening programs
Felling, chopping, splitting wood
Conservation hikes
Learning how to use an axe, saw, wedge
Map and compass hikes
Trapping animals
Cabin clean-up duties
Construction—carpentry
Weather study
Making check dams
Making posted signs
Pottery
Fishing

Outdoor cooking
Planting trees, grass, gardens
Farm chores
Camp maintenance projects
Trail blazing
Logging
Visit to the school farm
Swimming
Visits to community places of interest
Scavenger hunts
Lard making
Milking
Soap making
Sketching

Camping and outdoor living skills which should be included in the school program of outdoor education can best be taught in wooded areas. However, the following may also be taught on the play field or on a vacant lot:

CAMPING AND OUTDOOR LIVING SKILLS

A. **Campcraft**
1. Knife-selection, use, care, whittling, safety measures
2. Use of axe, hatchet, cross-saw, selection, use, care; splitting, chopping, cutting down trees; safety measures
3. Use of saws, shovels, picks, hammers, safety measures

B. **Fire Building**
1. Fixing a fireplace
2. Selection of wood and common kinds of fires for outdoor cooking
3. Fire safety hints

C. **Outdoor Cooking**
1. Menu planning—selection according to daily nutritional standards
2. Packing for hikes and overnights
3. Care of food—refrigeration, protection, waste disposal
4. Types of outdoor cooking devices
5. Preparation and serving of food

[1] Donaldson, George, *School Camping*, New York, Association Press, 1952, pp. 114–115.

D. Hikes and Outings

1. Kinds of hikes
2. Where to go, what to do, what to take, and what to do when you arrive
3. Hiking games, pacing
4. Camp site selection
5. Camp making and breaking; tent pitching, ditching and striking
6. Bed rolls and sleeping bags
7. Packing a knapsack, personal needs[1]
8. Light camping equipment

E. Knotcraft and Lashing

1. Rope whipping
2. Square knots, sheet bend, bowline, clove hitch
3. Ways to use knots
4. Square, diagonal, sheer, continuous lashing
5. Things to lash

F. Nature and Wood-lore Conservation

1. Common plants, edible and poison[2]
2. Common animals—harmful and friendly
3. Common insects and snakes—harmless and harmful
4. Common birds
5. Knowledge of astronomy
6. Knowledge of common myths and legends concerning the heavens
7. Common fossils, minerals
8. Fishing, hunting, and trapping skills
9. Forestry conservation
10. Trail blazing, map reading, use of compass
11. Weather casting
12. Improvised shelter, equipment, and rustic construction[3]
13. Soil conservation

G. Informal Group Activities[4]

1. Group singing
2. Simple dramatics, including stunts, skits, hand puppets
3. Story telling
4. Games—active, quiet, folk, nature

[1] Boy Scouts of America, *The Boy Scout Handbook*, 2 Park Ave., New York.
[2] Gaudette, Marie, *Leaders Nature Guide, How To Do Nature Before She Does You*, New York, Girl Scouts of America, 1946.
[3] Jaeger, Ellsworth, *Wildwood Wisdom*, New York, The Macmillan Company, 1935.
[4] Harbin, E. O., *The Fun Encyclopedia*, Nashville, Abingdon-Cokesbury, 1947.

5. Crafts—nature, junk, rise of native materials, sketching and painting, and others suitable for camp

Skills taught in campcraft should well terminate in a day, weekend, or summer camping. Activities included in the program must be geared to the interests, needs, and capabilities of the children. Fourth graders may not be as keen about knotcraft as sixth graders; they may, however, be thrilled with going on a vagabond hike or learning how to fry eggs on a heated rock.

HIKING

A hike is a walk with a purpose. It is one of the best of all outdoor activities, for it builds physical fitness through vigorous use of the big muscles of the body. There are many kinds of hikes ranging from early morning bird walks to mountain climbing.

Teacher and pupils should plan together where they want to hike, what each will take and how it will be packed or carried, what kind of clothes, and especially shoes and socks, would be the best to wear, what to do on the way, how to walk on the highway, or through the forest, and what to do when the group reaches its destination.

Places to hike might include going to some local park, to a nearby lake or forest, to see some one's farm, to visit some place of local interest, to see the local zoo, or some camp nearby. Group singing or round-robin story telling will add to the fun along the way.

Gradually hiking distances should be increased as the pupils become more expert in covering more ground with a minimum of fatigue and more adept in seeing interesting treasures along the way. Cookouts can add to the joy of the hike's end. Simple meals such as fried bacon and egg sandwiches, carrot sticks, cocoa, and fruit are easily prepared and great fun to do.

Types of hikes suitable, some suitable for class time, others for longer periods:

1. *Nature Hike*—to collect, study, or see as many kinds of wild flowers, birds, insects, or animals as possible.
2. *Treasure Hunt Hike*—each squad is given a sealed envelope containing a list of cues leading to the hidden treasure. The first squad to find the treasure wins.
3. *Scavenger Hunt Hike*—each squad is given a sealed envelope containing a list of articles to be brought back to a certain spot in

a given time limit. The group which has found the most articles wins.

4. *The Lost Baby or Object Hike*—each squad searches for a doll hidden by the teacher or a squad.

5. *Exploration Hike*—a walk along back roads, through forests, or other places unknown to the children.

6. *Coin Flip Hike*—a coin is tossed in the air at every road crossing to see which direction the group will go.

7. *Star, Sun or Cloud Hike*—a trip to a hill to catch and hear legends about the stars, sun or clouds.

8. *Moonlight Hike*—a night's stroll to see and hear the beauties of night.

9. *Stream Hike*—the class follows a creek, river or stream as far as possible in a given time to see how it winds, turns, and changes.

10. *Trail Blazing Hike*—the class finds and clears a new trail or path.

11. *Compass Hike*—each squad selects a direction and hikes that way. The groups exchange news of their adventures upon returning.

12. *Walk Out-Ride Back Hike*—one group walks while the second one rides and vice-versa for the return trip.

13. *Overnight Hike*—the group hikes to and from the established camp where they will stay overnight.

What one wears upon a hike depends upon where he is going, when, and the kind of weather expected. However, a good general rule to remember is that old comfortable clothes are best. Blue jeans or slacks may be preferred by the group to shorts. Shoes worn must be appropriate with room enough in them for the hiker to wear one or two pairs of heavy socks. Both shoes and socks must be free from rips or holes. Sweaters, jackets, or flannel shirts can be tied around the waist, sandwiches wrapped in bandanas and tied to a stick carried over the shoulder will leave hands and arms free for easy rhythmic swinging a-tuned to easy rhythmic walking.

Hiking is one of the few cost-free physical activities left in our land. Children, who learn early the joy of strolling, seeing, and absorbing the beauty and wonder of life which ever surrounds them, can well be started on a life-long pleasurable hobby.

FIREBUILDING

Fire has many uses: to cook, heat, burn rubbish, and give off warmth. The appeal to fire is omnipresent among all peoples of the earth, for everyone, regardless of age, is drawn to it. Children can be taught how to use fire—the desire for this knowledge can be constructively channelled.

Types of wood best for cooking are:

1. For fast flames needed for boiling purposes use pine, spruce, balsam fir, red maple, basswood, or elder.

2. For even flames and coals needed for frying or broiling use the hickories, oaks, birches, sugar maple, white ash, eucalyptus, locust, beech.

Points to remember about fire building are:

1. Clear the ground around the area.

2. Use small match-size twigs, shavings, or bark for the foundation.

3. Add finger-size dry sticks laid crisscross or tepee-shaped over the foundation.

4. Have all wood ready before starting the fire.

5. Light the fire with the wind at your back remembering that fire needs air.

6. Build the fire by adding wood of graduating size.

7. Be sure the fire is out before you leave it; water is best to use.

TYPES OF FIRES

TEPEE FIRE

1. Teepee or Wigwam

Used for boiling purposes. Place the wood in a teepee formation.

CRISSCROSS

2. Crisscross

A slow burning fire best for frying, baking, or heat. Start with a foundation of tender. Make a crisscross of sticks placing larger ones at the bottom.

REFLECTOR FIRE

3. Reflector

A slow burning fire used for baking. Bank the wood against larger pieces of green wood so that the heat is thrown forward. Have the baker in place before the fire is lighted.

INDIAN FIRE

4. Indian Star or Lazy Man's Fire

A slow burning fire which can be used for heat, comfort, and slow roasting. Start with a teepee fire. Use long poles, which are pushed into the fire as their ends burn.

HUNTER-TRAPPER FIRE

5. Hunter-Trapper Fire

Used for slow boiling, stewing. Two heavy logs of slow-burning wood are laid parallel, with the narrowest end placed facing the wind. Sticks of green wood are laid across the two to be used for supporting pans. Start from a teepee fire which will catch other tinder laid between the two big logs.

BEAN HOLE FIRE

6. Bean-Hole Fire

Used for cooking a one pot meal. Fire is laid in a hole 1 foot wide and 8 to 10 inches deep. Green sticks are laid across the top of the hole for supporting pans.

BACKLOG FIRE

7. Backlog Fire

Used for frying and boiling. Fire is built in front of a backlog for boiling purposes. Coals are raked forward between the two logs for frying purposes.

SUGGESTED EASY TO PREPARE OUTDOOR MEALS

Menu planning will aid children to learn the essentials of good nutrition. Outdoor cooking is great fun! Roasting wieners, and burning marshmallows is easy, but real outdoor cooking takes skill. Simple one-pot meals are best for young children to cook.
Each meal should include:
Meat, fish, cheese, beans, or eggs.

Milk for cooking or drinking.

Some kind of fruit.

One vegetable, preferably two—one cooked, one raw.

Enriched bread.

If the children are to be at camp all day the three meals eaten there will include:

At least 1 pint of milk per person.

Fruit of some kind for two meals.

Cereals or enriched bread.

Two vegetables—one raw of the green leafy variety, one cooked.

One potato, in addition to the other vegetables.

Meat, fish, cheese, beans or eggs.

Butter or fortified margarine.

Various types of outdoor cooking will be fun to try.

TENNIS RACKET BROILER

Tennis Racket Broiler

Toasting bread on sticks is an easy beginner. Broiling meat on green sticks shaped like snow shoes is more advanced and more fun to do.

TIN CAN STOVE

Tin Can Stove

Pan broiling, frying, and stewing can be done individually over tin can stoves made from large size number 10 coffee cans with a V shaped wedge cut out of the end from which the lid has been removed.

FLAT ROCK COOKING

Flat Rock Cooking

On-a-rock cooking is sheer delight to all who can do it. A flat rock is laid across several smaller ones and is used as a frying pan.

BAKING BREAD DOUGH

Baking Bread Sticks

Green stick cooking is an art, but also one not difficult to master. Prepared biscuit dough to which water or milk has been added is twisted around the end of a green stick and slowly toasted.

GREEN STICK COOKING

Green Stick Cooking

Barbecues are more advanced but sixth graders could cook small pieces of meat this way. Two V shaped sticks driven into the ground support a green stick on which the meat is speared through. A special sauce is used for basting the slowly-turned meat. Pans and skillets are used, too, but are not as novel for the novice as the ingenious methods suggested.

PLANKING

Planking

Planking, a method of cooking meat on a board by reflected heat is great sport especially for all Hopalong Cassidy fans.

PARAFFIN BUDDY BURNER

Paraffin Buddy Burner

Buddy burners made of tuna fish cans, paraffin, and cardboard are fun to make and use. One end is taken from the can, paraffin made from old candle stubs is dripped around a piece of cardboard wound in a loose spiral with one end pulled out as a wick. The burner can be used inside a tin can stove. It is ideal for egg frying or cooking pancakes.

Suggested things to cook by any of the mentioned methods are:

Green Stick or Green Stick Broiler

Steak, bacon, ham, liver
Bread twists
Kebabs

One Pot Meals

Chili
Corn chowder
Hunter's stew
Baked beans
Chop suey
Ring tum diddy

REFLECTOR OVEN

Reflector Ovens or Backlog Reflectors

Biscuits
Cookies
Cakes
Corn bread
Muffins

Fry Pans

Any meat that can be fried
Eggs—scrambled, fried
Toasted sandwiches
Pancakes
Fried potatoes

Coal Baking

Potatoes
Roast corn
Apples

Bean Hole Cooking

Stews
Beans
Cooked cereals

Plank Cooking

Fish
Steak
Chops
Liver
Ham

Barbecue

Pork
Beef
Chicken

Recipes for types of dishes which are unique to camping follow.

CHILI CON CARNE

Serves 8   One Pot

4 tablespoons of grease
4 chopped onions
1-1/2–2 lbs. chopped meat
2 cans tomatoes
2 cans kidney or red beans
salt
pepper

Fry onions and meat until brown. Season. Add tomatoes and beans.
Add chili powder or 2 tablespoons of Worcestershire sauce

CAMPFIRE STEW

Serves 8   One Pot

1-1/2–2 lbs. of hamburger
3 teaspoons of grease
2 cans of concentrated vegetable soup
Salt
Pepper

Make and fry little balls of hamburger. Fry onions in bottom of the pan until they and the meat balls are brown. Pour off excess grease. Add the soup. Cover and slowly cook until the meat is thoroughly cooked.

SAVORY BEANS

Serves 8   One Pot

6 wieners or 2 slices of ham
1 can of whole corn
2 cans of baked beans
1 can tomatoes
2 onions
Salt
Pepper

Fry onions and meat together. Add tomatoes, corn and beans. Cook slowly.

FISH IN A BAG

Individual   No Utensils

1/4–1/3 lb. of fillet fish per person
Salt
Pepper
Small piece of butter
Heavy wax paper
Newspaper

Wrap the seasoned, buttered fish in wax paper so it is all covered. Wrap again in wet newspaper. Leave in coals 20–30 minutes, turning it once. Keep paper wet enough to cook the fish by steaming. Season with lemon, if desired. Tin foil may be used instead of wax and wet paper.

CORN ROAST

Individual   No Utensils

2–3 ears per person
Salt
Pepper
Butter

Soak corn in husks in water 2–3 hours. Put in good bed of coals. Cook 20–35 minutes. Eat with lots of butter.

PIONEER DRUMSTICKS

8 persons   On-a-stick

2 lbs. of chopped beef
1 cup corn flakes crumbled fine
2 eggs
Pepper

Salt
2–3 onions
16 rolls or pieces of bread
8 green sticks thumb size

Mix beef, seasoning, eggs and cornflakes. Wrap around stick end, making it long and thin. Cook slowly over fire, turning frequently. Slightly twist to remove it from stick. Serve on bread.

KEBOBS
Individual   On-a-stick

1/4 lb. round steak cut in squares about 1 inch square
    and 1/4 inch thick
Small onion peeled and sliced
Partially boiled potato, sliced 1/4 inch thick
2 strips of bacon cut in squares
1 fresh tomato cut in thick slices
2 rolls or sandwiches

Alternate meat, onion, bacon, potato, and tomato on stick, leaving little space between pieces. Repeat in same order. Sear quickly all over. Then cook slowly away from coals, turning frequently. For variation try alternate pieces of lamb and onion, or bacon and liver, or oysters and bacon.

LOTS-MORES
Individual   On-a-stick

3 marshmallows
3 squares of chocolate
green stick thumb size

Split marshmallows and insert chocolate. Toast slowly.

MARGUERITES
Individual   On-a-stick

2 marshmallows
2 soda crackers
2 walnuts, pecans, or peanuts

Split marshmallows and place nuts on top. Insert between crackers and toast.

POTATOES BAKED IN TIN CAN
Serves 8   Baking

8 potatoes
No. 2 tin cans, with wire handles
Punch holes in sides of can near top to insert wire handles
Heavy wax paper

Scrub potatoes well and wrap in wax paper. Put a layer of sand or dirt in bottom of can, then put in potatoes with sand and dirt in between so no potato touches another. Cover well. Pile coals around can. Moisten sand or dirt occasionally. Cook 30–40 minutes over hot coals.

KNOTCRAFT

Although there are hundreds of knots with a specific use for each, the elementary school child should learn to tie a few basic ones well and know the unique value of each rather than trying to master the art of knowing how to tie many. The pupil should learn that a good knot is one which is easily tied and untied and one which will serve its purpose. Knots are used for: (1) joining rope or cord or string, (2) stopping the end of the rope, string or cord from slipping, (3) looping, (4) securing, (5) shortening other ropes, and (6) holding articles.

The teacher should have each pupil bring a piece of clothesline or small rope, demonstrate how the knot is tied or show a picture if she herself cannot tie the knot and have the pupils copy the instructions step by step. The pupils should tie the knot on a chair or box or tree, and practice until the skill is mastered.

Learning how to tie the following knots and their use might well be included in the program.

1. Square Knot

Used for joining two ends of rope or to tie a bundle, bandage, or shoestring, as well as to make a longer rope from several short ones.

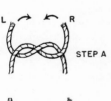

STEP A

STEP B

a. Take each end of the rope in each hand. Cross the end in the right over the end in the left, twisting it back down and up in front so that a single knot is made. The end you started with should now be in the left hand.

b. Take the end in the right hand and bend it over the left making a loop that lies along the knot already made.

c. Take the end in your left hand into the loop you have made.

d. Take hold of the knot on both sides, tighten by pulling the ends in opposite directions. To loosen, take hold in the same way and push toward the center.

SHEET BEND

2. Sheet Bend

Used to join two ropes of different size. Two ropes, one smaller, are needed.

a. Make a square knot with two ends. Take the end of the smaller rope (A) and cross it under the other piece of the rope at (B), then up and over the loop of the bigger rope at (C). This makes one end of the smaller rope on top and one underneath the loop of the larger rope. As you pull the knot tight the extra turn will secure the small end in place. The knot is completed after making the extra twist with the smaller rope.

3. Bowline

Used to make a loop in the end of a rope to slip over a hook or secure something to a post.

a. Take one end of the rope only but tie the other one to a tree or round object. Make a loop and judge the place where the knot will be. Let the rope lie in the palm of your left hand.

b. With the right hand, make a loop up and back of the fingers of the left hand, coming down in front, and catching the rope with the thumb as it crosses.

c. Slip your fingers out of the loop, take the end of the rope in the right hand with left thumb and finger. Pass the rope up from underneath to make a small loop.

d. Pull this end to make the main loop the size you want it, then pass the end in back of the standing part of the rope and back to the front and down into the small loop again so that it is beside itself.

e. Take these two pieces of rope in one hand and the main part of the rope in the other, pull the knot by pulling in opposite directions.

f. To make the loop around a tree or round object, pull around it before

BOWLINE KNOT

you pull through the small loop; pull tightly and proceed as in 1.

g. Try to tie the knot with one hand as sailors do but remember with even both hands you always should use just one end of the rope.

4. Clove Hitch

Used to tie something securely.

a. Take an end (A) around a tree or rung and cross it over its own part (B).

b. Take end around the tree or rung again and under the bend just made.

5. Slip Knot

Used to tether a horse, or attaching a rope to a bucket handle or for neck ties.

a. Draw end A (as shown in step a) around a tree or rung and make a small loop in it.

b. Bring A up behind and across the standing part of the opposite rope end as shown by D, then down through bight B, and then up around and down through bight B again (as shown in step b).

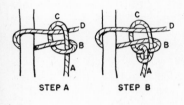

STEP A   STEP B

KNIFEMANSHIP AND TOOLCRAFT

Use of the knife can be taught to girls as well as boys. A Boy or Girl Scout knife is recommended. The pupils should be taught the parts of the knife, safety measures to use when opening and closing it, how to sharpen it, and how to care for it.

The group can be taught how to whittle useful articles from native materials including buttons, name tags, candle holders, letter openers, paper weights, lapel pins, napkin rings, knives, forks, and spoons.[1] How to make and use fuzz sticks and kindling wood might well be included.

[1] Ickes, Marguerite, *Arts and Crafts, A Practical Handbook*, New York, A. S. Barnes, 1943.

THE USE OF THE HATCHET AND AXE

1. The Axe

A hand axe is a good tool for general use. To use the axe properly, grasp the end firmly with the thumb around the first finger. Bring the axe down carried by its head and strike sharp direct blows on the wood. To cut a heavy log, strike diagonal blows, never cut square across. To fell small trees first clear the brush around it. Cut diagonally down the trunk and alternate this with blows up the trunk. To split a log, drive the axe into the wood, raise both together, striking on the edge of a block. Or lean the log against another log or block and strike in the center where it touches the block. Practice splitting larger logs into small pieces of kindling.

2. Axemanship

STEP 1

STEP 2

STEP 3

Teach your pupils to use first a light single headed axe. Have them first try to chop a log that is on the ground. To hold the axe, one grasps it easily, right hand with the palm under the handle of the axe and with left palm over the end. These positions are reversed for left-handed pupils. Balance weight easily and practice letting the axe fall from above your head on to the log. Then (1) raise the axe head with the right hand over your head while the left hand moves up slightly to the front. Keep elbows bent; (2) let the right hand slip down the handle to other hand as the axe falls but guide the handle and keep your eyes on the spot to hit; and (3) let the axe head do the swinging and the work, keep practicing until a rhythmic easy swing develops. Practice by cutting heavy logs before you begin chopping down small trees.

SLEEPING EQUIPMENT AND TENTS

1. The Bed Roll

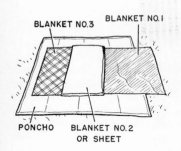

BLANKET NO.3   BLANKET NO.1

PONCHO   BLANKET NO.2
OR SHEET

Sleeping bags are ideal camping equipment. However, blanket rolls are simple to make and prove almost as good. First lay a poncho or raincoat on the ground. Place the first blanket on the poncho near the middle so that half of it extends out on the side. Place a second blanket on its end at the center of the first blanket so that it lies directly above the poncho. Lap each additional blanket over the underneath one. Fold a sheet and place it on last. Fold all blankets over in reverse order, 1, 2, 3, etc. Pin through all sides and the bottom with horse blanket pins. Snap the poncho over and tightly roll all the blankets into a bed roll. Carry the roll over the shoulder or on your back.

2. Tents

The simplest type of shelter is a poncho tent made by throwing a poncho over a rope stretched between two trees and pegging it down.

PONCHO SHELTER

A wall tent is also recommended. These can be bought at nominal cost at Army and Navy stores. The campers can be taught how to pitch and ditch these tents with skill as well as how to make wooden tables and chairs, brooms, waste baskets, and other housekeeping articles from native materials. Caches used for storing food and keeping it cool are also fun to make.

LASHING

This skill aids campers to use native materials for needed articles, for lashing is a way to bind sticks or poles together without nails. Its use serves to protect trees which would be damaged by nails and adds to the over-all rustic setting of camp. Since it requires only cord and sticks or poles, it is easily set up or taken down.

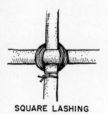

SQUARE LASHING

DIAGONAL LASHING

ROUND LASHING

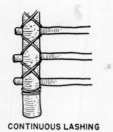

CONTINUOUS LASHING

1. Square Lashing

This type joins two sticks together at right angles.

A clove hitch is tied to the vertical stick at one end of the stick. Bring the standing part across the horizontal stick then around behind the vertical stick. Repeat until both sticks are secure.

2. Diagonal Lashing

This type joins two sticks at a diagonally formed X.

Tie a clove hitch around both. Make as many as six turns joining in one direction, then as many the other way. Finish off with a square knot.

3. Round Lashing

This type is used to join two short sticks to make one long one.

Tie a clove hitch around one then wrap the cord around both. Finish off with a square knot or half hitches.

4. Continuous Lashing

This type is used to make ladders or bridges.

Use small short sticks and long narrow ones. Notch the long sticks where the smaller ones will be lashed. Use a cord four times longer than the long sticks and start with a clove hitch at the end of the long stick at the middle of the cord, thus having equal lengths on either side of the long stick. The ends of cord will pull the knot tight as they come up from the under side of the long stick if the hitch has been properly placed. Next bring the cords around this knot over the first small stick following the lines of the long stick. Pull down and under, crossing the cord on the under side of the long stick. Pull cords over the second small stick, following the lines of the long stick by going under and crossing underneath the long stick, and coming up for the next one. The rope should always run parallel to the long stick on the top and cross on the under side. End with two half hitches and tuck ends of the rope under the last stick.

Lashing is fun to do. It is a useful camp skill, for the campers can learn to lash pieces of wood together to make coat hangers, mirrors, picture frames, tables, shoe racks, suitcase racks, a tripod for pots and pans, bridges, chairs as well as the other articles previously mentioned.

OTHER CAMP SKILLS

1. Finding Your Way

Knowing how to find one's way in the woods even when lost is a valuable skill. Teach pupils how to find their way by the sun, a watch, stars, tree moss, and a compass. At the same time introduce trail blazing by using trees, rocks, or grass. Map making and reading of places in the local community will be interesting to the students. Signaling by means of the Morse Code, or flags and smoke should also be included. Care should be taken, however, not to duplicate skill areas already covered by the pupils in their Girl and Boy Scout work. Use of a skill inventory sheet before classes begin will prevent any duplication.

2. Soil Conservation

The pupils can learn much in this area about our land and how to conserve our national resources. Learning how to build dams and understanding their use, soil erosion and correction, forest conservation, how to plant trees, shrubs, fruits, and vegetables will increase in each student a deeper appreciation of the soil and land which he lives. That we all live on the land is often forgotten in our modern world. Learning how to live simply in the out-of-doors, utilizing what is in one's environment, can add much to a child's wise use of present and future leisure time.

OUR AMERICAN HERITAGE

The early history of America is a brilliantly colored tapestry recording as its dominant pattern man's struggle to carve a unique life and culture out from a wilderness. Pictured there are Indians, explorers, trappers, prospectors, Pilgrims, lumberjacks, and ranchers—campers all, to whom life itself was camping—rugged human beings dependent upon the land, respectful of it, and seeing in it a good life. These dynamic pioneers, pushing beyond boundaries, blazing new trails into regions marked "unknown," left behind them rich sagas of daring courage. Today's youth needs to learn and appreciate this treasure.

Campfire programs should be built around folk themes. Songs and stories from all regions of the country will increase appreciation of other groups. Folk and square dancing, and party games will add much sheer fun. Games of low organization, including nature guessing games and contests in campcraft skills, will add much to build group unity and a spirit of good fellowship. Camping has no equal in bringing out and developing the best in youth and helping them find real adventure.

Suggested Readings

American Camping Association, *Marks of Good Camping: A Synthesis of Current Standards*, New York, Association Press, 1941.

Boy Scouts of America, *Scout Field Book*, New York, Park Avenue, 1944.

Clarke, James, *Public School Camping*, Stanford, Stanford University Press, 1951.

Donaldson, George, *School Camping*, New York, Association Press, 1952.

Girl Scouts, Inc., *Day Hikes*, New York, 1945, (#20-603).

Hammett, Catherine, *Campcraft A B C's for Camp Counselors*, New York, Girl Scouts, 1941.

Hammett, Catherine and Musselman, Virginia, *The Camp Program Book*, New York, Association Press, 1951.

Ickis, Marguerite, *Arts and Crafts, A Practical Handbook*, New York, A. S. Barnes, 1943.

Life Camps, Inc., *Extending Education Through Camping*, 369 Lexington Avenue, New York, 1948.

Manley, Helen and Drury, M. F., *Education Through School Camping*, St. Louis, C. V. Mosby Company, 1952.

Mason, Bernard, *Woodcraft*, New York, A. S. Barnes, 1939.

Masters, Hugh, "A Community School Camp," *Elementary School Journal*, January, 1941.

Mitchell, Viola and Crawford, Ida, *Camp Counseling*, Philadelphia, W. B. Saunders Co., 1951.

Nash, Jay B., "Why A School Camping Program?," *The Journal of Educational Sociology*, 23:500, May, 1950.

Rice, Rebecca, *Exploring God's Out-of-Doors*, New York, Association Press, 1934.

Shankland, S. C., *"The Need For Outdoor Education Today,"* *Bulletin of The National Association of Secondary School Principles*, 31:9–12, May, 1947.

Smith, Donnal, "Camping and Democracy," *Camping Magazine*, 46, February, 1951.

Studebaker, John, "Why Not A Year Round Educational Program?", *The Journal of Educational Sociology*, 22:8, September, 1948.

Vannier, Maryhelen, *A Manual For Camp Counselors*, Doctor's Dissertation, New York, New York University, 1948.

Wittenberg, Rudolph, *So You Want To Help People*, New York, Association Press, 1947.

Chapter 15

Restricted Programs for Atypical Children

No child should be excused from physical education classes because of a physical, emotional, or social handicap. Until recently, it has been the practice to allow the exceptional boy or girl to stay in the study hall or go to the library while his classmates had their physical education periods. Or, if the child were not too badly handicapped, he might have been allowed to be official score keeper during class athletic contests. Handicapped children need not and must not be mere spectators instead of participants regardless of their disability. For some, lying down resting is physical education, for still others playing cards or throwing darts is an activity which, when learned, may be the magic ticket that will admit them into peer groups. The unskilled child, if he is further handicapped by being physically crippled is, indeed, in for a lonely, isolated, miserable future. Children need to learn how to live successfully in our highly competitive society, how to mix with people, and how to use their leisure time wisely. Through individual help in corrective physical education handicapped children are increasingly being educated to face and recognize their limitations, and to learn how to work around them. They should be encouraged and required to learn how to play. Although no one group of children needs physical education more than any other, all groups must be included in the program.

Number of Handicapped Children

Out of 30,000,000 school children between the ages of 5–17. the following number have defects:[1]

    1. Cerebral palsy—106,560

[1] Stone, Eleanor and Deyton, John, *Corrective Therapy for the Handicapped Child*, New York, Prentice-Hall, 1951, pp. 7–9.

2. Post-poliomyelitis—62,160
3. Other orthopedic handicaps—168,720
4. Epilepsy—180,000
5. Rheumatic heart disease—300,000
6. Lowered vitality and delicate health—450,000
7. Blindness and partial sight—60,000
8. Deafness or impaired hearing—450,000
9. Speech, including cleft palate—1,500,000
10. Behavior problems—unclassified numbers

In addition to these figures the National Society for Crippled Children has estimated that between 25 to 50 per cent of all school children could be helped by better programs in corrective physical education.

Classifications

All atypical children fall into two classifications: (1) the physically handicapped, and (2) the socially handicapped. Within each of these groups each child differs widely, for no two of these children are alike any more than any two normal children are identical.

Types of physical handicaps among children are:

1. Postural defects
2. Crippling
3. Visual
4. Hearing
5. Speech
6. Respiratory
7. Cardiac
8. Nutritional

Types of social handicaps among children are:
1. Feeble-mindedness or mental retardation
2. Delinquents and/or those with remedial emotional maladjustments

Needs of Exceptional Children

The needs of exceptional children can be met if the following items are recognized:

1. Their needs are practically the same as those of normal children.
2. They can profit usually more from being with normal groups than from being segregated; they need to be encouraged to mix with those who are normal.
3. Normal children can often aid them toward helping them recognize their limitations and how to work around them. Although children are often cruel, they accept any handicapped child who

proves he has licked his problem and can do many other things better than they can.

4. Few children can be helped to any great extent who have been too sheltered by parents who have allowed them to remain helpless over a long period of time.

5. All children need to solve their own problems, to take and assume responsibilities, and to have good friends to help them become adjusted to their own limitations, environment, and society.

6. Work and play programs must be geared to their limitations, environment, and ability, yet be challenging enough so that the children can and will progress.

The Corrective Program

All exceptional children should be encouraged and required to take part in the physical education program, just as are all normal children. Points to be remembered by the teacher in charge of the corrective program are:

1. The program must be built upon the individual needs of each child.

2. The program must be conducted under the supervision and direction of a recognized medical authority.

3. The teacher should have specialized training to enable her to do this work successfully.

4. The parents' cooperation must be sought and secured.

5. The children follow the same procedures and rules in as many things as possible in normal groups, including class participation, costumes, and grading.

6. Classes for severely handicapped children should be kept small. The kind of defect will determine grouping possibilities. Malnourished children, for example, may have classes with those suffering from cardiac and respiratory defects.

7. Pupils should be assigned to special classes according to the amount of physical work permitted.

8. Complete records should be kept on each child including results of the physical examination, health history, observation and data from his family, reports sent to other staff members, a record of the child's behavior, and his personality rating.

9. The program should be set up in the gymnasium or chair-free room large enough for adequate equipment. The following minimum items are recommended:

   a. Stall bars
   b. Mats or mattresses with washable covers
   c. Scales

d. Individual benches without backs
e. Flying rings
f. One or more large triple mirrors
g. Bulletin boards
h. Individual exercise cards
i. Filing cabinet for records
j. Screens
k. Cots

Sample Letter Sent to the Family Physician

Cooperation with the family physician should be sought. The school doctor may wish to write to him and include a copy of the following blank to be filled out and returned, or this may be sent by the teacher.

DOCTOR'S BLANK
Physical Education Recommendations

Name of pupil_____ Sex_____

Address_____ School_____

Age_____ Grade_____

All pupils are required by the Education Law in this State to attend courses in instruction in physical education. Those pupils, who are unable to participate in the regular program because of defects, are required to take a corrective class built around their individual needs.

Special activities are provided for children who require special attention.

Check below the defect this pupil has according to your findings:

_____Postoperative   _____Defective posture

_____Convalescent   _____Flabby musculature

_____Cardiac   _____Foot defects

_____Malnutrition   _____Others

_____Chronic fatigue

Check below the activities you recommend that this pupil take part in:

_____Apparatus   _____Recreational sports (ping pong, shuffleboard, deck tennis)

_____Athletics

_____Stunts   _____Quiet table games

_____Rhythms (folk, square, social)   _____Corrective exercises

_____Swimming   _____Walking

_____Complete rest

This is to certify that I have examined __ _____ and recommended that he(she) participate only in these checked activities for a period of _____ weeks, _____ the whole semester.

Dr. _____   Phone _____

Date _____   Address _____

Additional comments or recommendations: _____

_____

_____

_____

Parent Cooperation

The teacher should gain the cooperation of the parents by helping them understand the importance of the corrective program. This may be done by a letter or by a personal conference. The teacher should explain the nature of the child's defect and what is being done to help him. A list of specific exercises recommended by the doctor to be done at home may be included in the letter to the parents, or be given to them at the conference.

Class Work

Corrective physical education classes must be as individual as possible. The program needs to be varied, stimulating, and challenging. Each pupil should be taught how to relax, how to do his own prescribed individual exercises, games and sports suitable for his handicap, and group activities. Additional work in the swimming pool is highly recommended for most cases. Whenever possible activities may be co-ed, for the social values of mixed group play are important.

A forty minute class period might include:

1. Relaxation   5 minutes
2. Light group exercises done to music   5 minutes
3. Individual exercises done to music   10 minutes
4. Group games   15 minutes
5. Relaxation   5 minutes

Exercises might well be incorporated into games whenever possible, or games made out of the exercises. Progress charts should be kept with the aid of the pupil. The teacher should also have individual talks with each child to help him gain insight on his own condition, and to encourage him to grow in skills. Together they might work out specific objectives toward which the pupil will work. This might be built around the following form:

STUDENT OBJECTIVE SHEET

IN

CORRECTIVE PHYSICAL EDUCATION

Name of student_____ Age_____

Defect_____ Grade_____

Things I want to accomplish this semester in Corrective Physical Education:

A. *Physical*

_____1. How to play one or more team games

_____2. How to play one or more individual games

_____3. How to do one or more social, folk, or square dance

_____4. How to increase my score on physical fitness tests

_____5. How to do one or more campcraft skill

_____6. How to swim

_____7. How to play longer without fatigue

_____8. How to gain or maintain the weight proper for my build

_____9. I can and will play after school

B. *Social*

_____1. Accept responsibilities

_____2. Cooperate more with others

_____3. Be more considerate of others

_____4. Be more tolerant of others

_____5. Be more able to see the humorous side of things

_____6. Get more people to like me

_____7. Get to know more about myself

Activities suitable for class work *upon the recommendation of a physician* are:

1. Games without equipment of the low organization type— (Simon Says, Still Water, I Spy, etc.)

2. Games of high organization or isolated sport skills (soccer, soccer dribble relay, basketball, basketball goal shooting, football, football throw for distance)

3. Dancing (folk, modern, square, social)

4. Marching and moving to rhythm

5. Gymnasium apparatus work (stall bars, balance beam, the horse, etc.)

6. Golf, clock golf, putting, miniature golf, driving

7. Handball, hand tennis

8. Tennis, paddle tennis, deck tennis

9. Ping pong

10. Volleyball, sitting volleyball, newcomb

11. Archery

12. Darts

13. Standard gymnastic stunts (cartwheels, somersaults, head stands, etc.)

14. Swimming, water basketball, diving

15. Hiking and camping

16. Shuffleboard

17. Box hockey

18. Quiet card games

19. Table games (checkers, pick up sticks, jacks, etc.)

20. Self-testing activities—basketball and baseball throws for distance and accuracy, etc.

21. Fly casting and fishing

22. Skating

23. Horseshoes

24. Wrestling

25. Weight lifting

26. Rope spinning

27. Tenniquoit

28. Tether ball

29. Conditioning exercises

Teaching Methods

Teaching-learning situations which are natural and desirable will be the most productive. Pupil self-direction should be a goal to be reached. Gradually more and more responsibility should be given him concerning his own use of class time. Each child should assist in building the program and have a strong voice in selecting activities. A relaxed atmosphere of adventure, and friendliness should permeate the room. All children should be trained to practice habits of safety in order that they may feel secure in what they are going without the fear of being hurt.

Specific Cases
POSTURE

Posture is a result of habit of the mind as well as of the body. There are many postures each person assumes rather than the static ram-rod one our grandparents considered ideal, for postures vary according to what one does. In general, good posture means proper body alignment in standing, sitting, and lying positions— all done with the minimum of fatigue, with ease, grace, and efficiency. In short. good posture is the maximum result produced by minimum of effort of the body when moving or held stationary. The body is properly balanced, the step is buoyant, the movements zip rather than drag, the head is erect rather than drooped, the hips are tucked under rather than thrust out, and the shoulders straight, not hollow. There are many postures the body assumes rather than one static posture, as each person moves about.

Causes of poor posture are:

1. *Poorly balanced diet*—muscles of the body are affected to such a degree that they do not have the power to hold the person up. An overweight child may have foot defects because the bones in his feet are not strong enough to support his body correctly.
2. *Environmental conditions*—poor lighting affects the posture habits of the child trying to do homework, as does a sagging bed mattress or the use of a large pillow.
3. *Rapid growth*—because different parts of the body may sometimes develop at faster rate, the child may slump. This is often true of adolescent girls who develop large breasts at an early age.
4. *Fatigue*—weary children droop because tired muscles are unable to hold the body in the best position. This fatigue may be the result of insufficient sleep, rest, food, and exercise.
5. *Mental and emotional tensions*—worry, strain, lack of security, fear, feelings of inadequacy, all tell on the bodies of their victims.
6. *Vision and hearing*—these defects sometimes cause one to assume incorrect body movements in order to see and/or hear what is going on in the world. Fixed habits of holding the head to one side or craning the neck forward may result.
7. *Structural and orthopedic defects*—some children are born with

non-remedial defects, such as a hunchback or short leg, others may acquire defects from accidents.

Types of Posture Defects

Three types of posture defects are the most common: (1) scoliosis or curvature of the spine, (2) lordosis or hollow lower back, and (3) kyphosis or round shoulders. Many deviations of a functional nature can be corrected, whereas defects due to a structural cause are difficult to correct by means other than surgery.

Posture Examinations

Posture examinations for elementary school children should be conducted wherever possible by an orthopedic specialist or a medical doctor. Serious defects in young children can be corrected more successfully than those found among secondary school students. The following suggested form may be used by the examining physician:

ORTHOPEDIC SCREENING EXAMINATION

————————————School

Name——————————————   Address—————————————

Age———————————————   Phone——————————————

Grade—————————————   Sex———————————————

Weight————————————   Race——————————————

Height——————————————

Body Type
1. Short and stocky ( )
2. Long and angular ( )
3. Athletic, broad shoulders and narrow hips ( )

Gait
Normal ( )
Abnormal ( )

Remarks:—————————————

Legs
Normal ( )
Bowed ( )
Knock-kneed ( )
Hyperextended ( )
Knee-caps normal ( )

Remarks:—————————————

Feet
Longitudinal arch
Normal ( )
Very low ( )
Very high ( )
Fallen ( )
Callouses ( )

Remarks:—————————————

Feet

Transverse arch

Normal ( )

Very low ( )

Very high ( )

Fallen ( )

Callouses ( )

Remarks:————————

Arms and Hands

Normal ( )

Deformity ( )

Bitten nails ( )

Tremors ( )

Remarks:————————

Posture

Good ( )

Superior ( )

Fair ( )

Poor ( )

Remarks:————————

Chest

Normal ( )

Hollow ( )

Deformity ( )

Remarks:————————

Toes

Normal ( )

Hammer ( )

Overriding ( )

Athlete's foot ( )

Corns ( )

Callouses ( )

Remarks:————————

Ankles

Normal ( )

Pronated ( )

Supinated ( )

Remarks:————————

Spine

Normal ( )

Kyphosis ( )

Lordosis ( )

Scoliosis ( )

Remarks:————————

Shoulders

Normal ( )

High (both) ( )

Low (both) ( )

High (one) ( )

Low (one) ( )

Winged ( )

Remarks:————————

Recommendations   *Describe*

1. Corrective exercises————————————————————

2. No correction needed—————————————————————

3. Condition not correctable————————————————

4. Rest————————————————————————————

5. Improved nutrition————————————————————

Name of Physician————————————————

Address————————————————————

Date————————————————————————

Records such as the above are only functional when used. The teacher in charge of the adaptive program needs to have a conference with the examining physician, the parents, and the pupil as soon after the examination as possible. A remedial program based upon the findings and recommendations made by the medical authority should be started as soon as possible.

Activities selected for the student with poor body mechanics due to functional reasons, may be learned from any course of study used for the other children.

Those selected for students having difficulties stemming from structural defects (lordosis, kyphosis, or scoliosis) may include the following:

1. Lead up games to basketball, football, softball, and volleyball
2. Speedball
3. Soccer
4. Tennis (regular, deck, paddle, hand)
5. Hand and Indian wrestling
6. All types of dancing except acrobatic tap
7. Individual stunts
   a. Cartwheel
   b. Head and hand stands
   c. Push ups
   d. Chinning and bar work
   e. Rope climbing
   f. Animal walks (crab, centipede, duck, and elephant)
   g. Human croquet
   h. Leapfrog
8. Hiking, camping, fishing, and bait casting
9. Archery
10. Golf (ten-pin, clock, regular)
11. Relays
    a. Throwing
    b. Passing
    c. Receiving
12. Recreational swimming

The Feet and Ankles

Defects of the feet and ankles include:
1. Flat feet

2. Weak feet
3. Ankle pronation (turned-in foot)
4. Ankle supination (turned-out foot)

Many parents and teachers have a mistaken idea that the child will outgrow a foot deformity or walking habit. This is rarely true. Children who complain of aching feet and legs and who quickly turn their shoes over to the sides should receive corrective devices to alleviate difficulties. Specially built shoes, arch supports, and ankle supports may be advisable.

Corrective exercises, along with instruction concerning proper shoe fitting, foot care, proper methods of weight bearing, and means of relaxing and refreshing tired foot muscles, can be most beneficial.

The adaptive program should be a broad one containing almost the same type of activities found in the regular program. Relays which involve picking up marbles with the toes, or moving objects with the feet as well as track and field events are especially recommended. However, those which call for heavy landing, or sudden twists and turns can be dangerous and should not be included. Aquatics are highly beneficial.

More serious foot defects, such as a shortened Achilles tendon or heel cord, rigid flat foot, as well as others due to structural causes, often limit participation in active games. If bearing the weight is painful, table and quiet games are more suitable.

Suggested activities for those having more serious defects include:

1. Foot marble games
2. Croquet
3. Bowling (lawn, duck pin, regular)
4. Shuffleboard
5. Tether ball
6. Simple rhythmical activities
7. Stunts and self-testing activities on mats and apparatus
8. Archery
9. Swimming, boating
10. Bicycling
11. Camping, fishing, fly casting

HEART DISEASE

Organic and functional heart disturbances are relatively common among young children. Rheumatic fever is more serious among school youngsters than has been formerly believed, for it often damages the heart of its victim. Even in lighter cases it is often referred to as the disease which is seldom cured, and as the disease that licks the joints and bites the hearts of children. Repeated attacks often follow lowered resistance and extreme fatigue. Over 70 per cent of all children suffer some degree of heart damage.

Signs and symptoms of the disease are: swelling, temperature, increased breathing rate, pallor, listlessness, irritability, frequent nosebleeds, and often tenderness and swelling in the joints of the body. Some cases are so slight that parents thinking their child is just hot, tired, and cross fail to call the doctor or even to put the child to bed. Leakage of the heart or heart murmur due to the toxins of the disease and fever are the result of both mild and severe attacks, although the chances of serious heart damage are greater in the more serious cases. No known cause of the disease has been found as yet. No child can be immunized or protected against the malady and to date no specific cure has been found for it. All children are potential victims of the disease.

Restricting these children entirely from any kind of physical activity can cause negative emotional reactions. Children want and need to play with others; repeated warnings and threats from parents can produce harmful fears. Rather, the child should be taught activities in which he can safely participate, made aware of fatigue signs, and urged to drop out of activity when he wishes. The family physician needs to recommend not only the kind of activity to be played, but also the amount advisable.

Suggested activities from which the physician could make recommendations include:

Archery	Mild roller skating
Circle games	Rope spinning
Bag punching	Social dance
Croquet	Swimming and light water games
Camping	Shuffleboard
Fishing, hiking, hunting	Ping pong
Juggling	Paddle tennis
Horseshoes	Ring toss
	Volleyball

DEAF AND HARD OF HEARING

It is claimed that one out of every ten persons in our society has hearing difficulties or is completely deaf. Special schools are provided for advanced cases, but the majority of those affected are enrolled in public schools, or mingle with normally-hearing members of our society. Lip-reading instruction, voice training, hearing aids, and proper emotional channelling have aided afflicted persons.

Since children suffering from hearing impairment often isolate themselves from others and thus develop needless feelings of fear, frustration, and insecurity, normal urges for activity must be re-emphasized and directed. These individuals might well take part in practically all the activities in the regular program. Individual stunts, such as push and pull ups, gymnastics, the usual athletic games offered to other pupils, and individual sports, such as tennis, archery, badminton, and deck tennis, are recommended. Because the sense of balance may be damaged, rhythmical activities may offer too much of a challenge to any child who has not had many opportunities to play or develop good coordination. Social dancing may gradually be included in the program.

BLIND AND PARTIALLY SIGHTED

Special schools are provided for those totally or partially blind. Although the number of children attending public schools who have serious eye difficulties is small, there are some known cases. The physical education program for these children should stress good body mechanics, the development of courage, and happiness. Individual activities, such as body building stunts, self-testing activities, and camping activities, are recommended for the upper elementary group. Social, folk, and square dances can add much joy to the lives of these children along with games of low organization, simple stunts and self-testing activities.

POLIOMYELITIS OR INFANTILE PARALYSIS

This disease, believe⌐ ⌐ be caused by a filterable virus which attacks the spinal cord ι   ⌐rve centers, is often a crippler of young and old alike. Me   ιuthorities now have found that although many persons w   have contracted the disease are paralyzed as a result, still mɔre recover from it without any or few bad effects. In fact, it has now been discovered that many persons have had the disease in a mild form and have, consequently, built up an immunity due to repeated exposure to small virus doses. Some few people may even have a natural immunity.

Children crippled from the disease and who are able to be in school should be assigned to classes in physical education. Those who have mild defects may well have classes with normal children. Those wearing braces, using crutches, or who are in wheel chairs may be assigned to the special corrective class.

Although programs in muscle re-education for these children must be built almost entirely upon specific exercise prescribed by medical authorities, the child can often receive great benefits from functional activities found in sports and games. Recreational activities high in carry-over values need to be stressed.

The victims of this disease above all need to learn to do things for themselves. They should never be waited upon or pampered. They should mingle with normal children as quickly and as much as possible.

Suggested activities for those in wheel chairs include:

Table games	Card games
Darts	Archery
Bait and fly casting	Swimming

Activities suitable for those wearing leg braces, or using crutches include:

Archery	Horse shoes
Shuffleboard	Individual stunts and self-testing activities
Camping and outing	
Swimming	Tether ball
	Bait and fly casting

Activities suggested for those having paralysis of one arm are:

Social dancing	Swimming
Running and other relays using the legs	Individual stunts and self-testing activities
Camping	Roller skating
Rope jumping	Hiking

CEREBRAL PALSY

Brain injured children, the victims of cerebral palsy, often have keen intelligence. Authorities claim that approximately 60,000 out of the half million children affected are highly educable. Formerly, many persons believed that many of the children were feeble-minded because they looked that way. We now believe that if the child is mentally capable of learning, is emotionally stable, and can get around well enough without a special attendant, he will be better off in a public school than in a special one. Often when cerebral palsied and other exceptional children are too carefully shielded by their parents they become spoiled and maladjusted. For these children especially the value of attending a public school is great.

Types of cerebral palsy most common include: (1) the *spastic*, which makes up the largest number, (2) the *athetoid* which is characterized by involuntary, uncontrollable, jerky movements and which makes up between 25 to 30 per cent of all cases, and the (3) *ataxic* which is characterized by disturbance in balance and posture, inability to control direction, and proneness to perform a multiplicity of eye movements and which makes up 5 to 10 per cent of all cases. Muscle rigidity and tremor often is found in all three types. Speech disorders and seizures are also common. Deafness is found in some cases of the athetoids.

Children who have cerebral palsy often possess intensified fears of falling, repeated failure, and resulting frustration. Timidity, self-consciousness, and resentfulness may be marked. Many are courageous, happy, and well adjusted, especially if they have had friendly, determined, patient parents. Most of those able to be in school have contributed greatly to the school in the way of spirit and talent.

The teacher needs to explain to all physically normal children and adults the nature of the child's defect, enlist their cooperation to accept him, and help him to help himself. Consideration should be the right of this pupil, just as it is for all others.

The child, if his condition is not too serious, may well be placed with a class of normal children. Since games are the normal outlet of all children it is important for the exceptional child to receive special aid in learning to do a number, or even a few, with average or above skill. Play activities should be adapted to meet the pupil's own limitation. Highly competitive games and relays need to be avoided, for under stress the child may be hurt more than helped.

Those children suffering from more serious injuries should be segregated from the group of normal children and placed in special corrective classes. However, they may well be assigned to classes in which are found those with heart, posture, or other defects previously mentioned. Games stressing balance, timing, and relaxation should be included in the program.

The teacher at all times needs to work not only with the doctor but also the parents. Special exercises recommended by the physician must be carried on at home. Parent training, in the case of the cerebral palsied child, is often almost as important as pupil training.

Suggested activities other than corrective exercises and techniques in relaxation include:

Simple folk dances	Simple singing games
Social dance	Camping and outing
Rhythmical activities	Games of low organization
Simon Says	Horse shoes
Yo-yo or Hi-Li	Shuffleboard
Going to Jerusalem	Target throwing
Swimming	Rope skipping

EPILEPSY

A pupil suffering from epilepsy has the same desires, interests, and drives for play as any other child. But, unlike others, he is faced with the great problem of living in a society or group where his affliction is met with great prejudice, ignorance, superstition, and fear. Even the word epilepsy carries great stigma. Fear of rejection from the child's peers and adult associates is constant and may be greatly magnified.

Epilepsy is caused by irritative injuries to the brain. The specific symptoms depend upon which part of the brain has been irritated. The symptoms vary from seizures lasting only a few seconds (Petit Mal or "Little Sickness") to those by twitching and convulsions in which the person becomes unconscious (Grand Mal or "Big Sickness").

Accurate statistics on the number of cases are not available, due primarily to concealment and stigma. It is, however, a major health problem, for from the standpoint of numbers, it occurs as frequently as active tuberculosis and diabetes, and four times as frequently as infantile paralysis.[1] Some medical authorities now

[1] International Council on Exceptional Children, Special Committee on Epilepsy, "Education for All American Children, Do We Really Mean It," 130 North Wells Street, Chicago, Illinois.

state that one out of every 100 persons in the United States has some form of epilepsy.

Children, whose seizures are mild, may and do attend public schools. Those with more serious difficulties are in special classes in public schools, or in private schools. Afflicted persons are educable, many are extremely intelligent, but a few are feeble-minded and non-educable in the usual sense.

Increasingly medical authorities are turning their attention to epilepsy. The new drugs dilantin, tridione, paradione, mesantoin, and phemerone have been found to be most effective; proper use of these medications have reduced the number of seizures in about one half of the cases. Diagnostic techniques are being improved constantly. The electro-encephalograph, a new instrument for measuring electrical impulses of the brain, has proved to be of great diagnostic value.

If the epileptic child is in school he can be helped by understanding teachers who can help the other teachers and pupils to realize that, with the exception of a possible seizure, the child is normal in other ways. Should a seizure occur the teacher can help the child by not showing fear, horror, or repulsion at the sight. By setting this pattern the pupils will copy, the teacher can then explain to the others that Johnny or Mary is having an attack which does not hurt him, that he is temporarily asleep or unconscious and when he wakes up he will not even know what happened but will be very tired. The child, after the attack, should be taken to the first aid room and be allowed to sleep or rest until he wants to get up. When he regains consciousness following a seizure, the first sight that he beholds should not be a circle of classmates and the teacher standing over him terror-stricken. During the seizure the teacher should place a tightly-rolled handkerchief between the child's back teeth, and place him on the floor where he cannot injure himself from convulsive reactions.

Epileptic children placed in school with normal children must be under the care of a physician, who should work closely with the physical education instructor in selecting activities suitable for them. Since they rarely have seizures while engaging in play activities, group participation with the normal should be encouraged. Activities which call for concentration might well be stressed. The controlled epileptic may benefit greatly from competitive sports and team relays which require physical conditioning and much concentration. Swimming, rope climbing, and other activities in which the child would be in danger if an attack might occur must be avoided at all times.

Suggested activities include as many as possible which other children do, and increased rhythmical activities calling for concentration, such as learning intricate tap, social, or folk dance steps.

LOWERED VITALITY

Children who are underweight, overweight, anemic, or who have had operations, rickets, tuberculosis, or other chest ailments fall into this group. All should be given modified school programs, little if any homework, and few responsibilities in both the home and school. Regular physical check-ups, an increased balanced diet, sleep and rest, and proper amounts as well as kinds of exercise should be recommended to the pupil and parents by the teacher and the physician. Allowing the pupil to rest or sleep during his physical education class may be for this person the type of physical education he most needs. However, the child should also learn quiet games and take part in modified sports as a part of this program.

Suggested activities include:

Archery
Bait and fly casting
Building games
Hiking
Camping and outing
Games of low organization
Marbles
Singing games

Jacks
Tables games, such as checkers, pick up sticks, etc.
Table card games
Ping pong
Self-testing activities
Social, folk and square dance
Swimming

OTHER DEVIATIONS

Other deviations of school children include:

Diabetes
Birth injuries
Congenital deformities
Speech defects
Hernia
Emotional disturbances

Each child requires individual attention. Recommendations made by the physician concerning the type and amount of physical activity best suited for each pupil must be followed to the letter by the teacher. Whenever possible the child should be placed in classes with normal children.

Physical education has much to contribute to the enrichment of the lives of all children. No child with defects need be restricted or denied the opportunity to learn how to play skillfully, or the joy of playing with his classmates and friends. In as much as possible, afflicted children should play the same games as their peers, but the teacher should have the approval of a physician of the suggested individual program for each such child in her group.

Suggested Readings

Drew, Lillian, *Individual Gymnastics*, Philadelphia, Lea & Febiger, 1935.

Everhardt, F. H. and Riddle, Gertrude, *Therapeutic Exercise*, Philadelphia, Lea & Febiger, 1947.

Hansson, K. G., "Body Mechanics and Posture," *Journal of Health, Physical Education and Recreation*, 16:549, December, 1945.

Karpovich, M. P. E. (originally by Schneider, E. C.), *Physiology of Muscular Exercise*, Fourth Edition, Philadelphia, W. B. Saunders, 1953.

Kelly, Ellen, *Teaching Posture and Body Mechanics*, New York, A. S. Barnes, 1949.

Lee, Mabel and Wagner, Miriam, *Fundamentals of Body Mechanics and Conditioning*, Philadelphia, W. B. Saunders, 1949.

Nash, Jay B., *Physical Education: Interpretations and Objectives*, New York, A. S. Barnes, 1949.

Neilson, N. P. and Cozens, F. J., *Achievement Scales in Physical Education Activities for Boys and Girls in Elementary Schools and Jr. High Schools*, New York, A. S. Barnes, 1934.

Rathbone, Josephine, *Corrective Physical Education*, Fourth Edition, Philadelphia, W. B. Saunders, 1949.

Stafford, George, *Preventive and Corrective Physical Education*, New York, A. S. Barnes, 1928.

Stone, Eleanor and Deyton, John, *Corrective Therapy For The Handicapped Child*, New York, Prentice-Hall, 1951.

Chapter 16

Intramural and After School Activities

Class Competition and Tournaments

Competitive class tournaments are suggested for grades, squads, teams, and individuals. Basically and in itself, competition for children is good if conducted under the proper conditions of good leadership and too much stress is not placed upon winning. Children like to compete, to match and test their skill with others. However, games and athletic activities best suited for their own age groups must be selected for competitive purposes. Types of competition possible are: (1) Elimination Tournaments, (2) Winner-Loser Tournaments, (3) Ladder Tournaments and (4) Round-Robin Tournaments.

ELIMINATION TOURNAMENTS

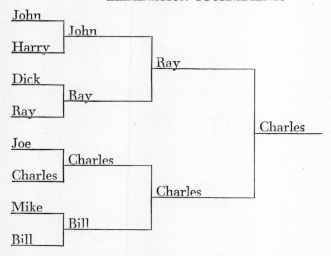

If the original number of contestants is a perfect power of two, no modification of this diagram is necessary. When the number of contestants is not a perfect power of two, byes are added until this is reached. The number of byes should equal the difference between the number of competitors and the next higher power of two. When fifteen are entered there will be one bye (16—15=1) etc. The number of byes should be divided so that one half of them appear at the top of the drawing and the remaining half at the bottom.

WINNER-LOSER TOURNAMENT

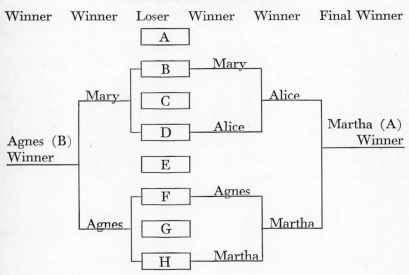

The principle for adding byes in this type of tournament is the same as in the elimination tournament. Winners move out to the right of the chart: losers move out to the left in the second round, and winners continue to move out to the left or right in all continuing rounds.

LADDER TOURNAMENT

Individuals or teams are arranged in ladder formation. Any player may challenge another player directly above. If the challenger is successful in defeating the opponent, his name takes the place of the defeated team, and vice versa. The final winner remains in the first position at the completion of the tournament.

Team 1
Team 2
Team 3
Team 3
Team 4
Team 5
etc.

ROUND ROBIN TOURNAMENTS

In this type of competition the revolving column is the simplest for pairing opponents. Numbers are given to teams or individuals. Bye is used in the place of teams or individuals if there is an uneven number of competitors. Pairing of competitors is done by placing them in two columns. Once teams or individuals are given a number; once the numbers appear on the tournament chart, that order must be maintained. Competitors are arranged in the following manner:

1 Jack	bye Ray
2 Agnes	7 Peggy
3 Martha	8 Bill
4 Alice	9 Catherine
5 Harry	10 Greg
6 Charles	11 Betty

Players are moved either clockwise or counterclockwise to meet their opponents. If there is a bye it remains stationary, each number jumping over it to the next place:

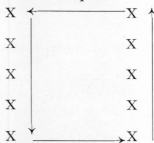

One fewer round is played than the number of teams or individuals entered. The pairings and series for a round robin tournament for eight teams are given below:

First Round	Second Round	Third Round
1————8	1————7	1————6
2————7	8————6	7————5
3————6	2————5	8————4
4————5	3————4	2————3

Fourth Round	Fifth Round	Sixth Round	Seventh Round
1————5	1————4	1————3	1————2
6————4	5————3	4————2	3————8
7————3	6————2	5————8	4————7
8————2	7————8	6————7	5————6

The pairings will be different in each round. The team winning the most games is declared the winner. The above procedure may be followed for any number of teams if a bye is used for an uneven number. When all players have played each other in each round, the tournament is completed.

TYPES OF COMPETITION SUITABLE FOR CHILDREN

Suggested games and sports for tournament competition for young children include:

Athletic games—(Soccer dodge ball, kick ball, newcomb, base football, touch football for grade 6, circle goal shooting, softball, etc.)

Hopscotch
Jump rope
Kicking soccer balls for distance
Kite making and flying
Marbles
Relays of all kinds
Running races
Stunts and self-testing activities (individual)
Target throws

CLASSIFICATION OF PLAYERS

Intramural activities are those physical activities conducted between groups of students within one school. A successful program depends upon equality between competing teams or individuals.

It is advisable to classify students according to a plan which includes the factors of age, height, weight, and sex. For safety reasons, boys and girls should be separated for most competitive sports after ten years of age, for boys at this age tend to surpass girls in strength, flexibility, endurance, and speed. However, because of social values inherent in team play opportunities should be provided for boys and girls to be members of the same team as many times as possible during each semester.

Younger children of primary age should be classified in different groups according to their capacity to enter into different levels of graded activities. Physical examinations and skill tests are the best way to determine this capacity.

Individual players may be classified for all competitive events according to age, height, and weight or a combination of these factors.

The teacher, aided by squad leaders, might well select team members, who in turn will elect their captains. This provides for a more reliable equalization of team skill, for children tend to chose their best friends rather than skillful players. Often the class ugly duckling or motor moron is either left out or is usually the last one chosen. Children, like adults, want to be first; it is ego damaging to always be last.

Another suggested way for selecting teams is for the group to select the needed number of captains. These chosen leaders stand facing the class, who will count off according to the number of captains. As each one calls out his number he goes and stands behind the captain having the corresponding number. This method is often superior to having circled groups number off in teams, for some pupils will be wise enough to count ahead and change places with one or two others in order to be on the desired team. Another method is selecting captains by pupil vote, having each player draw a number out of a hat, and stand behind the numbered captain drawn.

If the major emphasis is placed upon fun rather than winning the children will gradually select the method which to them seems fairest for classifying and forming teams. They should be encouraged to experiment with as many methods as possible. We learn to know what we want by finding out from experience what we do not want. Experience is not only the best teacher, it can also be an ideal way for learning how to make good judgments.

CLUB ORGANIZATION

Pupils may be organized into clubs for competitive purposes. Class, grade or team and home room teams are suggested. Group or physical education class groups may compete with members from other classes in after-school play. Interest groups may be organized into teams or individuals to compete against each other. Whatever sub-division or organizational plan is followed, the teacher should stress 100 per cent group participation and work toward that end.

An after-school leader's club might well be developed. Members may be either teacher selected or pupil elected. These pupils can be trained to organize competitive groups, assist in officiating, scoring, and record-keeping as well as planning and evaluating the complete program for a season, term, or year. The club might also be responsible for issuing, caring for, and checking in equipment. Bulletin board publicity, loud speaker announcements, and newspaper reports offer splendid means for integrating the total program with English as well as other subjects.

THE SEASONAL PROGRAM

The total after-school program should be organized around seasonal sports and games. Kite flying contests, marble, jack, or jump rope tournaments are best in the spring. Lead up games to football are best in the fall season, whereas basketball-type games are most ideal for the winter.

The following seasonal program might serve as a guide around which the leader could make additions:

FALL SEASON

Line soccer .... grade 4
Shuttle-pass soccer relay .... grades 5, 6
Simplified soccer .... grades 5, 6
Pin soccer .... grade 4
Relays .... grades 1, 2, 3, 4, 5, 6

WINTER SEASON

Dodgeball .... grades 4, 5, 6
Basketball shuttle relay .... grades 4, 5, 6
Newcomb .... grades 2, 3
Keep away .... grades 2, 3

Captain ball ....grades 4, 5, 6
Relays ....grades 1, 2, 3, 4, 5, 6

Spring Season

Base kick ball ....grades 3, 4
Kickball ....grades 3, 4, 5, 6
Jacks ....grades 1, 2, 3
Hopscotch ....grades 1, 2, 3
Jump rope ....grades 1, 2, 3
Kite flying ....grades 4, 5, 6
Relays ....grades 1, 2, 3, 4, 5, 6
Camping skill contests ....grades 4, 5, 6

A seasonal program provides a logical progression from lesson to lesson and season to season. Simple games which use the basic skills of running, throwing, catching, jumping, hopping, creeping, and hanging should be stressed through grade 4. More advanced games into which these fundamental movements are integrated should be stressed beginning at the fifth grade level.

Special Events

PLAY DAYS

Play days or community get-together days are excellent ways to get parents to come see what their children have learned. The primary purpose of the play day is to provide mass participation in all the games, stunts, rhythmical activities, hunting games, campcraft skills, and individual events. Every student should take an active part, not just the best from each school or class.

Play days may be organized for all the children (1) within one school, (2) in two or three neighboring schools combined, (3) from all schools in the district, or (4) for the whole county. Small play days organized at the close of the fall, winter, and spring program offer incentive for teachers and children to plan and carry out a systematized progressive program.

Suggestions for conducting a successful play day include:
1. Have a definite theme such as a rodeo day, national airplane, car or horse race, the olympic games, a popular holiday, etc.
2. Separate pupils from each school or class so that each team will be made up of members from different schools or classes.

3. Divide the players into teams built around the chosen theme:
   a. Rodeo—bronchos, mustangs, cowboys, etc.
   b. Airplane race—T.V., Braniff, American, United, etc.
   c. Olympic games—U.S., Germany, England, Italy, etc.
   d. Popular holiday (Christmas)—trees, toys, reindeer, etc.
4. Have each team wear a favor or symbol representative of the theme.
5. Play games known to all but change their names to fit the theme.
   a. Rodeo—a running race becomes a wild horse race across the plains, etc.
   b. Airplane—a running race becomes a non-stop flight from Los Angeles to New York, etc.
   c. Olympic games—a running race becomes a foot race of contestants bringing a lighted torch from Mt. Olympus to Helsinki, etc.
   d. Popular holiday—a running race becomes a race for reindeers for an honored place on Santa's Christmas team, etc.
6. Have each group make up a team yell, team motto, or song.
7. Have each group compete in other areas too, such as singing, charades, dancing, guessing games.
8. If refreshments are served change the name of the food to fit the theme.
9. Award simple prizes to winning team members, such as magazine pictures, ribbons, tin cups, etc.
10. Have a definite beginning and ending to the entire program and to each event.

OTHER SPECIAL EVENTS

Assembly programs, demonstrations, field days, special exhibits, motion picture films and colored slides, special programs prepared for community groups, festivals, along with other such events are rich opportunities for selling physical education to the public. People support the things in which they believe. They can see values in a football game. They rarely have an opportunity to see a good physical education program. Special events call for hard work, but values gained from extra hours of labor pay great dividends in increased student-parent interest and support to the teacher and what she teaches!

DEMONSTRATIONS

An annual public demonstration should be the outgrowth of the regular physical education program. It should be the best of the year's program but never its goal. All children should participate rather than the few selected best. Demonstrations may show (1) a typical class period, (2) a survey of all activities covered during the year, (3) pupil-parent activities in which the pupil demonstrates first, then the parent, or (4) a program centering around a general theme.

Rehearsals of the demonstration should be held largely during class period and little after-school time should be taken up with practice. Mass rehearsals held one or two days before the performance aid in smoothing out rough spots. These practices should include the procession and recession order, the finale and large numbers, each separate number on the program taken up in order, plus a check of the general effect of costumes, music, etc.

Scenery and costumes should be of secondary importance but should be made, in as far as is practicable, largely by the pupils. A scarf tied around the regulation uniform can do much to change its appearance.

The sample program which follows may serve as a suggested guide for a demonstration program showing the work done in six elementary classes.

A. Entrance march   all pupils

B. Singing games   grades 1, 2
   Hickory, Dickory, Dock
   Little Jack Horner
   The Muffin Man
   Did You Ever See A Lassie

C. Stunts and Tumbling   grades 3, 4
   Inchworm Walk
   Elephant Walk
   Forward and Backward Somersaults
   The Merry-Go-Round
   Pyramids

D. Relays   grades 4, 5
   Wheelbarrow Relay
   Ropejump Relay

Ten-pin Relay
Forty Ways to Get There Relay

E. Grade Games   4th grade boys
    Line Dodge Ball
    Line Soccer
    Hit Pin Baseball

F. Grade Games   4th grade girls
    Newcomb
    Shuffleboard
    Kickball

G. Square Dancing   grades 5, 6
    Old Dan Tucker   boys and girls
    Virginia Reel
    Starlight Schottische
    Butterfly Polka

H. Gymnastic Drill   grades 4, 5, 6
    Five minutes of exercises done to command.

I. Departure March   all pupils

School Assembly Programs

Special programs given in assembly can be a rich educational experience. It can be an excellent means of educating the principal and other teachers, and can lead to better understanding and appreciation on the part of the pupils.

The presentation may be (1) a general orientation type, (2) a recognition assembly, or (3) a special subject assembly.

The general orientation assembly is best held at the beginning of the new year. It is a grand means of acquainting newcomers with the objectives and activities included in the physical education program. Pupils can demonstrate games, dances, and other activities. Films might be shown which stress good sportmanship, or playground safety. The program can also be used to stimulate interest in coming events. Outside speakers may give illustrated talks or demonstrations.

The recognition assembly is the time leaders are given public acclaim for skill, leadership ability, or some contribution made to the school. Pupils can give short speeches stressing values of good health, fair play, or team loyalty. Songs or short poems may be interspersed in the talks. Awards given to outstanding pupils may be in the form of verbal recognition or actual presentation of a tangible inexpensive object.

The special subject assembly is often used to introduce new activities to the pupils or re-acquaint them with familiar ones. Posture, safety, Indian dancing, games from other lands might be used.

Exhibits

Although exhibits are often associated with a large occasion, such as National Education Week, or National Safety Week, the school exhibit can be a separate type of demonstration. A corridor, bulletin board, or room may be used for the display. Pupils should make, gather, and assemble all materials to be shown, working under the guidance of the teacher. Emphasis may be placed around such themes as the total physical education program, safety, good health habits, leisure-time, play, posture, or illustrated materials showing the work done in the department or class. Snapshots taken of pupils on the playground might be attractively arranged on a bulletin board. Mimeographed material may also be laid out for free distribution. Samples of toothpaste, cereal, soap, etc., may be obtained from companies interested primarily in using this type of advertising. Hobby samples often make an interesting exhibit and sometimes start new enthusiasts on a pleasurable pursuit of developing a new skill or interest.

Programs for Community Groups

The physical education department or classroom teacher is frequently asked to prepare programs for civic groups. As far as possible these programs should be drawn from the actual program in the school and be a fair representation of it. Spectacular performances given by a few should be kept at a minimum. Preferably as many pupils as possible should take part. Such programs often make a valuable contribution toward developing better understanding and appreciation between the school and community, the teacher and parent.

In conducting all special events the teacher should assume the responsibility for the organizing, conducting, and evaluating them. Student chairmen and their various committees should assist with all aspects of the event. Questions to be answered honestly both by the teacher and pupils when evaluating the outcome of each program are:

1. What changes were made in pupil growth in developing desirable attitudes, new skills, new knowledges?

2. To what degree did the program acquaint others with the real purpose and content of our physical education classwork and program?

3. What increased opportunities should be given to students next time in planning, conducting, and evaluating the program?

4. How many school people commented favorably on it? How many parents? What did other pupils say about it?

Football, Baseball, and Basketball Competition

One major problem facing the elementary teacher is when to allow boys and girls to compete on a sponsored school team against other schools. When the question is raised as to whether elementary school children should compete against others or not, teachers take sides on this issue, almost all immediately thinking of competition in basketball and football. Increasingly, competition in these two sports and its place in American schools is being questioned on all levels, but especially in high schools and colleges. Some believe too much emphasis is placed on these major sports and on too few players instead of the majority of students. Actually, competition in itself is not undesirable, it is only what one does when competing that may be negative, in how one feels when winning or losing. In reality, children compete for family status the day they are born. A group of boys playing marbles are competing against each other, as are a group of girls playing jacks for fun. Certainly we, as educated adults, must avoid stereotype thinking, realizing that we all must guard against thinking all policemen are "dumb," all detectives "smart," all teachers "old maids," all professors "absentminded," or all competition "bad." But at the same time, as educated adults, we must be cognizant that increasingly outside groups are putting greater pressure on teachers to allow sixth, fifth, and in some schools even fourth grade children to play competitive athletic sports. There are many pro and con arguments to this highly debatable question.

Arguments For

Some sporting goods salesmen, sport writers, parents, physical educators, coaches, and teachers argue that:

1. Since children will play these games anyway in sand lots

and streets, why not teach them how to play so fewer will get hurt.

2. Since these are our national games children should learn how to play them well early in life.

3. We will develop better high school and college players if we can teach players earlier in life and thus the game will be more thrilling to play and to watch.

4. The individual player who is beyond his age in growth and skill should not be held back by being forced to play baby or sissy games.

5. It is better to be skilled in one or two sports than just an average player in several.

Arguments Against

Some physicians, leading physical educators, coaches, teachers and parents argue that:

1. Children may receive permanent bone and ligament deformities from playing these adult games while they are in a period of rapid growth and body change.

2. There is little carry-over value in these games, for the modern world offers little opportunity to play these games throughout life. Few will play them when they are 28, 48, 68, 88.

3. The games are superimposed upon children by adults, often for their own selfish gains.

4. The games tend to reward professionalism by demanding ever increasing specialization and thrills.

5. Children should learn to do things set aside for children, to have something toward which to look forward when they become adult.

Since a challenging varied program in a wide range of physical activities should be provided for every child of grade school age, the above pro and con arguments should be viewed in this light. The American Association of Health, Physical Education and Recreation, The American Medical Association, and The American Society for State Directors of Health, Physical Education and Recreation have all taken definite stands against regularly scheduled inter-scholastic competition below the senior high school level.[1] Any school therefore, or any grade or junior high school

---

[1] Scott, Harry, *Competitive Sports in Schools and Colleges*, New York Harper Brothers, 1951, pp. 480–481.

teacher which bases its physical education on after-school programs in football, basketball or any other competitive athletics
limits participation to those of certain physical size, strength,
ability and/or all three, and does so without the approval of the
physical education profession, leaders in this field, or those in
medicine.

Suggested Readings

American Association for Health, Physical Education and Recreation,
Desirable Athletic Competition For Children, 1201 Sixteenth St.,
N.W., Washington, D. C., 1952.

Anderson, C. F., "Practical Hints On Demonstrations," *Journal of
Health and Physical Education*, Vol. 7, No. 3, March, 1936.

Crosier, Frank, "Play Days for Boys," *Journal of Health and Physical
Education*, Vol. 3, No. 5, May, 1932.

Davis, Elwood, C. and Lawther, John D., *Successful Teaching in Physical Education*, New York, Prentice-Hall, 1941.

Elsbree, Willard S., *The American Teacher*, New York, American Book
Company, 1939.

Evans, Mary, *Costumes Through The Ages*, New York, J. B. Lippincott
Co., 1930.

Gray, Miriam, *Physical Education Demonstration*, New York, A. S.
Barnes, 1947.

Hinman, S., *Physical Education In The Elementary Grades*, New York,
Prentice-Hall, 1939.

Jackson, C. O., "Suggested Programs For Demonstrations and Exhibi-
tions," *Journal of Health and Physical Education*, Vol. 8, No. 2,
February, 1937.

LaSalle, Dorothy, *Physical Education For The Classroom Teacher*, New
York, A. S. Barnes, 1937.

Murray, Josephine and Bathhurst, Effie, *Creative Ways For Children's
Programs*, Chicago, Silver Burdett Company, 1938.

National Section for Women's Athletics, *Special Events In The Physical Education Program*, 1201 Sixteenth St., N.W., Washington, D. C.,
American Association for Health, Physical Education and Recreation,
1939.

Scott, Harry, *Competitive Sports In Schools and Colleges*, New York,
Harper Brothers, 1951.

Shambaugh, Mary, *Folk-Festivals For Schools and Playgrounds*, New
York, A. S. Barnes, 1932.

Solomon, Ben, "The Little League," *Youth Leaders* (Entire Issue),
April, 1953.

Williams, Jesse Feiring, Dambach, John I., and Schwendener, Norma,
Methods in Physical Education, Second Edition, Philadelphia, W. B.
Saunders, 1937.

INDEX